A CONCISE
DICTIONARY
OF MUSIC

A CONCISE DICTIONARY OF MUSIC

An Introductory Reference Book by

JACK M. and CORINNE WATSON

Illustrated with musical examples

and line drawings

DODD, MEAD & COMPANY

NEW YORK

PRINTED IN THE UNITED STATES OF AMERICA

A

A. The letter A has many uses in music: (1) A is the name given to one pitch in each octave throughout the musical range. The orchestra usually tunes to the A above Middle C,* which has a frequency* usually of 440 cycles per second. (2) The name given to a scale* or key* whose first note is A. A composition may be written in the key of A major or A minor, or in the key of A-flat major or A-flat minor. (See also *Key signatures.*) (3) On the piano keyboard A is the white key that lies between the second and third black keys in each group of three black keys; A-flat is the black key just below A; A-sharp is the black key just above A. (4) A is used as a symbol for the first section of a piece that has two or more sections. For example, Chopin's *Minute Waltz* has three sections, the first and last being alike. The symbol for this form is ABA (called also ternary*). (5) A is used as the abbreviation for *alto* to indicate the alto voice in choral arrangements. For example, SAB means *soprano, alto,* and *bass.*

ABSOLUTE MUSIC. As opposed to program music* which tells a story or describes a scene, absolute music depends on nothing but itself. It consists of organized sounds that in themselves make up a composition. A Bach invention* or fugue* or a Beethoven quartet* or symphony* is an example of absolute music.

ABSOLUTE PITCH (Sometimes called "perfect pitch"). The ability to recognize simply by hearing the exact note that is being played or sung or to sing any desired note (within the range of the voice). A person with absolute pitch can tell at once whether an instrument is tuned too high or too low. Through practice many musicians acquire a sense of pitch that is relatively accurate, but a true sense of absolute pitch is rare.

1

ABSTRACT MUSIC. Another name for Absolute Music.*

A CAPPELLA (ah kah PELL ah). An Italian word meaning "in the chapel style," that is, without accompaniment. Choral music that consists of voices alone with no piano or instrumental accompaniment is *a cappella*.

ACCELERANDO (ah chay lay RHAN doh). An Italian word meaning "go faster." In music it means to gradually pick up the speed with which a particular passage is being performed. (See also *Tempo*.)

ACCENT. The rhythm of music is made clear by accent. In a waltz, for example, the 1-2-3, 1-2-3 rhythm is brought out by stressing slightly the first beat in each measure. In music written in 4/4 time the first and third beats of the measure are accented, the first (primary accent) being a bit stronger than the accent on the third beat (secondary accent). In most music, however, accents occur in other places as well. In such cases this mark (>) is usually placed above the notes to be accented. (See also *Rhythm*.)

ACCIACCATURA (ah tchah kah TOO rah). An Italian word meaning "a crushing." An ornament used in keyboard music of the seventeenth and eighteenth centuries. It consists of one or more dissonant* notes within a chord. When the chord is struck the dissonant note (or notes) is released at once, leaving the consonant* notes to sound. (See also *Ornaments*.)

ACCIDENTALS. These are the five signs used to show that a note is raised or lowered temporarily; or that a note returns to its normal position. A sharp* (♯) raises a tone one half step; a double sharp (𝄪) raises it two half steps (or one whole step); a flat* (♭) lowers a tone one half step; a double flat (♭♭) lowers it two half steps (or one whole step). A natural* sign (♮) cancels a previous change. An accidental affects one pitch only in a given measure, and not in the measures which follow.

ACCORDION. The accordion is a member of the reed organ family. It consists of a rather large bellows between two rectangular-shaped head-boards. The headboard on the right has a piano-type keyboard with a range of from one to two and one-half octaves, depending upon the size of the instrument. When the keys are pressed, they open valves which allow air to rush across metal reeds to produce tones. The headboard on

the left has a number of buttons that are pressed to get bass notes and chords. The player plays the melody with his fingers on the keyboard and plays the chords by pressing the buttons on the left headboard. At the same time he expands and contracts the bellows by pulling and pushing the headboards. Although it is not often used in orchestras, the accordion is a popular "social" or folk instrument.

ACOUSTICS. The science of sound, which includes the basic scientific principles of musical tone.

All sounds are caused by air waves set in motion by vibrating substances. Irregular and unsteady vibrations result in noise; regular and constant vibrations result in tone. Tones are usually produced by four different means: (1) a tightly stretched string, as on a guitar or violin; (2) a hollow tube in which air is confined, as a flute or tuba; (3) a membrane or skin stretched tightly over a hoop, as on a drum; (4) a resonant solid, such as the hardwood bars of the xylophone. When any of these is plucked, bowed, blown, or struck, they create vibrations which are carried through the air and set up sympathetic vibrations as they strike the eardrums.

The "highness" or "lowness" of a tone depends entirely upon the frequency (the speed) of its vibrations: the faster the vibrations, the higher the pitch; the slower the vibrations, the lower the pitch. Longer, thicker, and heavier substances vibrate more slowly than short, thin, and light substances. For this reason, the tone produced by a bass viol is much lower than the tone on a violin, and the tones possible on a flute are much higher than those on a tuba.

The intensity (loudness, as we usually think of it) of a tone is not affected by the number of vibrations of a tone. It depends upon the amplitude (width) of the vibrations: the greater the amplitude, the more intense the tone. For example, the stronger one strikes the key on a piano, the wider the piano string is caused to move during its vibration, and the more intense (louder) the tone will be.

Each instrument or voice has its own peculiar tone quality or timbre.* Yet any tone, whether sung or played by any instrument, always has exactly the same number of vibrations. What sounds like a single tone is actually many tones—a main or fundamental* tone plus varying numbers of additional sounds called overtones,* upper partials,* or harmonics.* Because the overtones are much weaker than the fundamental tone we are not usually aware of them. But their number and strength determine the particular tone quality of a sound. These upper partials that vibrate sympathetically with a fundamental tone are called the harmonic series.* (See also *Tone Color.*)

ADAGIETTO (ah dah ji ET toh). An Italian word meaning "slow," but not quite as slow as adagio.* (See also *Tempo.*)

ADAGIO (ah DAH jio). An Italian word meaning "leisurely" or "slow." (1) A piece or section of a piece that should be performed at a slow tempo. (2) A whole composition or movement* of a large work such as a symphony* that has a slow and perhaps tender character. (See also *Tempo.*)

AD LIB. An abbreviation of the Latin term *ad libitum,* which means "at pleasure." (1) Strict time is not required—the performer may vary the time to suit himself. (2) A particular instrument or voice does not necessarily have to be included in an ensemble.* (3) Certain notes may be played or omitted, as the performer wishes.

AFFETTUOSO (ah fet too OH zoh). An Italian word meaning "with feeling" or "affectionately." (See also *Expression.*)

AGITATO (ah ji TAH toh). An Italian word meaning "excited." When it is used alone, without any indication of speed, *agitato* usually means that the passage should be performed in a rather agitated way, and perhaps at a slightly faster tempo.

AGNUS DEI (AHN yoos DAY ee). A Latin term meaning "Lamb of God." It is the final portion of the Roman Mass* set to music and ends with the words *dona nobis pacem* (Grant us thy peace).

AIR. A tune with a simple melody for voice or instrument. *Londonderry Air,* a folk tune that has been used by a number of composers in songs and instrumental pieces, and *Air on the G String,* an arrangement for violin and piano of the second movement of Bach's Suite in D for orchestra, are examples. (See also *Ayre.*)

ALBENIZ (ahl BAY nith), **Isaac.** Spanish composer, born in Camprodón on May 29, 1860; died in Cambo-les-Baines on May 18, 1909.

At the age of four, Albeniz astonished an audience in a Barcelona theatre with his piano playing. When he was seven he wrote a composition excellent enough to be played by a military band in Barcelona. He was only thirteen, a student at the Madrid Conservatory of Music, when he ran away from home. He eventually came to the United States, where he supported himself for some time with his piano playing. He returned to Europe and studied with several well-known musicians, including Franz Liszt* in Budapest. He made many concert tours as a virtuoso pianist, and finally settled in Paris, where he devoted the remainder of his life to teaching and composing.

Most of Albeniz's music has strong rhythmic features of a Spanish nature. His works include several operas and operettas, a number of songs, and a great many piano pieces. Among the most popular of his works for piano are *Iberia,* a cycle of twelve pieces, and the well-known *Tango in D.*

ALBERTI BASS. A rather monotonous figuration of notes used as an accompaniment for the left hand in keyboard music. It is named for Domenico Alberti, an Italian composer of the sixteenth century who used the figuration frequently in his sonatas. The following example is from Alberti's sixth sonata:

ALBORADO (ahl bo RA doh). A popular type of morning tune performed in rural areas of northwest Spain. The alborado is usually performed by two musicians—one playing the melody on a rustic bagpipe, the other drumming an accompaniment on a small side-drum. The French composer Ravel* used this type of folk music effectively in his *Alborado del Gracioso* (Jester's Morning Song), a piece for piano, later transcribed for orchestra.

AL FINE (ahl FEE nay). An Italian term meaning "to the end." Al fine is used most often in the phrases *da capo al fine* (from the beginning to the end) and *dal segno al fine* (from the sign to the end). (See also *Da capo* and *Dal segno*.)

ALLA (ah lah). An Italian word meaning "in the manner or style of." For example, *alla marcia* means that a piece or section of a piece should be played in the style of a march.

ALLA BREVE (ahl la BRAY vay). An Italian term meaning "in a concise manner." The symbol for *alla breve* is a letter C with a vertical line drawn through it (₵). The sign indicates that the music is to be performed twice as fast as the notes written; that is, instead of four beats to a measure there should be only two beats. *Alla breve* is also called "cut time."

ALLARGANDO (ahl lar GHAN doh). An Italian word meaning "broader." It indicates a slower speed and a more dignified style.

ALLEGRETTO (ahl lay GRET toh). An Italian word meaning "rather lively." It indicates a speed not quite as fast as *allegro*.* (See also *Tempo*.)

ALLEGRO (ahl LAY groh). An Italian word meaning "lively." It indicates a rather fast speed, though not as fast as *presto*.* *Allegro* may also be used in a title to indicate the style of a piece or a movement, as Ravel's* *Introduction and Allegro*. (See also *Tempo*.)

ALLEMANDE (ahl MAHND). A French word meaning "German." (1) An old German folk dance in moderate duple* time. Late in the eighteenth century the term was used in South Germany for a fast waltz-like dance in 3/4 or 3/8 time. Examples of this type of dance are heard in Beethoven's *Twelve German Dances* for orchestra. (2) In suites* by certain composers, principally Bach and Handel, the *Allemande* is the name of the first movement. It is usually written in 4/4 time and is rather gay and sprightly in character. An example is the first movement of Bach's Suite No. 1 in C.

ALPHORN. A primitive type of wind instrument made of wood and often bound with bark. The alphorn, which is sometimes curved and sometimes straight, may be as long as ten feet, in which case the horn end rests on the ground when the instrument is played. Swiss mountaineers and herdsmen from some other European countries use the alphorn to call their cattle and to play simple melodies called *ranz des vaches.** In his Pastoral Symphony Beethoven* used the *ranz des vaches,* but had it played by more conventional instruments.

ALTO. An Italian word meaning "high." (1) The lowest female voice, in which case it means the same as *contralto.** (2) The lowest unchanged boy's voice. (3) A high kind of singing by men, achieved by an unnatural kind of vocal production called falsetto.* (4) Parts written for these voices in vocal or choral music. (5) Instruments with a range similar to the alto voice, as the alto flute. (6) The alto clef* (|₿) which is used principally in music for the viola.* (7) The French name for the viola.

ALZATI (ahl ZAH tee). An Italian word meaning "raised." For stringed instruments played with a bow, *alzati* means that the mute* should be lifted from the strings.

AMATI (ah MAH tee). Name of a famous family of violin makers who lived in Cremona, Italy, during the sixteenth and seventeenth centuries. The family produced hundreds of instruments of the finest kind, many of them for members of royal families all over Europe. The most celebrated member of the family, Nicolo Amati, was the teacher of another famous violin maker, Antonio Stradivari.* Most of the violins made by the Amati family that have survived to the present day are in museums and are almost priceless.

AM FROSCH (ahm FROSH). A German term meaning "at the frog." For stringed instruments played with a bow, *am Frosch* means that the part of the bow nearest the right hand should be used.

AM GRIFFBRET (ahm GRIFF bret). A German term meaning "at the fingerboard." For stringed instruments played with a bow, *am Griffbret* means that the instrument should be bowed near the fingerboard.

AM STEG (ahm SHTAKE). A German word meaning "at the small bridge." For stringed instruments played with a bow, *am Steg* means that the instrument should be bowed near the bridge.*

ANDANTE (ahn DAHN tay). An Italian word meaning "going." Andante indicates a rather slow rate of speed. It is also used to designate a movement* of a symphony* or sonata,* or sometimes a whole piece, as Beethoven's solo piece for piano, *Andante Favori*. (See also *Tempo*.)

ANDANTINO (ahn dahn TEE noh). An Italian word meaning "a little *andante*."* Modern composers use *andantino* to indicate a tempo that is a little faster than *andante*; composers of the Classic period sometimes used it to indicate a slightly slower tempo. *Andantino* has been used also as the title of pieces that are to be performed at an andantino tempo. (See also *Tempo*.)

ANIMATO (ah nee MAH toh). An Italian word meaning "lively." Music marked *animato* should be performed in a lively, animated way at a rather fast tempo.

ANSWER. In music that is written according to strict rules of counterpoint,* as in a fugue,* an answer is the repeating of a previously stated theme* or subject.* In the following three bars from Fugue No. 1 of Bach's *Well-Tempered Clavier*,* for example, the subject, which begins on C, is answered by the same theme beginning on G.

When the notes in the answer follow exactly the same pattern as those in the subject, as in the example above, the answer is called a *real answer*. If the answer is slightly different it is called a *tonal answer*. (See also *Counterpoint* and *Fugue*.)

ANTHEIL (ahn TILE), **George.** American composer, born in Trenton, New Jersey, on July 8, 1900; died on February 12, 1959. A talented young pianist, Antheil won the Guggenheim Fellowship when he was only twenty-two years old. For the next five years he traveled through Europe as a concert pianist. One of his earliest works, written when he was twenty-four, was called *Ballet Mécanique*. This ballet, in which he used airplane propellers, motor horns, and other non-musical sounds, caused quite a stir. Later his compositions became less daring, although he continued to use jazz idioms frequently. He spent several years in Hollywood, where he wrote music for many films. In addition, he wrote three operas, six symphonies, four sonatas, two concertos, and a large number of compositions for orchestra.

ANTHEM. A short choral song of a serious nature, with or without solo parts, and usually with an organ accompaniment. The words are of a religious character, often taken from the Bible or other sacred works. The anthem is sung in most Protestant churches. (See also *National Anthem*.)

ANTIPHON. Part of the service in the Roman Catholic and Greek Orthodox Churches. It is sung or intoned as responses between a solo voice and a group of singers, or between two groups of singers before and after a Psalm or Canticle.

ANVIL. A percussion* instrument that has no definite pitch. A real blacksmith's anvil is sometimes used in the orchestra, but more often a heavy metal bar with a striker takes its place. Anvils are called for in a number of works, most notably Wagner's* *Das Rheingold,* which is scored for eighteen anvils. Perhaps the best known work which makes effective use of anvils is the "Anvil Chorus" from Verdi's* opera, *Il Trovatore.*

APPOGGIATURA (ahp poh djah TOO rah). An Italian word meaning "leaning." There are two kinds of appoggiaturas, long and short. The long appoggiatura appears before the main note, but is played on the beat and takes away some of the value of the main note, as in this example:

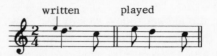

The short appoggiatura (sometimes called a *grace note*) is played very quickly just before the main note. Both kinds appear as smaller notes, but the short appoggiatura usually has a small diagonal line running through it, as in this example:

ARABESQUE (eh rah BESK). A word often used as the title of a musical selection that is graceful and rather light and gay in character. The name has been borrowed from architecture, in which it is a kind of ornate design carved in wood or stone and used frequently in Arabian architecture and art works. Robert Schumann* used the title for one of his piano pieces. A number of later composers, including Debussy,* have also written pieces they called *Arabesque.*

ARCO (AHR koh). An Italian word meaning "bow" (of a stringed instrument). Either alone or as *coll' arco,* it means that the player should use the bow again after a *pizzicato* passage (where the strings are plucked with the fingers).

ARIA (AH ree ah). An Italian word meaning "air." However, the elaborate kind of solo song called an *aria* is quite different from the rather simple type of song called an *air.* In most operas and oratorios each of the leading characters has one or more arias, many of which call for the most expert kind of singing. Examples of famous arias are the "Toreador Song" from *Carmen* by Bizet,* the "Bell Song" from *Lakmé* by Delibes,* and "He Shall Feed His Flock" from Handel's* oratorio *The Messiah.* (See also *da capo aria.*)

ARIETTA (ah ree AY tah). An Italian word meaning "little aria." An arietta is a shorter and less elaborate solo song than an aria. An example is Barbarina's solo in Mozart's opera, *The Marriage of Figaro.*

ARIOSO (ah ree OH soh). An important feature of some oratorios* and some operas* which combines the narrative character of a recitative* with the song-like character of the aria.* The baritone* solo "For the Mountains Shall Depart" from Mendelssohn's oratorio *Elijah* is an example of the arioso.

ARNE, Thomas Augustine. English composer, born in London in March, 1710; died there on March 5, 1778.

Arne's father was opposed to his son's becoming a musician and sent him to Eton with the idea of his studying law. The boy managed, however, to study music privately and proved to be so successful as a composer that his father finally gave his consent to his adopting music as a profession. Arne's first opera, *Rosamond,* was produced in London when he was just twenty-three years old, and from then on he proceeded to compose a great many works, most of them for the stage. The famous English patriotic song, "Rule Britannia!" occurs in one of his masques,* *Alfred.* In 1759 he was awarded a Doctor of Music degree by Oxford University, and subsequently became known as Dr. Arne.

ARPEGGIO (ahr PAY djoh). An Italian word meaning "harp-like." An arpeggio is a broken chord;* that is, a chord whose notes are sounded in rapid succession beginning with the lowest note. Arpeggios may be written out or indicated by a vertical wavy line in front of the chord.

In piano music, arpeggios may be marked for both hands. In that case, if the chords for the left and right hands have separate wavy lines, the notes for the left and right hands are played at the same time. If there is one wavy line continuing through both staffs,* the notes in both chords are played successively, beginning with the lowest note in the bass.*

ARRANGEMENT. The rewriting of a composition originally intended for one instrument, voice and/or ensemble, for a different one. For example, a symphony* written originally for orchestra* may be "arranged" for band.* Since the band does not include any stringed instruments, the parts intended for violins,* violas,* cellos,* and bass viols* must be scored* for other instruments that are normally included in a band. An example of a good arrangement is the one for piano and orchestra made by Beethoven from his own violin concerto in D major (Op. 61). Another is any one of the Vivaldi* violin compositions that Bach arranged for the clavier.* Folk songs* and composed songs are often arranged for two or more voices, and many vocal compositions written originally for one voice have been arranged for glee clubs and choruses. (See also *Transcribe*.)

ART OF FUGUE, THE. An important, but unfinished, work written by J. S. Bach during the year before his death. In this work Bach teaches the art of fugue* and counterpoint* by a unique method. Instead of using rules, he uses examples, all of which are built from a single theme.* In some twenty fugues and canons* based on that one theme, Bach used every possible device of imitative counterpoint. Although no instruments were specified for performing them, the fugues and canons are so beautiful that they have been arranged for organ, harpsichord, piano, string quartet, small orchestra, and other combinations.

ART SONG. A song in which there is artistic unity between the vocal part, the words, and the accompaniment. The art song is the work of a single composer (often set to words by someone else). It differs in many respects from the folk song,* which consists simply of a melody and words and whose origin is unknown. Two examples of beautiful art songs are *An die Musik* (To Music) by Schubert,* and *Après un rêve* (After a Dream) by Fauré.*

ASSAI (ahs SAH ee). An Italian word meaning "very." It follows another expression or tempo mark, as in *lento assai* (very slow) or *piano assai* (very soft).

A TEMPO (ah TEM poh). An Italian term meaning "in time." It indicates that the tempo* indicated at the beginning of a piece should be resumed after it has been interrupted by a faster or slower section.

ATONAL MUSIC. Music in which the notes and chords are not related to a tonic* or key center. Almost all the music we hear is written in one of the major or minor keys. It may include notes or chords of other keys, but these always "resolve" to the basic key of the composition. This is called tonal music. In atonal music each note of the chromatic scale* (twelve notes in all) is given equal emphasis, and there is no attempt to relate them to any specific key center. The first attempts at writing atonal music were not successful, and eventually a twelve-tone technique* was worked out. Music written according to this technique has more unity than earlier atonal music. It should be recognized, however, that not all music employing twelve-tone technique is atonal; but a great deal of the music written according to that system rejects traditional tonality, and on that score could be described as atonal.

ATTACCA (aht TAHK kah). An Italian word meaning "attack." In works of more than one movement, such as symphonies* and concertos,* the word *attacca* means that the following movement* should be started at once, without the pause ordinarily taken between one movement and the next.

AUGMENTATION. A way of treating a theme so that the time value of the notes is lengthened; for example, quarter notes become half notes, half notes become whole notes. Augmentation is used occasionally in fugues and in the development* sections of sonatas,* symphonies,* and so on.

AULOS (AU loss). A wind instrument popular with the ancient Greeks. None of the instruments have survived to the present day, so historians have had to depend on written descriptions and carvings to figure out what kind of instrument the aulos really was. They believe that the aulos was a double reed instrument somewhat similar to the oboe,* and that two auloses were played at one time by the performer. They believe also that the tone of the aulos was shrill and somewhat like the drone* of the bagpipe.*

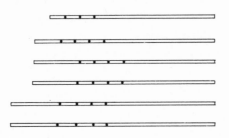

AUTOHARP. A stringed instrument that resembles the zither,* with strings tuned like those of a piano. Cross bars marked with the names of certain basic chords* have "dampers" which shut out the sounds of all strings except the ones needed for those particular chords. The Autoharp is played by pressing the bars for whichever chord is desired with one hand while strumming across the strings with the other hand. Because it is easy to play and yet provides an effective accompaniment for singing, the Autoharp has become a popular instrument for both school and home use.

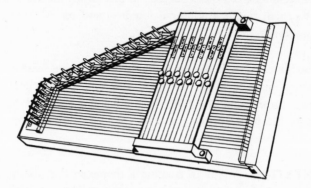

AVE MARIA (ah vay mah REE ah). A Latin term meaning "Hail, Mary." The *Ave Maria* is a prayer to the Virgin Mary, used in the Roman Catholic church. It has been set to music by many composers, but the two most popular versions are those by Schubert* and by Gounod.* Gounod's *Ave Maria* is made up of his own melody, the words of the prayer, and an accompaniment consisting of the first Prelude from Bach's *Well-Tempered Clavier.** It is known as the Bach-Gounod *Ave Maria.*

AYRE. A simple kind of song popular in the sixteenth and seventeenth centuries in England. An ayre consisted usually of a voice part that carried the principal melody, and an accompaniment to be played by such instruments of the period as lutes* or viols.* The accompaniment was sometimes sung by other voices.

B

B. The letter B has many uses in music: (1) B is the name given to one pitch in each octave throughout the musical range. It is one whole step higher than A.* (2) The name given to a scale* or key* whose first note is B. A composition may be written in the key of B major, B minor, B-flat major, or B-flat minor. (See also *Key Signatures*.) (3) On the piano keyboard, B is the white key that lies just above each group of three black keys. (4) B is used as a symbol for the second section of a composition that consists of two or more sections. For example, Bach's *Minuet in G* has two sections, the second being different from the first. The symbol for this form (called binary*) is AB. (5) B is used as the abbreviation for *bass* to indicate the bass voice in choral arrangements. For example, SAB means soprano, alto, and bass.

B. MUS. (Sometimes written Mus. B.) The abbreviation for Bachelor of Music, an academic degree earned by students when they complete a definite four-year course of study in a college or conservatory of music.

BABBITT, Milton. American composer, born in Philadelphia, Pennsylvania, on May 10, 1916.

In addition to studying music at New York University and Princeton University (he received degrees in music from both institutions), Babbitt studied composition privately with Roger Sessions.* He was only twenty-two years old when he was appointed to the faculty of Princeton University. There he has taught not only music, but mathematics as well. Babbitt is a gifted composer whose music has been performed widely in Europe and America. His works include compositions for piano, strings, brass instruments, and music for a film, "Into the Good Ground."

15

BACH, Anna Magdalena. Second wife of the great German composer, Johann Sebastian Bach. She was born in 1701 and died in 1760, ten years after the death of her husband. Anna Magdalena was just twenty years old when Bach, a widower with several children, married her. Busy as she was with housekeeping on a limited budget and seeing to the welfare of her own and her stepchildren, she still found time to study music. Her husband compiled for her a collection of his own pieces and those of others to help her in her studies. Known as *Anna Magdalena's Notebook,* its charming marches, minuets, polonaises, and songs are as spritely and fresh today as they were when Anna Magdalena studied them.

BACH, Carl Philipp Emanuel. Son of the great German composer Johann Sebastian Bach and his first wife, Maria Barbara. He was born March 8, 1714 in Weimar and died on December 14, 1788 in Hamburg.

Carl Philipp showed great musical talent at an early age. When he was only eleven he could play the difficult music his father was writing, and even before he entered the university he had composed a number of works for the clavier.* In 1740 he was appointed to the position of court musician to Frederick the Great of Prussia. He remained there for twenty-seven years, then accepted the post of church organist in Hamburg.

During Carl Philipp's lifetime the piano gradually took the place of the clavier and the harpsichord* and he adapted his music to the new instrument. The techniques he developed and the music he wrote entitled him to be called the "father" of modern pianoforte playing. He wrote an enormous number of works, including piano concertos and sonatas, symphonies, chamber music, oratorios, and church music. Many of his compositions are studied and performed today.

BACH, Johann Christian. German composer, born in Leipzig on September 5, 1735; died in London, England, on January 1, 1782.

Johann Christian was the youngest son of the great Johann Sebastian and Anna Magdalena Bach. As a boy he studied music in Leipzig, probably with his father. After his father's death in 1750, Johann Christian was taken to Berlin, where he studied for a number of years with his half brother, Carl Philipp Emanuel Bach.* At the age of twenty-one he went to Italy for further study in Bologna, and there he remained for six years writing a great deal of music for the church and several operas that were produced with a good measure of success. In 1762 he accepted an invitation to go to England as composer to the Italian Opera in London. He remained in England until his death twenty years later, becoming known as "the English Bach." In addition to his church music and operas, he wrote an enormous number of works. These include English and Italian arias and songs, orchestral works, chamber music, military marches for wind instruments, and a great many sonatas and other works for the clavier* and the piano.

BACH, Johann Sebastian. One of the greatest musicians of all time. He was born in the town of Eisenach, Germany, on March 21, 1685, and died in Leipzig on July 28, 1750.

Johann Sebastian's early childhood was a happy one. He attended school, sang in the church choir, and studied the violin and viola under the direction of his father, who was the town musician of Eisenach. But before Sebastian was ten years old his mother died, and less than a year later his father died. An older brother, Johann Christoph, took Sebastian into his own home. He was a fine organist and teacher and began at once to give Sebastian lessons on the clavier.*

Sebastian lived with his brother until he was fifteen, an age when boys of his class were expected to provide for themselves. Fortunately, he had a well-trained voice and had sung for several years in church choirs, so, when an opening occurred in the choir at Lüneburg, famous for its fine church music, he applied and was accepted. This position not only gave him a little spending money, but it also furnished his room and board and an opportunity to continue his studies. After just a year at Lüneburg his voice began to break and he could no longer sing in the choir. However, his fine musical training and his ability to play the violin, the viola, and the clavier made it possible for him to stay on as an instrumentalist.

As a musician, Sebastian grew enormously during his three years at Lüneburg, but his great desire was to become a church organist and choirmaster. When he heard of an opening at Arnstadt, where a fine new organ was being installed, he applied for the position. Although he was only eighteen years old, he so impressed the officials with his organ playing and his talent for composition that they hired him at once. Two years later he was offered a position at a bigger church in the larger town of Mühlhausen, and accepted. About this time an uncle died and left him enough money to marry and set up housekeeping. His wife was his cousin, Maria Barbara.

Less than a year later Sebastian accepted an appointment as chapel organist and concertmaster of the orchestra in the court of Duke Wilhelm

Ernst in Weimar. There he stayed for nine years, composing a steady stream of cantatas. His next post was that of *Kapellmeister** at the court of the Prince of Anhalt-Cöthen.

During the five years that Sebastian stayed at Cöthen he composed a large number of instrumental works for the small but excellent court orchestra. During that time, too, his wife died unexpectedly, leaving him with several young children. His second wife was Anna Magdalena.* Interested now in teaching music to his own children, Sebastian composed for them some exercises that contributed greatly to fingerboard technique. Up till then, players of the clavier used only the fingers and not the thumb. The hands were held flat, so the thumbs did not reach the keys. Sebastian had the fingers curve so the thumbs could be used. This exercise book for one of his sons was called *Clavierbüchlein von Wilhelm Friedemann Bach*. A little later he compiled a set of clavier pieces and songs to help his wife with her music—the famous *Anna Magdalena's Notebook*.

In 1723 Sebastian accepted the position of Cantor* of the Leipzig Thomasschule. For the remainder of his life he served the school and church of St. Thomas in Leipzig, finally becoming blind the year before his death.

Bach wrote a vast quantity of music which includes:

(1) Church music: almost two hundred cantatas, six motets, *The Magnificat, Passion according to St. John, Passion according to St. Matthew, Christmas Oratorio, Mass in B minor*.

(2) For orchestra: six Brandenburg concertos; four suites; two violin concertos; a concerto for two violins; a concerto for harpsichord, flute and violin; concertos for harpsichord.

(3) For organ: fugues, toccatas, preludes, fantasies, sonatas, and many chorale preludes.

(4) Chamber music: sonatas for solo violin, for solo cello, for *viola de gamba,* and a work for flute, violin, and continuo* called *Das Musicalisches Opfer*.

(5) For keyboard instruments: fifteen two-part inventions, fifteen three-part inventions, six French suites, six English suites, toccatas, partitas, the Goldberg variations, the Italian concerto, and his two famous works written primarily for instructional purposes: *The Well-tempered Clavier** and *Die Kunst der Fuge* (The Art of Fugue*).

BACON, Ernst. American composer, conductor, and pianist, born in Chicago on May 26, 1898.

Following his earlier study of music in Chicago, Bacon went to Europe where he studied piano, composition, and conducting, mainly in Vienna. His principal works are an opera, *A Tree on the Plains*; a musical comedy, *Take Your Choice*; a cantata, *From Emily's Diary* (with words by Emily Dickinson); two symphonies; a quintet for two violins, viola, cello, and piano; and several other compositions for orchestra.

BAGATELLE (bah gah TELL). A French word meaning "trifle." A bagatelle is a short, rather light piece, usually for piano. François Couperin* gave the title to a harpsichord piece; Beethoven used the name for his well-known *Seven Bagatelles,* Op. 33, and for three other sets; and a number of later composers, including Dvořák, have used the title *Bagatelle* for pieces in various forms.

BAGPIPE. One of the oldest known instruments, the bagpipe was used in ancient Rome, where the emperor Nero is said to have played on it. In writings of the Middle Ages, there are frequent references to the instrument.

The most familiar type, the bagpipe played by the Scottish Highlanders, consists of an airtight leather bag which the player fills with wind through a blow pipe. The wind is then forced through reed pipes. One of the pipes, called the chaunter, provides the melody. The chaunter may have one or two reeds and is provided with fingerholes by which the pitch is varied to produce the melody. The other pipes, called drones,* are each pitched to a single note. The sound is a rather thin, reedy melody accompanied by a droning accompaniment that never changes pitch.

Many countries have variations of the bagpipe, some of them very picturesque. The Irish bagpipe is equipped with a bellows which is placed

under the arm so the air can be forced through the reed pipes by pressure. The Russian bagpipe has a goatskin bag, often with the hair left on, a carved goat head for the chaunter stock, and a highly ornamental chaunter. The Spanish bagpipe, called a *gaita,* has a rubber-lined cloth bag, carved wooden pipes, and colorful decorations of silk ribbons and fringe.

Not much music has been composed for the bagpipe except in Scotland. In most countries it is used principally as a folk instrument, providing accompaniment for folk songs* and music for native dances.

BALAKIREV (bah LAHK ee reff), **Mily Alexeyevich.** Russian composer, pianist, and teacher, born in Nizhny-Novgorod on January 2, 1837; died in St. Petersburg (now Leningrad) on May 29, 1910.

Balakirev received his first music lessons from his mother, and proved to be so talented that at the age of ten he was taken to Moscow to study piano. When his mother died, he was befriended by Karl Eisrich, a German musician who was employed by a wealthy landowner to arrange musical evenings in his home. Balakirev was only fourteen when he helped Eisrich prepare a performance of Mozart's *Requiem* and did such an excellent job that he was hired as Eisrich's assistant. A year later he was allowed to conduct rehearsals of several Beethoven symphonies with a professional orchestra. His first compositions were written about the same time. Most of his life was devoted to teaching and composing, although from time to time he had to take other jobs in order to make enough money to support himself and his two sisters.

Balakirev's works include two symphonies, the symphonic poem *Tamara,* a great many piano pieces, some lovely songs, and arrangements of folksongs that he discovered during trips to various remote parts of Russia. (See also *The Five.*)

BALALAIKA (bah lah LIKE ah). A guitar*-like instrument popular in Russia. It is triangular in shape with a long fretted neck and three gut strings. It is played by plucking the strings with a plectrum.* Balalaikas

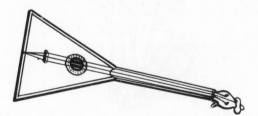

are made in various sizes, some being so large they rest on the ground when they are played. The instrument is used mostly by country folk as accompaniment for dancing and singing. Sometimes as many as six balalaikas are used to form a kind of band.

BALLAD. A song whose words tell a story. Folk ballads often tell a romantic, sometimes tragic, story in a series of verses, the same music being repeated for each verse. *Barbara Allen,* a very old folk ballad that originated in England, is an example of a ballad that is found in hundreds of versions. *Casey Jones* is an example of an American ballad. Some of the most beautiful art songs* follow this same ballad style. Such songs as Loewe's* *Edward* and *The Earl King* are examples.

BALLAD OPERA. A type of musical play with spoken dialogue and songs, often making use of folk tunes. The ballad opera became popular in England during the eighteenth century, the most popular one being *The Beggar's Opera* by John Gay. Two examples of ballad opera that have been produced successfully in recent years are Kurt Weill's* *The Threepenny Opera,* based on the same plot as *The Beggar's Opera,* and Douglas Moore's* *The Ballad of Baby Doe.*

BALLADE (bah LAHD). An instrumental piece, usually fairly long, that is lyric and romantic in style. Sometimes the ballade is based on an actual folk ballad or romantic writings. Examples are the first of Brahms' *Four Ballades for Piano,* Op. 10, which is based on the Scottish ballad *Edward,* and the four ballades that Chopin wrote for the piano, which are thought to have been inspired by the poems of a Polish poet, Mickiewicz.

BALLET. A form of entertainment in which costumed dancers perform to music, usually provided by an orchestra.

The ballet, in the broad sense of the term, is one of the oldest art forms, having been popular in ancient days. In the Middle Ages ballet played a prominent part in festivals and even in religious pageants. During the Renaissance ballet performances were important in the festivities at the French and Italian courts, where the dancers were usually the ladies and gentlemen of the nobility. One of the most important composers of ballet music during the seventeenth century was the great French composer Jean-Baptiste Lully,* himself a dancer, who introduced ballet into the opera. In varying degrees, the association of ballet with opera has continued ever since.

Nevertheless, ballet has continued to develop as an art form by itself.

During the nineteenth century the center of ballet moved from France to Russia, where the Imperial Ballet School had been founded a century earlier. In 1847 a Frenchman, Marius Petipa, went to St. Petersburg to take charge of the Imperial Ballet, and it was he who persuaded the Russian composer Tchaikovsky* to collaborate in writing three famous ballets that are among the favorite ballets performed today: *Swan Lake, The Sleeping Beauty,* and *The Nutcracker.*

In 1909 a Russian, Sergei Diaghilev, formed a ballet company with the great dancer Fokine and brought the art to new heights of perfection. They gave their first performance in Paris. Diaghilev encouraged such outstanding composers as Igor Stravinsky* and Maurice Ravel* to write music especially for the ballet. The later ballets of the Diaghilev company are said to have been influenced by the ideas of an American dancer, Isadora Duncan, who believed in a natural form of dancing that was quite different from the strict formality and "toe technique" of the Russian school.

In the United States, beginning in the 1920's, interest in the ballet increased, and a modern dance form that is typically American gradually developed. The ballets are based on realistic themes, and often combine classic and jazz styles most effectively in the music. *Billy the Kid* and *Rodeo,* both with scores by Aaron Copland,* are examples of the modern American ballet.

BAND. A group of musicians playing brass,* woodwind,* and percussion* instruments. A band does not have violins,* violas,* or cellos,* which are dominant in an orchestra.* Instead, wind instruments such as flutes,* oboes,* clarinets,* and cornets* are used as melody instruments, lower brass and woodwinds are supporting instruments, and percussion instruments provide the strong rhythmic element that is so characteristic of band music. A *symphonic band* has a greater proportion of woodwind instruments and may even use bass viols. A *military band* may have fewer woodwinds in comparison with the brass and percussion instruments. Although any band may be used for marching, timpani,* string basses, and any other large and cumbersome instruments cannot be used.

Band music, traditionally, is of a "lighter" nature than orchestral music. The most famous American composer of band music was John Philip Sousa,* but other well-known composers have written music for band, and a great many works for orchestra have been transcribed or arranged for band.

BANJO. A stringed instrument used widely in popular and folk music* and jazz.* The body consists of a membrane such as white calfskin stretched tightly over one side of a hoop. The long neck is made of hardwood and fitted with a fingerboard with raised metal frets* which divide the fingerboard into half-tones.* The most popular banjo has five or six strings, but a tenor banjo with four strings is occasionally used in jazz bands. Most banjos are played with a plectrum,* but there is a type of banjo played with the fingers. The tone of the banjo is hard, sharp, and short, which makes the instrument suited primarily to a jazzy, rhythmic type of music.

BAR. (1) A vertical line drawn across a staff* or staffs to mark the division between two measures of music, more properly called a *bar line*. (2) The music between two bar lines. In the second sense, bar has the same meaning as *measure.**

BARBER, Samuel. One of America's most important composers. He was born in West Chester, Pennsylvania, on March 9, 1910.

Barber began to study music when he was only six years old, and by the time he was seven had already begun composing. At thirteen he was admitted to the Curtis Institute of Music in Philadelphia, where he studied composition, piano, and singing. He later won three important awards for composition—the *Prix de Rome** and the Pulitzer Prize, the latter for two years in succession, 1935 and 1936.

Four years after his graduation from the Curtis Institute his Symphony No. 1 was played in Rome. Since then he has composed a steady stream of works, including many songs, orchestral works, choral works, *Adagio for Strings,* the ballet *Medea,* the opera *Vanessa,* and a cantata, *The Prayers of Kierkegaard,* based on some of the writings of a famous Danish philosopher of the 19th century.

BARCAROLLE. The song sung by the gondoliers of Venice, Italy, or a piece of music that imitates the gondoliers' songs. The characteristic 6/8 time with alternating strong and light beats gives the effect of a boat rising and falling with the waves or the steady strokes of the oars.

Many composers have written barcarolles; Fauré* wrote thirteen for the piano. The most familiar are probably Chopin's* (Op. 16) for piano, and the Barcarolle from Offenbach's* *Tales of Hoffmann.*

BARD. A poet-singer or minstrel of Medieval Ireland, Scotland, and Wales. Bards were hired by noblemen to provide entertainment in their castles and even to accompany their small armies into battle. They composed their own songs, usually to do honor to their patrons, and accompanied themselves on lyre-like instruments called crwths.* Later on they used harps.* Bards continued to exist until the early eighteenth century.

BARITONE. (From the Greek: *barys*—deep—and *tonos*—tone.) The male singing voice that is lower than a tenor and higher than a bass. The range is roughly two octaves, from low G to E above Middle C. However, many trained baritones can sing both lower and higher tones. Because of the power and brilliant quality of the baritone voice, many important roles in opera have been written for it. Some examples are Escamillo, the toreador in Bizet's* *Carmen*; Don Giovanni, the leading character in Mozart's* opera *Don Giovanni*; Tonio, the clown who sings the famous Prologue in *I Pagliacci* by Leoncavallo.*

BARITONE INSTRUMENTS. The baritone saxophone* and the baritone saxhorn* have been so named because they are smaller and have a higher compass* than the bass sizes. The brass instrument called a baritone horn has the same pitch as a euphonium* and is similar in size and shape, but its tone is not as rich and impressive. (See also *Brass Instruments.*)

BAROQUE (bah RAWK). A French word borrowed from the Portuguese word *barroco,* which means an irregularly shaped pearl. "Baroque" was originally applied to a kind of highly ornamented style of architecture and decoration that was fashionable in the seventeenth and early eighteenth centuries in Europe, but has been borrowed by music historians to identify music that was written during the same period. Roughly, the Baroque period in music begins with the Italian composer Monteverdi,* who was born in 1567, and ends with the German composer Handel,* who died in 1759.

The Baroque period was a fertile one in the development of musical forms, both vocal and instrumental. Notable examples are opera,* oratorio,* cantata;* the aria* and recitative;* the fugue,* concerto,* suite,* variations,* chorale prelude,* toccata,* passacaglia,* chaconne,* and rondo.* Some of the important composers of the Baroque period, in addition to Monteverdi and Handel, were Schütz,* Buxtehude,* Corelli,* Purcell,* Vivaldi,* and J. S. Bach.*

BARTÓK (BOR tawk), **Béla.** Hungarian pianist and composer, born March 25, 1881, in Hagyszentmiklós, Hungary; died in New York City on September 26, 1945.

Bartók, who became one of the most important composers of the twentieth century, showed musical talent at an early age. He began to take piano lessons from his mother when he was five years old. He gave his first public performance when he was ten, playing a movement from a Beethoven sonata and a composition called *The Danube* that he himself had composed. When he was thirteen his mother took him to Pozsony where he was able to hear opera and orchestral concerts and to study seriously. Although he was offered a scholarship at the famous Vienna Conservatory of Music, he decided to remain in Hungary and attend the Budapest Academy. He became known as a brilliant pianist, but at the same time he became more and more interested in composition.

Realizing that what was being accepted as Hungarian music was not the real folk music* of his country, Bartók began to study the music of the peasants and, with his friend Zoltan Kodály,* another outstanding composer, collected and published *Twenty Hungarian Folksongs,* the first of a vast number of native folk works that were to follow. These folk songs influenced his own compositions greatly, freeing him from what he called "the tyrannical rule of major and minor keys."* He found that most of the folk music was based upon primitive pentatonic* scales and filled with a variety of unusual rhythms.

Bartók came to the United States in 1940 and remained here for the rest of his life, teaching and composing. His compositions cover a wide field: ballets, a one-act opera, choral works, orchestral works, chamber music, and pieces for solo instruments and voice. He composed many graded teaching pieces for young piano students. *Mikrokosmos,* for example, consists of 153 pieces and exercises published in six books, beginning with Grade I. Another collection of eighty-five pieces in four books is titled simply *For Children.*

BARYTON. A bowed stringed instrument popular in the eighteenth century in Germany, but no longer played except by groups that specialize in playing old instruments. It resembled a bass viol with six strings that were bowed and a number of additional strings that vibrated in sympathy, but were not played.

Haydn* composed more than 120 pieces for baryton, viola, and cello, because his employer, Prince Esterházy, was fond of playing the baryton.

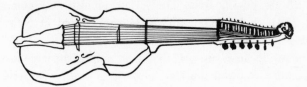

BASS. (1) The lowest adult male voice with a range of approximately two octaves, roughly from the second E below Middle C to the first F above Middle C. (2) The lower part of a composition is called *bass* to distinguish it from the upper part, or treble;* specifically, the bottom line, upon which the harmony is built. (3) A bass instrument (as the double bass,* the bass flute, the bass clarinet) is an instrument that has a lower range and a deeper tone than other instruments of the same family; the string bass or double bass is sometimes called simply the "bass." (See also *Bass Clef.*)

BASS-BAR. A strip of wood about eleven inches long that is glued to the inside of the sounding board of violins and similar instruments, just under the left foot of the bridge. Its purpose is to distribute over the sounding board the vibrations produced by the strings on the bridge. It helps also to strengthen the sounding board and support the bridge.

BASS CLEF. In notated music the symbol for the bass clef is this familiar sign: (𝄢). Normally the bass clef is used for the left-hand part of piano music, for bass and baritone voices, and for the lower pitched instruments. The upper curve of the sign begins on the line of the staff that indicates the F below Middle C, and thus it is sometimes called the *F Clef.*

BASSET HORN. An instrument similar to the clarinet but lower in pitch. It was invented in the 18th century and used by Mozart in his opera *The Magic Flute.* Although such late composers as Richard Strauss* and Roger

Sessions* have written parts for it, the basset horn is rarely heard today except with groups that specialize in playing old music on the original types of instruments.

BASSO (BAH soh). An Italian word meaning bass.* A *basso cantante* (singing) is a bass voice with a lyrical, lighter quality than a *basso profondo* (deep), a voice that is lower and heavier.

BASSOON. A woodwind instrument, the bass member of the oboe* family. The bassoon is played with a double-reed and through a long wooden pipe doubled back on itself. The bassoon has a wide compass* and can play from the third B-flat below Middle C to the second D above Middle C. The wide range and the rich quality of the bassoon make it a valuable instrument in the orchestra and in bands. Its close relative, the *double bassoon,* has a compass an octave lower. The double bassoon has a tube so long (as much as 18 feet) that it is doubled back on itself four times. (See also *Woodwinds.*)

BASS DRUM. A percussion instrument without definite pitch, consisting of a large wooden cylinder with one or, usually, both sides covered with tightly stretched skin. It is normally played by being beaten with a stick that has a large, felt-covered knob on the end. It can, however, be played with regular drumsticks if a drum roll is required.

BATON. The stick used by conductors to beat time. Although usually made of some light-weight wood, batons are sometimes made of metal. Most conductors hold the baton in the right hand, leaving the left hand free to indicate matters of expression. Some conductors, particularly choral conductors, prefer to use no baton at all.

BAYREUTH (BYE royt). A town in Bavaria, Germany, famous for its yearly festival of Wagner's operas. Wagner,* who had made his home in Bayreuth, designed the festival hall himself, where the first season was devoted to his *Ring of the Nieblungs* in 1876. Music lovers from all over the world attend the Bayreuth Festival held each summer and managed today by Wagner's grandsons, Wolfgang and Wieland Wagner.

BEAT. (1) The unit of measurement of time in music. We say that music written in 3/4 time has three beats to the measure; one written in 4/4 time has four beats to the measure, and so on. (2) When two slightly different pitches are sounded together they create tiny pulsations (beats) that can be heard at regular intervals. The difference in pitch between the two sounds can be measured by the number of beats per second. This phenomenon of acoustics* is made use of in the tuning of certain instruments, as the piano. (See also *Down Beat.*)

BEETHOVEN (BAY toh fen), **Ludwig van.** One of the world's greatest composers. He was born in Bonn, Germany, on December 16, 1770 and died in Vienna, Austria, on March 26, 1827.

As a boy in Bonn, Beethoven led a poverty-stricken and unhappy life. His father, a musician at the court in Bonn, managed to add a little to his small salary by teaching the clavier* and the violin. However, he was undependable and wasted much of his income on drink. His mother was a sweet-tempered woman whom Beethoven adored. But she was not able to control her wayward husband.

Beethoven showed great talent at an early age, and his father was greedy to show him off as a prodigy. He forced him to practice for long hours when he was barely big enough to reach the keyboard, and insisted on his playing at a public concert when he was only seven. The boy had very little schooling, but he studied the piano, organ, violin, and viola. When he was about eleven he was lucky enough to begin study with a fine musician, the court organist Neefe. Under Neefe's guidance, young Ludwig made so much progress that he was soon given the responsibility of conducting orchestra rehearsals when Neefe was away. He was only fourteen when he was appointed assistant court organist.

Three years later he traveled to Vienna, then the musical capital of the world. While there he played for the great Mozart.* Mozart was so impressed with his ability that he predicted a great future for him, saying: "Keep an eye on that boy. Some day the world will hear from him." The visit was cut short by the news of his mother's serious illness. He returned to Bonn and reached her bedside before she died at the early age of forty.

Without a mother to keep the home together, matters went from bad to worse. The father lost his job at court. Although half his salary was added to Ludwig's salary so that he could care for his two younger brothers, this still was not enough and he had to earn more money by teaching. Ludwig was only nineteen when he became legally responsible for the family.

Ludwig stayed in Bonn, first as court organist and later as viola player in the court theater, until he settled in Vienna for good in the fall of 1792. He had been composing steadily almost from the time when he first learned to play the clavier, but he did not consider his early compositions of much value, and not until 1795 did he put *Opus 1* (first work) on three trios he had written during the two preceding years in Vienna. Beethoven scholars have tended to classify his subsequent works into three periods. During the first period, which lasted until about 1803, he composed some fifty works including the first and second symphonies, the Kreutzer sonata for violin, and six string quartets. All the compositions of this first period show marked individuality, but they offer only a little evidence of the important innovations in style that were to come later. The second period included the years from about 1803 to 1815, during which he composed most of his best-known works. It is in these works that Beethoven's great power and originality began to show up so clearly. The third period included the years from about 1816 until his death in 1827. The great Mass, *Missa Solemnis,* the powerful Ninth Symphony, and some of his greatest quartets belong to this last period of his life. During these later years, Beethoven was caused much grief by his nephew, whose guardian he had become in 1815. The boy was hard to manage and rebelled against his uncle, who tried to be kind and was certainly generous. On the other hand, it was undoubtedly hard for the boy to live with a man who was always worried about money, whose temper was short, and who was becoming more and more deaf. Beethoven's hearing had begun to fail when he was not yet twenty-eight years old, and by the time he was thirty-nine he was completely deaf—an agonizing tragedy for a musician whose life was composed of sounds.

Nevertheless, he continued to compose, though some of his latest and greatest works he heard only in his mind; never as they were performed.

Beethoven wrote an enormous number of works, the most important of which are:

(1) For orchestra: nine symphonies; a violin concerto; five piano concertos; two romances for violin and orchestra; a concerto for piano, violin,

and cello; a fantasia for piano, orchestra, and chorus; and several overtures, including the famous *Coriolanus* and *Leonore,* No. 1, 2, and 3.

(2) For chamber groups: a septet; a quintet for piano and wind instruments; a string quintet; sixteen string quartets; four string trios; six piano trios; trio for clarinet, cello and piano; a serenade for flute, violin, and viola.

(3) For the stage: the opera *Fidelio*; a ballet, *The Creatures of Prometheus*; incidental music for a number of dramatic productions, including Goethe's *Egmont,* Kotzebue's *The Ruins of Athens* and *King Stephan.*

(4) For piano: thirty-two sonatas; twenty-one sets of variations; five sets of bagatelles; and numerous rondos and minuets.

(5) For other solo instruments: twelve sonatas, a rondo, six allemandes, and a serenade for violin and piano; five sonatas and a number of variations on works of Mozart and Handel for cello and piano; a nocturne for viola and piano; a sonata for horn.

(6) For voice: one song cycle and more than seventy single songs.

BEL CANTO (bell KAHN toh). An Italian word meaning "beautiful singing." The term is used to describe a style of singing that originated in Italy in the seventeenth century and has remained a model for singers in many parts of the world ever since. *Bel canto* stresses beautiful tones, fine phrasing, evenly sustained notes, and clear diction.

BELL. (1) The curved, spreading end of a wind instrument. The shape of the bell affects the tone quality; for example, the small spread of the bell

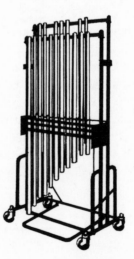

on a bugle causes the tone to be brilliant, while the wide spread of the horn bell makes for a more mellow tone. (2) An instrument of the orchestra. It consists of a metal tube that hangs from a hook. It is played by being struck with a metal hammer. A full set of bells usually covers the notes in one octave.

BELLINI (bell LEE nee), **Vincenzo.** Italian opera composer, born in Catania on November 3, 1801; died in a small town near Paris, France, on September 23, 1835.

Bellini died young, but in his brief life he composed eleven operas, only one of which, *Norma,* is widely performed today. *Norma* and two other operas, *La Sonnambula* and *I Puritani,* have been favorites of many great singers of the nineteenth and twentieth centuries because of the beautiful, lyrical style of Bellini's writing.

BELLY. The upper surface, sometimes called the *table,* of the soundbox of such stringed instruments as the violin,* cello,* and guitar.* The tone quality of an instrument with a curved belly (such as the cello) depends greatly upon the age of the wood from which it is cut and the size of the grain. The belly is thickest in the middle, under the bridge,* and thins out to the edges of the instrument.

BENNETT, Robert Russell. American composer and conductor, born in Kansas City, Missouri on June 15, 1894.

Bennett began his study of music when he was nine years old. He studied later in Paris, London, and Berlin, and by the time he was sixteen he was able to earn his living as a pianist, composer, and conductor. Bennett became well known through his work in motion pictures and radio. He has made many arrangements for film music, conducted the music on several popular radio shows, and has made the orchestrations for a number of musicals, including some by Richard Rodgers.*

Bennett's compositions include an opera-ballet, *Endymion;* two one-act operas, *An Hour of Delusion* and *The Enchanted Kiss;* concertos; works for chorus, chamber groups, and band; and six symphonies, one of which is called the *Symphony in D for the Dodgers,* composed in honor of the famous baseball team, the Brooklyn Dodgers (now the Los Angeles Dodgers).

BERCEUSE (behr SEUS). A French word meaning "lullaby." A berceuse is a composition for piano or other instrument which is characterized by a melody and an accompaniment with a soothing, rocking rhythm that suggests the motion of a cradle. Many composers have written pieces of this kind, but probably the best known is Chopin's* *Berceuse,* Opus 57, for piano.

BERG (bairg), **Alban.** Austrian composer, born in Vienna on February 9, 1885; died there on December 24, 1935.

Berg was born into a musical family in a musical city, and at a very early age showed great talent. By the time he was fifteen, before he had studied music seriously, he had already composed some seventy pieces. As a boy he had been sensitive and rather dreamy, and his early compositions reflect his nature. However, when he was nineteen he began to study music theory and composition with Schoenberg* and from then on his attitude about music and his own aims as a composer underwent a complete change. He adopted the twelve-tone technique* of his teacher and began composing in the new idiom. In 1921 he completed the opera *Wozzeck,* which had its first performance in Berlin in 1925 and created a great stir. It has remained a major work in the repertoire of opera theaters in Europe and America ever since.

Berg's principal works include a piano sonata; a string quartet and *Lyric Suite* for string quartet; three pieces for orchestra; a chamber concerto for piano, violin, and wind instruments; a violin concerto; and two operas, *Wozzeck* and *Lulu.* The opera *Lulu* was not complete when Berg died, but it nevertheless has received numerous performances in recent years.

BERLIN, Irving. American composer, born in Temun, Russia, on May 11, 1888.

Berlin, whose real name was Israel Baline, was brought to America when he was five years old, and was educated in the public schools of New York City. He began his musical career as a singing waiter in New York cafes, and in 1911 succeeded in getting his song, *Alexander's Ragtime Band,* published. The great success of the song established him as a writer of ragtime tunes, and from then on he composed a steady stream of popular numbers. He wrote the music and the lyrics for numerous musical comedies* and revues, among them the *Ziegfeld Follies, As Thousands Cheer, Annie Get Your Gun,* and *Call Me Madam.* Among his many popular songs, some of them from the motion pictures for which he wrote the music, are "Always," "Remember," "Easter Parade," "I'm Dreaming of a White Christmas," and "God Bless America." In 1955 he was awarded a medal by President Eisenhower for his contribution in composing patriotic songs.

BERLIOZ (BARE lee oze), **Louis Hector.** French composer and conductor, born near Grenoble on December 11, 1803; died in Paris on March 8, 1869.

Berlioz' father, a doctor, wanted his son to study medicine. Both he and the mother considered music to be an unsuitable career for their son and tried hard to turn him against it. However, even as a young boy, Hector was fascinated by music and studied the piano, the guitar, and the flute. At a very early age he composed little pieces which he insisted on playing for his friends. At the age of fifteen he wrote a quintet for flute and strings and several songs.

When he was about eighteen he was sent to Paris to study medicine, which he detested. However, he kept at his studies for a while, spending as much time as possible at the Paris Opera and in the library of the Paris Conservatory. Finally he managed to enter the Conservatory, where he studied first with Lesueur, and later with a fine teacher, Reicha. In 1830 he won the *Prix de Rome** and spent several years in Italy, a country that he took to immediately.

Berlioz' highly temperamental and romantic nature was reflected in his music. He enjoyed some successful tours as a conductor, mainly of his own works. On some occasions his works were not received favorably.

Not many years ago Berlioz was regarded more as a genius at orchestration than as a great composer. More and more, however, musicians and music critics are recognizing his great gifts as a composer.

Of the many works that Berlioz wrote, those most often performed today are probably three of his choral compositions, *Romeo and Juliet, The Damnation of Faust,* and *The Childhood of Christ*; two orchestral works, the *Fantastic Symphony* and *Harold in Italy.* In recent years his opera *Les Troyens* (The Trojans) has been presented in Europe.

BERNSTEIN, Leonard. American composer and conductor, born in Lawrence, Massachusetts, on August 25, 1918.

Bernstein, one of the most talented musicians America has produced, graduated from Harvard University in 1939, then went on to the Curtis Institute of Music for further study. Some of the eminent teachers he studied with were Walter Piston, Fritz Reiner, and Randall Thompson. He later became the favorite pupil of Koussevitzky, taking over many conducting assignments at the Berkshire Music Center in Tanglewood. He was just twenty-five years old when he was appointed assistant conductor of the New York Philharmonic Orchestra, and shortly after that time he made musical history when he took over a conducting assignment from the guest conductor who had become ill, Bruno Walter. Without a rehearsal he gave a remarkable performance that was reported in newspapers all over the country. In 1958 he was appointed director of the New York Philharmonic —the youngest and the first American-born conductor ever to hold that post.

As a composer, Bernstein is no less gifted. Among his more serious works are two symphonies, a work for piano and orchestra called *The Age of Anxiety*, a one-act opera written to his own libretto and called *Trouble in Tahiti*, and a Serenade for Violin, Strings, and Percussion. His scores for Broadway shows include *On the Town, Wonderful Town, Candide*, and the "smash hit," *West Side Story*.

BILLINGS, William. American composer, born in Boston on October 7, 1746; died there on September 26, 1800.

Billings is considered today to be the first American composer to write music that was original. By trade he was a tanner of hides, but he was interested in composing and studied the few books about music theory that were available to him. He was especially interested in choral music and wrote many hymns* and anthems.* During the Revolutionary War he wrote a number of patriotic songs.

The first collection of his published songs, *The New England Psalm Singer*, appeared in Boston in 1770. It contained a new kind of song which he called "Fuguing Tunes," written in parts, on the order of the canon.* He later published five more books: *The Singing Master's Assistant, Music in Miniature, The Psalm Singer's Amusement, The Suffolk Harmony*, and *The Continental Harmony*.

BINARY FORM. A term used to describe the form of a piece of music (or a movement* of a longer composition, such as a suite*) that has two parts. It is sometimes called AB form. An example of a piece written in binary form is the familiar *Minuet in G* by Bach. A good deal of dance music of the seventeenth century was built according to this two-part form. Later, the pattern was used in music that was unrelated to dance forms.

BINCHOIS (ban SHWAH), **Gilles.** Burgundian composer, born in Mons (now in southeastern Belgium) about 1400; died in Soignies (near Mons) on September 20, 1460.

Binchois was first a soldier, then, when he was about thirty years old he became a chaplain at the court of Philip, the Duke of Burgundy. He remained at the Burgundian Court for the rest of his life, serving at the same time as canon* on several occasions at neighboring churches. In addition to more than fifty chansons* he wrote many religious works and twenty-two motets.*

BITONALITY. The use of two different keys* at the same time in a piece of music. An example of bitonality would be to play the right hand part of a piece in the key of C and the accompaniment in the key of G. This would sound extremely dissonant and unpleasant. However, some modern composers have used bitonality with a good deal of success in achieving certain effects, but they have been careful to use keys that are closely enough related to have certain chords in common.

BIZET (bee ZEH), **Georges.** French composer born in a suburb of Paris on October 25, 1838; died in Bougival on June 3, 1875.

Bizet was born into a musical family. His father was a teacher of singing and his mother a talented pianist. At the age of four he began to study music with his mother, and by the time he was nine he showed such talent that his father tried to enter him in the Paris Conservatory of Music. The classes were full and he had to wait almost a year, but in the meantime he was sent to a famous musician of the day, Marmontel, for instruction. He was just ten years old when he was admitted to the Conservatory as a regular student.

He did well in his studies and after only six months won the first of a series of prizes that led to the coveted *Prix de Rome** when he was not quite twenty years old.

As the winner of the *Prix de Rome,* Bizet's expenses were paid for three years of study and composing in Italy. He continued to show great promise, but on his return to Paris in 1860 he thought seriously of taking a position as a teacher at the Conservatory and of becoming a concert pianist in order to make a living. Instead, he decided to stick to composing, even though it meant doing "odd jobs" such as copying music, playing for opera rehearsals, and making orchestral arrangements of other people's music. Although he did some teaching, the remainder of his life was devoted to composition. He wrote many works—songs, piano pieces, operas, stage works of various kinds, works for orchestra and for chorus. He is best known in this country for his opera *Carmen.* Another well-known work of Bizet's is the suite of pieces for orchestra called *L'Arlesienne* (The

Girl from Arles), written originally to accompany a play of that name by Daudet.

BLITZSTEIN, Marc. American pianist and composer, born in Philadelphia on March 2, 1905; died in Fort Defiance, Martinique, on January 23, 1964.

Blitzstein showed great musical promise as a child and played his first public concert when he was just five years old. He began composing when he was seven, and appeared as soloist with the Philadelphia Orchestra when he was fifteen. Later he went to Europe, where he studied with Nadia Boulanger* in Paris and with Arnold Schoenberg* in Berlin.

Returning to the United States, he devoted his entire time to composing. During the second world war he served in the U.S. Air Force in England, but even then he composed a symphonic poem, *Freedom Morning,* and a symphony, dedicated to the 8th Army and Air Force, called *The Airborne.*

Although his works include songs, chamber music, choral music, and piano pieces, his most successful writing was for the stage and films. Of his eight operas, *The Cradle Will Rock* and *Regina* were especially well received. He also wrote two ballets, incidental music for several plays, and background music for many motion pictures. In 1954 he did an Americanized version of Kurt Weill's *Threepenny Opera,* a work that has enjoyed enormous success. At the time of his death, he was working on another opera, based on the famous Sacco and Vanzetti case, that had been commissioned by the Metropolitan Opera.

BLOCH, Ernest. Naturalized American composer, born in Geneva, Switzerland on July 24, 1880; died July 15, 1959 in Portland, Oregon.

Bloch began his study of music at an early age, with violin as his major instrument. In 1916 he came to America where he taught composition at the David Mannes School in New York City. After serving as director of the Cleveland Institute of Music and director of the San Francisco Conservatory, he was, in 1940, appointed a professor of music at the University of California.

Bloch's music is highly individual, much of it reflecting the strong emotional intensity of his Jewish heritage. Some of his major works are specifically Jewish: for example, his *Shelomo* (Solomon), a rhapsody for cello and orchestra; *Avodath Hakodesh* (Sacred Service) for baritone, chorus, and orchestra; and his symphony for voices and orchestra, *Israel.* Other works include a rhapsody, *America,* written in honor of his adopted country; an opera, *Macbeth,* based on the play by Shakespeare; *Symphony in C-sharp*; two works for piano and orchestra, *Scherzo Fantasque* and *Concerto Symphonique*; and a piano quintet in which he introduced quarter-tone passages.

BLUES. A style of jazz* based on early Negro folk songs,* particularly work songs. It became popular with its introduction in the song "Memphis Blues" written by W. C. Handy about 1909. Since then it has been used in many popular songs such as "St. Louis Blues," "Limehouse Blues," "Blues in the Night," and so on. Blues melodies have been used also in longer works by contemporary composers, for example, *Rhapsody in Blue* and *An American in Paris* by George Gershwin.*

BOEHM SYSTEM. A key mechanism for the flute,* invented in the early nineteenth century by the German flutist, Theobald Boehm. This system, which provided properly spaced holes with keys, made it possible to play trills and fast passages that had been impossible on flutes provided only with finger holes. The system was soon applied to other wind instruments.

BOLERO (bo LEH roh). A Spanish dance in moderate 3/4 time for one or two dancers, usually performed with castanets* marking the characteristic rhythm: (♩ ♪ or ♩ ♪). A good example is Chopin's *Bolero* for piano, Opus 19. Another is Ravel's *Bolero,* written as a ballet* score, rather than for solo dancers, but usually performed by an orchestra. It is an unusual work in that the melody is played over and over again to an accompaniment that varies very little except in orchestral color and dynamic* level. It begins softly with a few instruments and gradually builds up to a tremendous climax at the very end in which all the instruments of the orchestra are playing fortissimo.*

BOND, Carrie Jacobs. American song-writer, born in Janesville, Wisconsin, on August 11, 1862; died in Hollywood, California, on December 28, 1946.

Although untrained in music, Mrs. Bond had a gift for melody that made her songs very popular. She wrote more than 175 songs, most of which she published herself. Among her best known songs are *The End of A Perfect Day,* which sold several million copies; *I Love You Truly,* a favorite song for weddings; and *Just A-Wearyin' for You.*

BONGO DRUMS. Small Cuban drums, usually played in pairs. They are struck with the fingers rather than with sticks, and are often used in dance bands for playing rhumbas and other Latin-American dances.

BORODIN (bara DYEEN), **Alexander.** Russian composer and scientist, born in St. Petersburg (now Leningrad) on November 12, 1833; died there on February 27, 1887.

Borodin's mother, a beautiful and intelligent woman, saw to it that her son received a good education. By the time he was thirteen he could speak German, French, and English in addition to his native language, and he had become quite a good musician. He studied flute and piano, and at the age of nine he composed a polka for piano which he called "Helene" in honor of a little girl friend. He learned to play the cello in order to participate in chamber music with a group of his friends, and he proceeded to compose several trios and sonatas for the group to play.

Borodin's interest was about equally divided between science and music, and in 1850 he entered the Medico-Surgical Academy where he studied botany, zoology, anatomy, and chemistry. Six years later he graduated with honors and was appointed to a position in the Academy. This left him little time for music, but he spent as much time as possible playing and composing.

His meeting with the great composer Balakirev* stimulated him to take up music seriously, and he gradually made a name for himself in European music circles. He was a master of colorful orchestration, and most of his music has a distinct oriental flavor.

Borodin is probably best known for his opera *Prince Igor,* which he had not completed when he died of a heart attack in 1887. It was finished by Rimsky-Korsakoff* and Glazounov* together. The popular *Polovtsian Dances* are from that opera. Another well-known work is his symphonic poem,* *On the Steppes of Central Asia.* Other works include three symphonies, the third uncompleted; chamber music; a suite and several other pieces for piano; and fourteen songs, most of them to his own words.

BOULANGER (BOO lahn zhay), **Nadia.** Famous French teacher, born in Paris on September 16, 1887.

Although not a composer herself, Nadia Boulanger has taught a great many musicians who became famous composers. Among leading American composers who studied with her are Roy Harris,* Walter Piston,* and Aaron Copland.* She studied composition with Fauré at the Paris Conservatory, and later became a lecturer there. She taught harmony* at the American Conservatory at Fontainebleau, and followed Paul Dukas* as a teacher of composition at the École Normale de Musique in Paris. In the United States she has given special courses at Wellesley and Radcliffe Colleges and at the Juilliard School of Music.

BOULEZ (boo LEZ), **Pierre.** French composer, born in Montbrison on March 26, 1925.

Boulez graduated from the Paris Conservatory when he was twenty years old, and three years later became a theater conductor in Paris. As a composer, he belongs to the extremely advanced group. His works are derived from the twelve-tone technique* of composition, but they exhibit highly individual rhythmic and dynamic effects based on mathematical calculations. He has written compositions for voices and orchestra, piano and orchestra, a *Polyphony* for seventeen instruments, a flute sonata, a work for two pianos, piano sonatas, and a string quartet.

BOURÉE (boor RAY). A French word meaning "a bundle of firewood." In music, the Bourée is a dance in quick double time that begins on the last quarter of the measure. It may have originated in France, possibly as an old woodcutters dance, but it was adopted in Germany and occurs often in the suites* of the eighteenth century, especially those of Bach. It consists of two parts, each of which is repeated. An example is the Bourée from Bach's Suite No. 3 in D Major.

BOW. A slender wooden stick with horsehairs stretched the length of it. The bow is used for playing the violin,* viola,* cello,* and double bass.* Originally, bows were curved, somewhat like the bows used in archery, hence the name. The modern bow tapers toward the end away from the hand and is equipped with an adjustable nut that can be turned to tighten the hair. The bows used for the viola, cello, and double bass are similar to the violin bow, but the viola bow is slightly heavier, the cello bow is shorter as well as heavier, and the double-bass bow is the shortest and heaviest of all.

BOWING. The technique of playing a stringed instrument with a bow. Different ways of using the bow are indicated on the music by certain signs and terms. Some of the most important are these:

  ⊓ *down-bow,* with the arm moving from left to right.
  V *up bow,* with the arm moving from right to left.
  ⌒*slur,* two or more consecutive notes played without changing the direction of the bow.
  – *détaché,* a note played separately from its neighboring notes, but without changing the direction of the bow.
  • *staccato,* played with short, quick strokes of the bow.
a punta d'arco, playing with the point of the bow.
am Frosch, playing with the end of the bow nearest the hand.
am Steg or *sul ponticello,* playing near the bridge.
col legno, bouncing the stick on the strings instead of playing with the hairs of the bow.
legato, playing with smooth up and down strokes of the bow.
martelé or *martellato,* playing with heavy up and down "hammered" strokes with the point of the bow.
ricochet, making the bow bounce several times on a down stroke.
saltando, sautillé, or *saltato,* bouncing the bow lightly on the strings.
spiccato or *piqué,* a light staccato played with the middle of the bow.
sul tasto, playing near the fingerboard.
tremolo, playing with short, rapid up and down strokes of the bow.

BRACE. (1) A curved line used to connect the two manual staffs in music for a keyboard instrument. (2) A straight bracket used to connect two or more staffs for instrumental and vocal ensemble* music to show which staffs are to be read simultaneously.

BRAHMS, Johannes. One of the great composers of the nineteenth century. He was born in Hamburg, Germany, on May 7, 1833; died in Vienna, Austria, on April 3, 1897.

At a very early age young Johannes showed a strong liking for music. His father, a double-bass player in the city theater orchestra, hoped that he would become an orchestra player. He gave his son lessons on the violin and cello, but Johannes liked the piano much better. He practiced hard and made excellent progress. By the time he was thirteen he had begun to earn a little money by composing light pieces under an assumed name, and for several years he played the piano at night in taverns and dance halls for the entertainment of sailors. During the day he continued to study and compose music, and by the time he was twenty years old he had developed remarkably, both as a composer and as a pianist.

About this time he met a talented Hungarian violinist, Remenyi, with whom he set out on a concert tour. On the tour he met the famous violinist, Joseph Joachim,* and through him he met Robert Schumann,* at that time one of the most influential composers in Europe, and his wife Clara, a famous concert pianist. The Schumanns encouraged young Brahms and helped to promote his compositions. Brahms became an intimate friend of the Schumann family, and when Schumann suffered a mental breakdown and died in a home for the insane, Brahms did everything possible to comfort Clara and the children.

Brahms spent a number of years conducting, playing, and composing, all the time becoming better known in the musical circles of Europe. In 1871 he accepted a position as director of the *Gesellschaft der Musikfreunde* (Society of the Friends of Music) in Vienna. He kept the job for just three years, feeling that it left him too little time for composing. He remained in Vienna, however, for the rest of his life.

Brahms was a hard worker and one of his own severest critics. He destroyed everything he had written before he was nineteen years old because he felt the music was not worth publishing. Even so, he left an enormous number of works in practically every field of composition except opera, which he never attempted. Among his masterpieces are two great choral works: *A German Requiem* and the *Alto Rhapsody*; for orchestra: the *Academic Festival Overture, Tragic Overture, Variations on a Theme of Haydn,* and four symphonies; two piano concertos; a concerto for violin and cello; sextets, quintets, quartets, trios, and sonatas for chamber groups; many piano solos and duets; eleven choral preludes for organ; and nearly two hundred songs.

BRASS. The name given the group of musical instruments that are made of brass or other metals and that are played by being blown into directly through a cup-shaped or funnel-shaped mouthpiece. Normally, the brass instruments of the orchestra* are horns,* trumpets,* tenor and bass trombones,* the tuba,* and sometimes the cornet.* Other brass instruments, found more often in bands, are the Flügelhorn,* B-flat bass,* baritone,* euphonium,* and mellophone.*

BRASS BAND. A band made up largely of brass* instruments and percussion* instruments. Ordinarily a brass band consists of alto saxhorns,* B-flat basses,* baritones,* cornets,* trombones,* drums,* and cymbals.* Some brass bands use trumpets,* bugles,* and timpani.*

BRIDGE. (1) The thin piece of wood that stands on the belly* of stringed instruments such as the violin,* cello,* and guitar,* and which supports the strings. The bridge carries the vibrations of the strings to the body of the instrument. In stringed instruments of the violin family the bridge is held in place by the strings. On the Spanish guitar and some other plucked instruments the bridge is glued to the belly. The fretwork, or carving, on bridges of violins, violas, and cellos helps to make the bridge lighter and more flexible, which in turn improves the quality of the tone. (2) The term *bridge* is used also to describe a connecting passage, usually involving a change in key, between the more important sections of a composition, as in a sonata* movement.*

BRIO (BREE oh). An Italian word meaning "spirit" or "fire." It is usually used in the phrase *con brio,* which means that a passage so marked should be played with dash and spirit.

BRITTEN, Edward Benjamin. Outstanding British composer and pianist, born in Lowestoft, England, on November 22, 1913.

Britten became interested in composing at a very early age and wrote a string quartet when he was only nine. He was a gifted pianist also, and is well known in Europe and America as the accompanist for Peter Pears, one of England's leading tenors, for whom he has written many songs.

To American school children, Britten is a familiar composer because of two of his works, *The Young Persons Guide to the Orchestra* and *Let's Make an Opera.* He has been most successful in writing music for voices, and is one of the best known contemporary writers of opera. His highly dramatic *Peter Grimes* has been presented at opera houses all over the world. Other operas of his that have enjoyed great success are *Albert Herring, Billy Budd,* and *A Midsummer Night's Dream.* His other works include music for motion pictures, radio, and numerous stage productions; music for choral groups, one of which, called *Friday Afternoons,* is scored for children's voices and piano; another, his large work for chorus and orchestra, *The War Requiem*; several compositions for orchestra; chamber music; and a great many songs and arrangements of folk songs.

BROKEN CHORD. A chord* in which the notes are played one after the other instead of all at one time. This example shows the C-major chord written to be played as a broken chord:

BRUCH (brookh), **Max.** German composer, born in Cologne on January 6, 1838; died in Friedenau on October 2, 1920.

Like many other noted composers, Bruch showed a decided talent for music at an early age. His mother was a well-known singer and watched over her son's early musical training carefully. He studied with some of Europe's finest teachers, and became a noted teacher himself. His first opera was produced when he was only twenty years old. Although Bruch wrote almost a hundred choral works, three symphonies, and a number of songs, he is best known in America for two compositions—his Concerto No. 1 in G minor for violin and orchestra, and his setting of the Hebrew melody *Kol Nidrei* for cello and orchestra.

BRUCKNER (BROOKH nair), **Anton.** Austrian composer and organist, born in Ansfelden on September 4, 1824; died in Vienna on October 11, 1896.

Unlike many other gifted composers, Bruckner matured musically rather late in life. He did compose some organ preludes while he was still a school-boy, but his first great works did not appear until he was in his forties. His early training was at the great monastery of the Augustinian monks at St. Florian. Later he spent several years as a village music teacher in several small Austrian towns. In 1856 he went to Linz, where he became court organist, and where he composed a number of large works—two Masses and three symphonies in addition to a good many smaller choral works. At the age of forty-four he settled in Vienna, became a professor at the Conservatory, and continued to compose.

Bruckner wrote nine symphonies (the ninth was not complete when he died), several great Masses, and an enormous number of smaller choral works for the Roman Catholic church, of which he was a devout member.

BUFFO (BOOF foh). An Italian word meaning "comic." An *opera buffa* is a comic opera. A *buffo* singer is one who specializes in comic roles, usually a bass.

BUGLE. The simplest of the brass instruments, usually made of copper or brass, with a conical tube and a cup-shaped mouthpiece. It has no valves, so the tones it can produce are limited to the overtone series. Although the bugle is sometimes used in brass bands, its chief use is for military calls and signals.

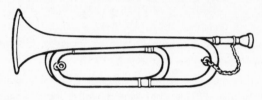

BULL, John. English composer and organist, probably born in 1562 (the exact place and date are not known); died in Antwerp, Belgium, on March 13, 1628.

Bull was educated in Queen Elizabeth I's Chapel and at Oxford University, where he earned the degrees of Bachelor of Music and Doctor of Music. In 1596 Queen Elizabeth recommended him for the first music professorship at Gresham College. In those days college professors were required to give their lectures in Latin. Bull's skill as a composer and organist was so great that an exception was made in his case, and he was allowed to lecture in English. He held the Gresham College post until his marriage, which disqualified him for the position. Shortly afterward he moved to Belgium, and in 1617 he became organist of the Cathedral of Notre Dame. Bull's fame rests largely on the contribution he made to the development of contrapuntal* keyboard music. His works, which number around two hundred, consist mainly of church music, madrigals,* and pieces for keyboard instruments.

BURLA (BOOR lah). An Italian word meaning "joke." In music, a *burla* is a short, lively, and frequently humorous, piece. The word *burlesque* is derived from the word *burla*. An example of a *burla* in classical music is Mozart's *Ein musikalischer Spass* (A Musical Joke) for two horns and strings, K. 522.

BUSONI (boo ZOH nee), **Ferruccio Benvenuto.** An Italian pianist and composer, born near Florence on April 1, 1866; died in Berlin, Germany, on July 27, 1924.

Busoni's father was a clarinet player, and his mother was a singer. As a child he studied with his parents, and with practically no outside instruction became such a piano virtuoso* that he was considered a prodigy. He appeared as a pianist in Vienna at the age of nine, and he made a successful concert tour of Italy while still in his teens. His early compositions, however, were not of much value.

Busoni became famous as a pianist and teacher, and taught in such widely scattered places as Helsingfors, Moscow, Boston, Vienna, and Berlin. His arrangements for piano of J. S. Bach's* keyboard works are well known to piano students everywhere. As a composer in his own right, he is best known today for his three operas, *Arlecchino, Turandot,* and *Doctor Faust.* *Dr. Faust* was not completed at the time of his death, but was finished later by one of his students.

BUXTEHUDE, Dietrich. Danish composer and organist, born in Helsingborg in 1637 (the exact date is not known); died in Lübeck, Germany, on May 9, 1707.

Buxtehude probably studied organ with his father, who was for many years organist in a Helsingborg church. Not much is known about his activities as a young man, but he was talented enough to obtain one of the most lucrative positions in northern Europe when he was thirty-one years old—that of organist at the Marienkirche in Lübeck. He soon became famous as an organist, musical director, and composer; so much so that J. S. Bach,* at that time a very young man, travelled some two hundred miles on foot to hear his concerts. In addition to his many church cantatas and organ works, he wrote sonatas for instrumental groups and a number of pieces for harpsichord.*

BYRD, William. English composer and organist, born about 1543 (the exact date is not known) probably in Lincoln; died on July 4, 1623, probably in Stondon (Essex).

When he was about twenty years old, Byrd became organist at Lincoln Cathedral, and later was appointed organist of the Chapel Royal. Queen Elizabeth granted to Byrd and Tallis,* the other organist of the Chapel Royal, the sole right to publish music in England. Although Byrd was a

Roman Catholic he wrote music for the Anglican church as well as his own. In addition, he wrote an enormous number of madrigals,* rounds,* and solo songs; many pieces for the virginal* and other instruments of the day. He is considered one of the masters of polyphonic music of the sixteenth century and, in fact, one of the greatest composers the world has known.

C

C. The letter C has many uses in music. (1) C is the name given to one pitch in each octave throughout the musical range. (2) C is the name given to a scale* or key* whose first note is C. A composition may be written in the key of C major, C minor, C-sharp major, or C-sharp minor. (See also *Key Signatures.*) (3) On the piano keyboard C is the white note that lies just below each group of two black notes. The C closest to the middle of the piano keyboard, called Middle C, serves as a "point of reference" in locating notes above and below it on the staff and on the keyboard. (4) The C clef is used in two different positions to indicate Middle C: The alto clef shows that Middle C is on the third line. It is used for the viola and other instruments of the same range. The tenor clef shows that Middle C is on the fourth line. It is used for the tenor trombone and the upper register of the bassoon, cello, and double bass. (See also *Clef.*)

CACCINI (cah TCHEE nee), **Giulio.** Italian singer and composer, born in Rome about 1545; died in Florence in December, 1618. (The exact dates of his birth and death are not known.)

Not much is known about the boyhood of Caccini, only that he was educated as a singer and lute* player. In 1578 he joined the court of the Duke of Tuscany in Florence, and about the same time became associated with a famous group of Florentines who were interested in recreating the musical dramas of ancient Greece. Caccini wrote and published a number of songs of a type that was new for his time: songs for solo voice with accompaniment by a single instrument (usually the lute). *Amaryllis,* often sung today, is one of those songs.

CADENCE. The conclusion of a phrase, a section, or a piece which gives a feeling of rest or repose. Harmonically there are two types of perfect cadence—the *perfect authentic* cadence and the *perfect plagal* cadence. With the perfect authentic cadence, the last two intervals* or chords must be the dominant (which is always built on the fifth degree of the scale) and the tonic (always built on the tonic or first degree of the scale). Furthermore, the top part (soprano voice) of the final triad or chord and the bottom part (bass voice) must be the tonic note. With the perfect plagal cadence, the last two triads or chords must be the sub-dominant (always built on the fourth degree of the scale) and the tonic, and the topmost and bottom parts must also be the tonic. When the top note or bottom note of the final triad or chord of either an authentic or plagal cadence is not the tonic, then the cadence is *imperfect*.

Two other types of cadence that occur frequently are the *half cadence* and the *deceptive cadence*. A half cadence occurs when a phrase ends on the dominant triad or chord instead of the tonic. A deceptive cadence occurs when the chord progression at the end of a phrase is from the dominant to the submediant (the triad or chord built on the sixth degree of the scale), the mediant (built on the third degree of the scale), or some other chord (except the tonic).

CADENZA. A passage near the end of a vocal or instrumental solo or a section of a composition that gives the performer a chance to display his technical ability. It occurs most often in the concerto, often near the end of the first movement or before the recapitulation.* Originally, cadenzas were improvised by the performer. In most music played today the cadenza is written out, either by the composer or (in the case of early music) by a music editor.

CADMAN, Charles Wakefield. American composer and organist, born in Johnstown, Pennsylvania, on December 24, 1881; died in Los Angeles, California, on December 30, 1946.

As a boy, Cadman studied music in Pittsburgh and taught himself to play the organ. By the time he was twenty-one he had already become known as a fine organist. He also conducted a famous male chorus, and for some time was the music critic on the *Pittsburgh Dispatch*. He became interested in Indian music and devoted himself to study of the music of various tribes. He made records of the music and toured widely in the United States and Europe lecturing on Indian customs and music. Almost all of his compositions are based on Indian themes.

Cadman wrote more than three hundred songs, the most famous of which are *The Land of the Sky Blue Water* and *At Dawning*. One of his operas, *Shanewis* (The Robin Woman) was performed in two successive years by the Metropolitan Opera Company in New York; another, *A Witch of Salem*, was produced in Chicago. His other works include piano pieces, a violin sonata, chamber music, and a number of choral and orchestral compositions.

CAGE, John. American composer, born in Los Angeles, California, on September 5, 1912.

Cage began his study of piano when he was four years old, first with a local teacher, next with his aunt, and then with Fanny Dillon. After graduation from high school he attended Pomona College for two years, then went to France. In Paris he studied briefly at the Conservatory, then began studying and experimenting on his own with ultra-modern musical ideas. After a year and a half he returned to the United States and continued his study of composition with Henry Cowell,* and later with Schoenberg* and Varèse.* Cage's compositions consist mainly of noises and silences, and bear little relationship to traditional concepts of music. One of his most startling innovations was the "prepared piano," achieved by inserting such objects as large wooden bolts, pieces of glass, rubber, and other materials between the strings of a grand piano, thus transforming the piano into a kind of percussion* instrument. On a number of occasions he has organized his own orchestra for the express purpose of performing his works. These orchestras have been largely made up of performers whose instruments consisted of such unorthodox materials as hub caps, brake bands, pie tins, and whatever could be found to produce the variety of sounds that Cage needed for his compositions. At the opposite extreme is his three movement work, *4 Minutes and 33 Seconds* for piano, during which the pianist sits at the piano without playing, the idea being that the audience becomes more acutely aware of the ordinary noises that constantly assail his ears. Although Cage's works have been performed by such outstanding organizations as the New York Philharmonic Orchestra, his audiences have been sharply divided between admirers and severe critics.

CAMPANELLA (cahm pah NELL la). An Italian word meaning "little bell." It is sometimes used as the title of a composition in which the sounds of bells are imitated. A well-known example is Liszt's *La Campanella,* a brilliant piece for piano, based on the finale (*Rondo alla campanella*) of Paganini's Violin Concerto in B minor. (See also *Glockenspiel.*)

CANCAN. A French word meaning "scandal." The cancan dance is based on the quadrille* and is performed in fast 2/4 time. Its chief characteristic is high kicks. The traditional cancan costume consists of a headpiece made of plumes, a low-necked dress with a tight bodice and full, ruffled skirt. Long stockings, held up by garters, and brightly colored high-heeled shoes are usually worn with it. The cancan originated in Paris, France, where it became popular in music halls during the latter part of the eighteenth century. Offenbach* used the cancan in his operetta *Orpheus in the Underworld.*

CANON. A piece, or portion of a piece, in which one part is imitated by one or more other parts. Each part enters in such a way that it overlaps the one that precedes it. The old round* *Three Blind Mice* is an example of one type of canon. It can be repeated over and over until the singers drop out part by part, leaving one part to be finished alone. This type is called a "perpetual" canon. Most canons, however, end with a short coda,* a section in which all the parts come together.

CANTABILE (cahn TAH bee lay). An Italian word meaning "singable." It indicates that the music should be played in a smooth, flowing style, as though the notes were being sung.

CANTATA (cahn TAH tah). A work for singers and instruments which may contain arias* for soloists, duets, recitatives* (speech-like sections), and instrumental interludes. The text, or story, of the cantata may be either religious or secular (non-religious). The religious cantata is similar to the oratorio,* but is shorter and less elaborate. The secular cantata is usually narrative like opera, but it is performed without scenery, costumes, or action. Bach's *Christ Lay in Death's Bonds* is an example of a religious cantata; his *Coffee Cantata,* a satire, is an example of a secular cantata. Bach wrote some two hundred sacred and about twenty-five secular cantatas. Originally, the cantata was a secular composition for voice, developed in Italy in the seventeenth century. Many composers have written cantatas, among them Mendelssohn,* Liszt,* Brahms,* Berlioz,* and Samuel Barber.*

CANTOR. In the German Protestant church the director of music is called the *Cantor.* Bach, for example, was for many years Cantor of St. Thomas's Lutheran Church in Leipzig. In Jewish synagogues and in some Roman Catholic churches the chief male singer is called Cantor.

CANZONA (kahnt ZOH nah). An Italian word meaning "song." (1) A lyrical type of song, especially of the kind found in Italian opera. (2) A kind of instrumental music popular in the sixteenth and seventeenth centuries. Rather light and lively in character, canzonas sometimes were written for keyboard instruments, as Bach's* organ canzonas, or for instrumental ensembles.

CAPRICCIO (cah PREE choh). An Italian word meaning "caprice" or "whim." It is generally applied to a light, gay piece in which the composer writes according to his own fancy rather than any particular form. Bach,* Mendelssohn,* Brahms,* and many other composers have written pieces they called *Capriccio.*

CARILLON. A set of bells usually hung high in a tower. The bells are tuned to the chromatic* scale, so it is possible to play melodies on them. Each bell's clapper is set in motion when the player strikes a key or pedal that is connected with the bell. Two famous carillons in the United States are the carillon in the Bok Singing Tower in Lake Wales, Florida, and the carillon in the tower of Riverside Church in New York City. The Riverside carillon has seventy-four bells, making it the largest in the world.

In recent years an electro-mechanical carillon has been invented. It consists of tiny bars which are struck by hammers set in motion by a keyboard mechanism. The sound is amplified electronically so the tones produced are as loud as those of the largest carillons with cast bells.

CARISSIMI, Giacomo. Italian composer, born in Marino in 1605 (exact date is not known); died in Rome on January 12, 1674.

Almost nothing is known about Carissimi's boyhood, but it is certain that he must have studied music and exhibited great talent, for he was appointed *maestro di cappella* (Chapel Master) at Assisi when he was only twenty years old and four years later was offered the same position at the Church of Saint Apollinaris in Rome. There he remained until his death, devoting his life to the music of the church, to teaching, and to composition. As a composer, he is considered one of the "immortals." He did a great deal in the development of the solo cantata and the oratorio with recitative. Young vocal students today often study his works, especially such songs as *No, No, Non Si Speri* and *Vittoria, Mio Core,* both of which are included in modern collections of old Italian songs.

CAROL. A song of joyous character sung today mainly for religious holidays such as Christmas and Easter. Old carols, such as "Good King Wenceslas," are associated mainly with sixteenth-century England, but they were popular all over Europe during the Middle Ages. Although some carols originated as folk songs or dances, others, such as "Silent Night," were composed for special occasions.

CARPENTER, John Alden. American composer, born in Chicago on February 28, 1876; died there on April 26, 1951.

Carpenter's first music teacher was his mother. He continued to study with her until he was twelve, then studied with a pupil of Liszt,* Amy Fay. He entered Harvard College when he was seventeen, and during his four years there he continued to study music. Although he was intensely interested in music, he entered his father's business—a shipping supply firm—after graduating from Harvard, and remained in business until his retirement in 1936. During that time, however, he continued to compose.

Carpenter wrote three ballets. The most successful, *Krazy Kat,* was a comic ballet based on the cartoon series of the same name. He also wrote two choral works, a string quartet, a piano quintet, and a number of songs. Of the seven orchestral works he composed, *Adventures in a Perambulator* is probably the best known.

CARTER, Elliott. American composer and music critic, born in New York City on December 11, 1908.

Carter studied music at Harvard University with Walter Piston,* then went to Paris for further study with Nadia Boulanger.* After returning to the United States he devoted most of his time to composing music and writing music criticisms for various newspapers and magazines. Twice he was awarded a Guggenheim fellowship, first in 1945 and again in 1950, and in 1960 he received the Pulitzer Prize for his String Quartet No. 2. Other compositions that have brought him acclaim are his ballets, *Pocohantas* and *The Minotaur*; his Symphony No. 1; Sonata for Cello and Piano; *Eight Etudes and a Fantasy* for woodwind quartet; Variations for Orchestra; and Double Concerto for Harpsichord, Piano, and Orchestra.

CASTANETS. A percussion instrument made of two hollowed-out pieces of hard wood held together by a cord. The player holds the castanets with the cord over the thumb and first finger and strikes them together with the other fingers. Castanets originated in Spain and are used mainly to accent the rhythm of Spanish music. Dancers often hold a pair of castanets in each hand and vary the rhythm and tempo of the "clicks" according to

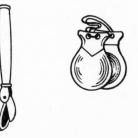

the particular dance. Flamenco* dancers are particularly skillful with castanets.

The castanets used in the orchestra are usually attached to a stick. The player shakes the stick to make the castanets click together.

CATCH. A round* for three or more voices, sung without accompaniment. During the seventeenth and eighteenth centuries, catch singing became so popular in England that a catch club for noblemen and high-ranking musicians was organized in 1761 to promote the composing and performing of catches, as well as glees* and canons.* Some of the catches were so elaborate that it took a good deal of study to be able to sing them.

CELESTA. A keyboard instrument with hammers that strike steel bars. Its range is from Middle C upward for four octaves, and its tone is pure and bell-like. The celesta was invented in 1886 and used for the first time a few years later by Tchaikovsky* in the "Dance of the Sugar Plum Fairy" from his ballet, *The Nutcracker*. It has since been used by a number of

composers in works for orchestra, but it is seldom heard as a solo instrument.

CELLO (CHEL loh). An abbreviation of *violoncello,* a stringed instrument of the violin family. The cello, which is shaped much like the violin, is twice as large. It has a peg on the lower end that rests on the floor, and the player plays from a sitting position. The four strings are tuned to the same notes as the viola,* but an octave* lower:

The cello is one of the most important instruments of the orchestra. Furthermore, its velvety tone and expressive qualities have made it a favorite among solo instruments, and many compositions have been written for it by some of the world's greatest composers. (See also *Violin Family.*)

CHABRIER (shah bree AY), **Alexis.** French composer, born in Ambert on January 18, 1841; died in Paris on September 13, 1894.

As a child, Chabrier was a gifted pianist, and although he studied music and began to compose when he was only ten years old, his father did not like the idea of his son's devoting his life to music. He studied law, and after graduation spent eighteen years in the French Ministry of the Interior. During that period he spent his spare time with his artist and musician friends and did considerable composing. He resigned his job as a lawyer when he was thirty-nine, and within a very few years had made a reputation as a composer.

Chabrier wrote five operas, two large choral works, a great many piano solos and duets. But he is best known today for his songs and for his colorful rhapsody for orchestra, *España.*

CHACONNE (sha KOHN). Originally, the chaconne was a rather wild Spanish dance in 3/4 time. It is better known now as a piece in slow triple time in which a short theme is repeated over and over again. The theme is either a series of chord progressions or a melody, in which case it is usually in the bass. (See also *Passacaglia.*) Many composers have used the chaconne in longer works. Bach used it as the final movement of his Partita No. 2 in D minor for violin; Beethoven's C minor Variations are in the form of a chaconne; Brahms wrote the last movement of his Symphony No. 4 as a chaconne.

CHADWICK, George. American composer and music teacher, born in Lowell, Massachusetts, on November 13, 1854; died in Boston on April 4, 1931.

Chadwick began his study of piano with his older brother, but he soon showed such talent that he was sent to Boston to study organ under Eugene Thayer. When he was twenty-three he left his position as director of music at Olivet College in Michigan and went to Europe for three years of study. He then settled in Boston, where he remained for the rest of his life, devoting his time to composition and to his job as director of the New England Conservatory of Music.

Chadwick was one of America's most skillful composers. His works, which include operas, chamber music, songs, piano pieces, choral compositions, and orchestral works, have been performed widely.

CHAMBER MUSIC. Music written to be played in a room or small hall rather than in an auditorium. Chamber music may be said to differ from orchestral music in that a single instrument plays each part, and each instrument is as important as any other in the performance of the music. Furthermore, chamber music is almost always played without a conductor.

Some of the more usual types of chamber music are the trio (for three players), the quartet (for four players), the quintet (for five players), the sextet (for six players), the septet (for seven players), and the octet (for eight players). By far the most popular chamber music combination has been the string quartet, composed of first and second violins, viola, and cello. Other popular combinations are the trio, made up of piano, violin, and cello; and the quintet, which frequently is the same as the string quartet with piano added.

Although much chamber music was written earlier, Haydn* and Mozart* were the first two composers to establish the true chamber music style. Since then, most noted composers have written chamber music. Many people consider chamber music to be the most refined and highest form of instrumental music.

CHAMINADE (shah mee NAHD), **Cécile.** French pianist and composer, born in Paris on August 8, 1857; died in Monte Carlo on April 18, 1944.

Chaminade began writing music when she was only eight years old. She studied piano also, and by the time she was eighteen had begun to give public concerts, often playing her own music. For the most part she wrote rather light and agreeable "parlor music," although she did attempt some works for orchestra, a ballet, and a comic opera. She is best known for her songs and piano pieces, including the well-known *Valse-Caprice, Arabesque, Impromptu,* and *Scarf Dance.*

CHANSON (shahn SOHN). A French word meaning "song." It is used as the name of a solo song or a song for a vocal ensemble in the French language. It is also used occasionally to describe an instrumental piece with song-like characteristics. The polyphonic* chanson, popular in the sixteenth century, was written in the imitative style of the period.

CHANT. Vocal music without accompaniment, used in church services. An example is the Gregorian Chant* used in the service of the Roman Catholic church. (See also *Plainsong.*)

CHAVEZ (CHAH vess), **Carlos.** Mexican composer and conductor, born in Mexico City on June 13, 1899.

Chávez is one of Mexico's most noted composers. His father was Mexican, of Spanish descent, and his mother was Indian, and his music reflects something of both backgrounds. He began writing music when he was very young, and by the time he was twenty he had written a complete symphony. In 1928 he was made Director of the National Conservatory of Music in Mexico, and the same year he founded the Mexican Symphony Orchestra. He has been its conductor since then. He has also appeared with some of the major symphony orchestras in the United States as guest conductor.

Chávez's compositions include four symphonies, four ballets, several choral works, chamber music, songs, and piano pieces.

CHERUBINI (keh roo BEE nee), **Maria Luigi Carlo Zenobio Salvatore.** Italian composer, born in Florence on September 14, 1760; died in Paris on March 15, 1842.

Cherubini, the son of a theater musician, began to learn music when he was six years old. By the time he was sixteen he had written three Masses,* an oratorio,* three cantatas,* and numerous other works. While on a visit to London when he was twenty-four, he was appointed composer to the King. Two years later he settled in Paris, where he spent most of his time for the rest of his life.

In all, Cherubini wrote twenty-four operas, twelve of them for performance in Paris. The only one of his operas that is performed today is *Medea,* which has been revived in recent years with a certain amount of success. It is said that Beethoven* admired *Medea* so much that he kept a score of it on his piano. In addition to opera, Cherubini wrote several string quartets, six piano sonatas, and a great deal of church music. As Director of the Paris Conservatory of Music, a post which he accepted in 1821 and held for twenty years, Cherubini influenced greatly the musical life of France and other European countries.

CHIMES. (See *Bells.*)

CHINESE BLOCK. A percussion instrument which consists of a hollow block of wood. When it is struck with a stick it gives a hollow sound that has no clear pitch. In dance bands, several blocks of different sizes are used to give the effect of higher and lower pitches.

CHOIR. (1) A group of singers ordinarily, though not always, made up of sopranos, altos, tenors, and basses. A choir is most often associated with a church. (2) The part of a church where the singers are seated. (3) A particular group of instruments in the orchestra, as the *brass choir.*

CHOPIN (show panh), **Frederic François.** Polish composer (French by adoption) born near Warsaw on March 1, 1810; died in Paris on October 17, 1849.

Chopin, who is generally considered one of the greatest of all composers of music for the piano, was a child prodigy. He was only four when he began to study the piano, and he advanced so rapidly that he was able to play at a concert in Warsaw by the time he was eight. He received a good education at the time he was studying music, something for which he was grateful in later years. His enormous talent for composition also showed itself early. He was just fifteen years old when his Opus 1, *Rondo in C minor,* was published. Even earlier he had written several mazurkas* and polonaises,* most of them published later.

Although Chopin's father was French, his mother was Polish, and some of his most important works reflect his early interest in the folk music of Poland. All his life he remained a Polish national, even though he left his native country when he was twenty and never returned.

As a young man Chopin became firmly established as one of the most important piano virtuosos of his day, but his health was poor and he eventually had to give up public performances. He was so well known and admired, however, that he was able to charge high fees for his lessons and his compositions and so could live comfortably without the need for exhausting concert tours.

Although Chopin was only thirty-nine years old when he died, he had written more than two hundred works, most of them for the piano. They include four *Ballades,* twenty-seven *Études,* fifty-one *Mazurkas,* twelve *Polonaises,* nineteen *Nocturnes,* twenty-five *Preludes,* and seventeen *Waltzes.* He wrote two concertos and several other works for piano and orchestra, as well as several works for chamber groups and seventeen "Polish" songs.

Chopin's harmonies were novel, daring for his time, and very beautiful, and they exerted a tremendous influence on the "Romantic" composers of his day.

CHORALE (cor AHL). A melody to which hymns are sung in church by the congregation. The chorale was introduced into the German Lutheran church in the 16th century by Martin Luther,* who believed that the congregation should take part in the music of the service. Luther himself wrote many chorales, one of the most familiar of which is *Ein' feste Burg ist unser Gott* (A Mighty Fortress is Our God).

CHORALE PRELUDE. A composition usually for organ, that is based upon, and uses as its chief melodic material, a church chorale. The most important organ chorale preludes were written by J. S. Bach.

CHORAL SYMPHONY. A symphony in which a chorus as well as the orchestra is used. The most famous choral symphony is Beethoven's Symphony No. 9 in D minor. Its last movement is a setting of the great poet Schiller's *Ode to Joy,* written for chorus, four solo singers, and orchestra.

CHORD. Three or more different notes sounded at the same time. The different kinds of chords and the way they are related to each other is an important part of the study of harmony.*

A three-note chord consisting of the first, third, and fifth notes built on any degree of a major or minor scale* is called a triad.* The diatonic* triads built on the tonic* in the scales of C major and C minor look like this:

maj.   min.

An *augmented triad** is one whose fifth is raised one-half step; a *diminished triad** is one in which both the third and fifth are lowered one-half step. In the key of C they look like this:

aug.   dim.

In any major key there are seven possible diatonic triads: three major, three minor, and one diminished:

maj.   min.   min.   maj.   maj.   min.   dim.

In any minor key there are thirteen possible diatonic triads: five major, four minor, one augmented, and three diminished:

min. dim. min. maj. aug. min. maj. min. maj. maj. dim. maj. dim.

A *seventh chord** is made up of the first, third, fifth, and seventh notes of a scale; the *ninth chord** is the same as a seventh chord with the ninth added. In the key of C, the seventh and ninth chords look like this:

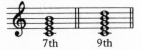

7th   9th

If the key note* of a chord is in the lowest position, the chord is in the *root** *position*. If the third is at the bottom, it is in the *first inversion.** If the fifth is at the bottom, it is in the *second inversion,** and so on:

root   1st   2nd
position   inversion   inversion

CHORUS. (1) A body of singers, usually divided into groups of sopranos, altos, tenors, and basses. A *mixed chorus* is composed of both male and female singers. An *all-male* chorus is usually divided into groups of first and second tenors, baritones, and basses, although an all-male chorus may include all voice ranges by the use of boy sopranos and altos, or boy sopranos and countertenors.* Such combinations were particularly important during the late Middle Ages and the Renaissance, before women were allowed to sing publicly. An *all-female* chorus may be divided into first and second sopranos and first and second altos. (2) The part of a song, sometimes called the *refrain,* that is repeated after each verse. (3) Music written for a choral group. (4) A group of people who dance as well as sing in a revue or in a musical play.

CHROMATIC. A term used to describe raised or lowered tones that do not occur in the diatonic* scale of the key. For example, in the key of F major, the diatonic scale is F-G-A-B♭-C-D-E-F. Notes, such as E♯, C♭, and B♯, which do not appear in the scale, are said to be chromatic, which means "colorful."

CHROMATIC SCALE. A scale made up completely of half steps:

CIMAROSA (chee mah ROH sah), **Domenico.** Italian composer of operas, born in Aversa on December 17, 1749; died in Venice on January 11, 1801.

Cimarosa, the son of a bricklayer, was orphaned at an early age and educated first in a charity school, then at the Conservatorio Santa Maria di Loreta. His first opera was produced in Naples when he was just twenty-three, and he rapidly became one of Italy's most important opera composers. Except for several years spent in Russia as chamber composer to Catherine II and several as *Kapellmeister** at the Austrian Court in Vienna, Cimarosa spent his entire life in Naples and Rome. *Il matrimonio segreto,* still produced, is the most famous of his sixty-five operas. He also wrote cantatas,* Masses,* and other works.

CLARINET. A woodwind instrument with a cylindrical tube made of wood or ebonite (occasionally of metal) and played with a single-reed mouthpiece. The single reed vibrates when wind is forced between it and the edges of the slot leading to the tube, creating the tone. The open end of the tube is bell-shaped. There are several different types of clarinet, but the most commonly used are the B-flat clarinet, the A clarinet, the E-flat clarinet, and the bass clarinet. The B-flat and A clarinets have a range of three octaves and a sixth, which can be extended higher by skillful performers. The bass clarinet has a range an octave lower than the regular B-flat clarinet. Its low tones are particularly rich in color, making the instrument a valuable one in the orchestra. The small E-flat clarinet, which is pitched a fourth above the B-flat clarinet, is used most often in bands. (See also *Basset Horn* and *Woodwinds*.)

CLASSICAL MUSIC. A term people sometimes use when they are referring to "serious" or "art" music, as opposed to "popular" music. To the musician, however, it is more apt to mean music of a certain period from about 1750 to about 1830, including the music of Haydn, Mozart, and early Beethoven. The difference between the Classical composers and those of the Romantic period* which followed is largely one of attitude. The Classical composers were more concerned with logic, form, and structure in their music than the Romantic composers; the Romantics usually concentrated on the expression of emotions, often extending the old forms or creating new ones to fill their needs.

CLAVECIN (CLAH va sahn). The French word for harpsichord.*

CLAVES (CLAH vehs). A percussion instrument consisting of two hardwood sticks which are played by being struck together. They originated in Cuba and are used frequently in dance bands to accent the rhythm of rhumbas and other Latin-American type music.

CLAVICHORD. A keyboard instrument popular in the sixteenth, seventeenth, and eighteenth centuries. It was a forerunner of the piano. In recent years it has been revived for the purpose of playing music that was originally written for it. The clavichord is oblong in shape, about two feet wide and four feet long, and is equipped with stretched strings that run parallel to the front of the instrument. When a key is pressed, a small T-shaped piece of brass attached to it strikes a string, causing it to vibrate.

The tone of the clavichord is soft and delicate, making it an excellent instrument for small rooms or for broadcasting, but not for the concert hall.

Both J. S. Bach* and his son, C. P. E. Bach,* wrote a great deal of music for the clavichord.

CLAVIER (clah VEER). A word taken from the French, meaning "keyboard." It applies to keyboard instruments with strings: the clavichord,* the harpsichord,* and the piano.* Bach used the word in the title of his famous work of forty-eight preludes and fugues, *The Well-Tempered Clavier.** In his time the term also included the organ. (The piano had not yet come into general use.)

CLEF. A sign used to locate the pitches on the lines and spaces of a staff. The clefs used most often in music today are the G (or treble) clef, the F (or bass) clef, and two C clefs.

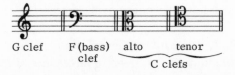

G clef   F (bass) clef   alto   tenor

C clefs

The G clef begins on the second line, indicating that that line is G. It is generally used for the right-hand or upper staff of piano music and for such high-pitched instruments as the violin and the flute. The F clef begins on the fourth line, indicating that that line is F. It is used for the left-hand or lower staff of piano music and for such low-pitched instruments as the cello and the bassoon.

The C clef is usually placed on the staff in one of two ways: When it is centered on the third line it indicates that the third line is Middle C. In that position it is sometimes called the *alto clef* or the *viola clef,* and is used mainly for viola music. When the C clef is centered on the fourth line it indicates that the fourth line is C. In that position it is sometimes called the *tenor clef.* It is used in music for the tenor trombone and the higher range of the bassoon, cello, and double bass.

CLEMENTI (cleh MEN tee), **Muzio.** Italian composer and pianist, born January 23, 1752 in Rome; died March 10, 1832 in Evesham, England.

Clementi, who is well known to generations of piano students for his collection of 100 studies called *Gradus ad Parnassum,* began to study music when he was very young. He made such rapid progress that he won an appointment as an organist when he was only ten years old. In addition to organ, he studied singing and counterpoint, and by the time he was fourteen he had written several choral works, one of which, a Mass, was performed with great success in Rome.

A wealthy Englishman became interested in the talented boy and talked his family into letting him go to England for further study. Clementi studied diligently, perfecting his skill as a pianist and continuing to compose. When he was introduced to musical circles in London at the age of twenty-one he created something of a sensation. From then on he enjoyed a career as one of Europe's outstanding pianists. When he died he was honored by a funeral and burial in the cloisters of Westminster Abbey in London.

In addition to his *Gradus ad Parnassum,* Clementi wrote a large number of sonatas, several symphonies, and other works.

CODA (COH dah). An Italian word meaning "tail." In music it is a section which concludes a piece, or a movement of a larger work. The coda follows the last section of the regular formal structure of the music, and is meant to bring the piece to a satisfactory conclusion. Many pieces have codas, though some may consist simply of a few final chords. Others may be quite long and elaborate. The final ten measures of Chopin's famous Nocturne, Opus 9, No. 2, in E-flat is an example of a brilliant coda.

COLOR. A term used in music to describe the tone-quality of instruments and voices. A tone color may be brilliant, soft, dark, bright, and so on.

COLORATURA (color rah TOO rah). A term applied to vocal works that contain trills,* rapid scales* and arpeggios,* and other types of difficult passages. An example of a coloratura aria* is the "Bell Song" from the opera *Lakmé*. A *coloratura soprano* is a singer with a light, flexible voice who has developed the technique necessary to sing such music.

COMIC OPERA. An opera whose plot is characterized by sentimental and often comic situations, and whose music is lighter and gayer than the music of grand opera. A comic opera usually has a happy ending. Examples of comic opera are *The Mikado* by Gilbert and Sullivan and *The Love for Three Oranges* by Prokofieff.

COMMON CHORD. A term that is used frequently for the major or minor triad* in root position. The common chords of C major and C minor are:

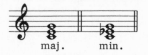

maj.   min.

COMMON TIME. A term sometimes used for 4/4 time (four beats to a measure), often indicated by a large C at the beginning of a piece, as:

COMODO (COH moh doh). An Italian word meaning "comfortable." In music it means that a passage should be performed at an "easy" rate of speed, neither very fast nor very slow.

COMPASS. (Sometimes called *range*.) The lowest to the highest notes that an instrument can play or a voice can sing. For example, the *compass* of the B-flat clarinet is from the D below Middle C upward more than three octaves to the third B-flat above Middle C; the normal *compass* of the tenor voice is from the second B below Middle C to the G above Middle C.

CON (kohn). An Italian word meaning "with." It is used with other words, as *con brio* (with spirit), *con affetto* (with affection), and so on.

CONCERT BAND. As opposed to a marching band,* a band which performs in a concert hall or auditorium, like an orchestra. It is made up of woodwind, brass, and percussion instruments, but usually has more woodwinds than does a marching or military band. It may have string basses, but it does not have violins, violas, or cellos. Its repertoire is likely to contain fewer marches and more arrangements of music written originally for orchestra than that of a marching band.

CONCERTINA. An instrument similar to the accordion,* but without a keyboard. It consists of a bellows with six-sided headboards at each end. Each headboard is equipped with handles and with a set of small studs that are operated with the fingers. The studs on the left are used for playing chords; those on the right for single notes.

CONCERTINO (kon chair TEE noh). An Italian word meaning "small concerto." (1) A composition shorter and less elaborate than a concerto,* often in one movement rather than three, which is usual for a concerto. An example is Weber's* *Concertino for Clarinet,* Op. 26. (2) The group of soloists in a seventeenth or eighteenth century *concerto grosso.**

CONCERTMASTER. The leading (first) violinist of an orchestra. He sits close to the conductor, and he often assists the conductor at orchestra rehearsals. Solo violin passages that occur in the orchestra's concerts are usually played by the concertmaster.

CONCERTO (kon CHAIR toh). An Italian word meaning "concert." A concerto is a work for a solo instrument, or a group of solo instruments, with orchestra. Solo concertos are usually in three movements, the first movement of which contains an elaborate cadenza* that gives the soloist a chance to show his skill in playing brilliant passages. The second movement is usually a slow movement, similar to the second movement of a symphony. The third movement is almost always in rondo* or variation* form, although it may be in sonata form.*

Concertos written for more than one solo instrument are called *double concertos* or *triple concertos.* Brahms wrote a double concerto for violin and cello; Beethoven wrote a triple concerto for violin, cello, and piano.

Mozart established the modern concerto form with his fifty concertos for various instruments. His lead has been followed by many composers, among them Beethoven, Schumann, Brahms, Chopin, Tchaikovsky, Ravel, Prokofiev, and Gershwin. (See also *Concerto Grosso.*)

CONCERTO GROSSO (kon CHAIR toh GROH soh). An Italian term meaning "great concert." The concerto grosso was the forerunner of the modern concerto, but differed from it considerably. Instead of calling for one soloist with orchestra, it was written for a small group of solo instruments (the *concertino*) and a larger group of instruments or full orchestra (called *concerto, tutti,* or *ripieno*). Two Italian composers, Corelli* and Torelli,* are credited with originatihg it in the seventeenth century. It is sometimes called the Baroque* concerto. Some twentieth century composers have written works modeled to some extent on the Baroque concerto grosso, among them Bloch,* Hindemith,* and Bartok.*

CONCERT PITCH. (1) The standard of pitch to which instruments are tuned. By international agreement in 1939, the A above Middle C on the piano was to be tuned to 440 vibrations per second. This standard of pitch has been adopted almost everywhere. Before an orchestra begins to play, the properly tuned A is sounded by the oboe, and all the other instruments are tuned accordingly. In the case of a piano concerto, the orchestra tunes to the A on the piano. (2) The term is used also to indicate the actual pitches of transposing instruments.* For example, the note C on the B-flat clarinet is B-flat "concert pitch."

CONDUCTING. The musical directing of such organizations as orchestra, chorus, band, opera, glee club, and so on. A conductor's chief responsibility is to lead his ensemble in the interpretation of the music. He indicates the correct tempo by motions of the right hand so that all the performers will begin at the same time, keep together properly, and end at one time. Sometimes he may use a baton;* sometimes only his hand.

With his left hand the conductor signals certain instruments or singers to "enter." He also shows by certain movements of the hand, by his facial expression, and even by movements of his whole body, all of the elements of expression that enter into the performance of a work.

A conductor must be thoroughly familiar with every detail of the score, and he must be able to communicate what he knows to the performers. This is a skill that demands an extremely high level of musicianship.

CONSERVATORY. A special school which offers instruction in all aspects of music. It originated in Italy in the sixteenth century as a *conservatorio,* a kind of orphanage where musically talented children were trained especially to serve as musicians in the churches and at the courts of the noble families. Later, the conservatory became more or less what it is today, a school where students pay for instruction or, in the case of exceptional talent, are granted scholarships for the study of music.

CONSOLE. The part of a pipe organ that is used by the player to control the sound—the keyboard, foot pedals, stops,* and so on. Some modern organs are controlled electrically, in which case the console is in a separate cabinet that can be moved from place to place.

CONSONANCE. Music in general is made up of consonant and dissonant sounds. Most people think of consonant sounds as being pleasant and dissonant sounds as being unpleasant or "discords." However, the difference between pleasant and unpleasant sounds depends largely on a person's taste in music as well as the historical time to which he belongs. Some contemporary music is filled with what in earlier times would have been considered extreme dissonances.

Traditionally, certain intervals* have been considered *consonant,* others *dissonant.* The so-called consonant intervals are the major and minor thirds, perfect fourths, perfect fifths, major and minor sixths, and the octave.

CONTINUO (kon TEE noo oh). See *Figured Bass.*

CONTRABASS. Another name for the Double Bass.*

CONTRABASSOON. See *Bassoon.*

CONTRALTO. The lowest female voice. The normal range of the contralto voice is roughly two octaves, from the G below Middle C to the second G above Middle C. Some contraltos are able to sing higher, and some lower. In choral music the contralto voice is referred to by the shorter term *alto.*

COPLAND, Aaron. One of the most influential of contemporary American composers, born in Brooklyn, New York, on November 14, 1900.

Copland was very young when he began to study the piano with his sister as teacher. He continued to study while going to school, and after he graduated from high school he took up counterpoint and harmony with the noted composer Rubin Goldmark.* During this period he wrote a number of compositions. One of the earliest was a scherzo for piano called

The Cat and the Mouse, a humorous work that was published in 1920. He was in his early twenties when he went to France for several years to study with Nadia Boulanger* in Paris. On his return to America he continued to compose and became extremely active in promoting the performance of compositions by American composers.

Copland's compositions include choral works, orchestral works, chamber music, piano solos, and songs. But he is probably known to a wider audience for his ballets, *Billy the Kid, Rodeo,* and *Appalachian Spring,* and for the background music he wrote for such outstanding films as *Of Mice and Men, Our Town, The Red Pony,* and *The Heiress.* Always interested in young people and their musical activities, he wrote an opera especially designed for school production, *The Second Hurricane.*

CORDA. An Italian word meaning "string." In piano music the term *una corda* means to use the soft pedal. On grand pianos the soft pedal causes a damper to close off the sound of two of the three strings that are usually struck for each note, so only one string sounds. This direction is cancelled by the terms *tre corde* (three strings) or *tutte le corde* (all the strings), which indicate that the soft pedal should no longer be used.

CORELLI, Arcangelo. Italian violinist and composer, born in Fusignano on February 17, 1653; died in Rome on January 8, 1713.

Corelli, who became one of the most admired violinists and composers of his day, was educated in Bologna and spent the better part of his life in Rome, mainly in the service of a Cardinal. His compositions were published throughout Europe, and violin students flocked to Rome to study with him. In his many works, mainly for the violin, he contributed greatly to the technical and expressive possibilities of that instrument, and is credited (with Torelli*) for having established the form of the *concerto grosso.**

CORNET. A brass instrument similar to the trumpet. Its mouthpiece is cup-shaped, and the end of the tube bell-shaped. It has three valves* which open into the bend of the brass tubing. The bore of the cornet, said to be "conical," is more sharply tapered than the bore of the trumpet,* and it is shorter. The cornet can be played with greater agility than the trumpet, but its tone lacks the brilliance and dignity of the longer instrument. Modern cornets are usually pitched in B-flat. They have a compass of a little over two octaves.

COUNTERPOINT. Music in which two or more distinct melodies or different parts of the same melody are played or sung at the same time, and which together make "musical sense." Compositions written according to the rules of counterpoint range all the way from rather simple pieces for piano, in which the right hand plays one part (or voice) and the left hand plays the other part, to extremely complicated works with several voices interwoven. A fairly simple example of counterpoint is this opening section from Bach's two-part Invention No. 10 in G-Major.

J. S. Bach,* a great master of counterpoint, wrote a great many works that have stood to this day as classic examples of contrapuntal writing, in addition to his great work *The Art of Fugue.**

COUNTERTENOR. The highest male voice, sometimes called "male alto." The countertenor is characterized by a high range and a brilliant, ringing tone produced by using the head register.*

COUNTRY DANCE. An old English dance that originated in rural areas and later became popular in more sophisticated society. Originally the music was performed on rustic instruments such as the bagpipe* and fiddle.* Later it was written for regular instruments of the orchestra. It was usually danced by groups of men and women facing each other. As the tunes changed, the dancers changed their steps in a variety of movements. The first published collection of country dances was printed in England in 1651.

COUPERIN (COO per ranh), **François**. Famous French organist and composer, born in Paris on November 10, 1668; died there on September 12, 1733.

Couperin was a member of a noted family of musicians who for almost two centuries were organists at the Church of St. Gervais in Paris. François was called "Le Grand" (*The Great*) because of his fame as an organist. He became better known, however, as a composer of harpsichord* music. His works include more than 200 harpsichord pieces and a famous book on harpsichord playing called *L'Art de toucher le Clavecin*.

COURANTE (coo RAHNT). A French word meaning "running." The *courante* is a lively dance with running steps that originated in the sixteenth century and became popular in the seventeenth and early eighteenth centuries. J. S. Bach* and other Baroque composers made it a part of their suites* along with other dance forms, as the *allemande,** the *gigue,** and the *sarabande.**

COWELL, Henry. American composer, born March 11, 1897, in Menlo Park, California.

Cowell began to study the violin when he was five years old, but by the time he was eight he decided that he wanted to become a composer and he switched to the piano. He became noted as a pianist and as a composer who liked to experiment with new ideas. He won a Guggenheim Fellowship in 1931, an honor that made it possible for him to study in Berlin. He later toured Europe on several occasions as a concert pianist.

Cowell invented the term *tone cluster,** which is used to describe a whole group of notes played with the elbow, the fist, or sometimes the forearm. Together with Leon Theremin he invented an instrument called the *rhythmicon,* an electrical device which produces different rhythms at the same time.

Cowell has written an enormous number of works which include thirteen symphonies, an opera, numerous pieces for the piano, and a work called *Hymns and Fuguing Tunes* based on the book by William Billings.*

CREDO (KRAY doh). A Latin word meaning "I believe." It is the third part of the Ordinary of the Mass.*

CRESCENDO (cray SHEN doh). An Italian word meaning "to increase." *Crescendo* means to get gradually louder. The abbreviation for *crescendo* is *cresc.*

CRESTON, Paul. American composer, born in New York City on October 10, 1906.

Creston, whose real name was Joseph Guttoveggio, came from a poor family. His parents realized, however, that he had unusual musical talent and they managed to have him take piano lessons. He later studied with some outstanding teachers, but he could not afford many lessons and was forced to learn a great deal by himself. His situation improved greatly when he won the first of two Guggenheim Fellowships in 1938. In addition to his work as a pianist, organist, and composer, he has done research in music therapy, acoustics, and aesthetics.

Creston's first published work was a set of five dances for piano, written when he was twenty-six years old. Numerous compositions followed, the most important of which are three symphonies, a piano concerto, and a ballet.

CROOK. A short piece of metal tubing that can be inserted between the mouthpiece and the body of a horn* or trumpet* to change the pitch. Before the invention of valves* or pistons,* crooks were necessary to enable the instruments to play in a variety of keys. Crooks were made in different sizes to give the different basic keys to the instrument. For example, a horn with an F crook would sound a major third lower than it would when the A crook was used. Crooks are rarely used today.

CROON. To sing softly, in a sentimental fashion, with a kind of sliding effect. Crooning became popular in the early 1930's when it was introduced by such entertainers as Bing Crosby and Rudy Vallee.

CROTCHET. The English name for the quarter note: (♩). The crotchet rest is the same as a quarter rest: (𝄽).

CRWTH (crooth). An ancient stringed instrument popular in the British Isles during the Middle Ages. It consisted of a rectangular wooden box with four (and later, six) strings stretched over a fingerboard, as on the violin. It was played with a bow.

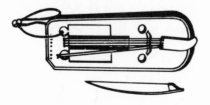

CSÁRDÁS (CHARR dahsh). A Hungarian dance that has two distinctly different parts. The first, called *lassú,* is slow and melancholy; the second part, called *friss,* is very fast and lively. A good example of the *csárdás* is Liszt's *Hungarian Rhapsody* No. 2.

CUI (kyoo EE), **César Antonovich.** Russian composer, born in Vilna on January 18, 1835; died in Petrograd (now Leningrad) on March 24, 1918.

Cui was the son of a French officer who remained in Poland after Napoleon's retreat and married a Lithuanian lady. As a child, César showed a marked talent for music and was given lessons in piano and theory. However, when he was fifteen he entered a military school and he subsequently graduated as a military engineer. He became an expert in fortifications, and it was not until 1857, when he was twenty-two years old, that he found time to turn again to music.

Cui's first published work, a scherzo, was written in 1858 and dedicated to his bride. He wrote eleven operas, several choral works, orchestral works, and a number of compositions for solo instruments and orchestra. However, he is best known today for his piano solos and songs. (See also *The Five.*)

CUIVRÉ (kwee VRAY). A French word meaning "brassy." Cuivré is a direction to horn players to play with a harsh, brassy tone.

CYCLE. A name given to a group of compositions, usually songs, that are related in some way and are meant to be performed together. An example is Schumann's famous *Dichterliebe* (Poet's Love). It consists of sixteen songs, all set to poems by the famous German poet, Heine.

CYMBALS. Percussion instruments, usually made of brass and resembling two large round plates. They are held by knobs or by leather straps that pass through holes in the center, and are played by being struck together. Sometimes only one cymbal is used, in which case it hangs from a frame (or

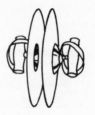

is attached to a bass drum) and is played by being struck with a stick. Cymbals vary in size, but those used in the orchestra are usually at least fourteen or fifteen inches in diameter.

CZERNY (CHAIR nee), **Karl.** Austrian pianist, composer, and teacher, born in Vienna on February 20, 1791; died there on July 15, 1857.

Czerny's father, a gifted musician, began to teach his son to play the piano when he was a small child, and by the time Karl was ten years old he was a skilled pianist. Beethoven was so impressed with his talent that he offered to teach him, and Karl studied with him for three years.

Czerny might have been one of the virtuoso pianists of his day. He preferred teaching, however, and built a remarkable reputation. Liszt* was one of a number of famous musicians who studied with him.

Czerny wrote almost a thousand works, but he is remembered today almost entirely for his technical studies and exercises, still used by piano students all over the world.

D

D. The letter D has many uses in music: (1) D is the name given to one pitch in each octave throughout the musical range. (2) The name given to a scale* or key* whose first note is D. A composition may be written in the key of D major, D minor, or D-flat major. (See also *Key Signatures.*) (3) On the piano keyboard D is the white key that lies between the black keys in each group of two black keys.

D.C. An abbreviation for *da capo.**

D.MUS. (Sometimes written Mus.D.) The abbreviation for Doctor of Music, a degree sometimes earned by completing a definite program of graduate study in music. More often the D.Mus. degree is conferred by a college or university on a person who has made an outstanding achievement in the field of music.

D.S. The abbreviation for *dal segno.**

DA CAPO (dah CAH po). An Italian term meaning "from the beginning." It indicates that the performer is to go back to the beginning of a piece and repeat. *Da capo al fine* means to go back to the beginning and repeat to the word *fine* (end). *Da capo al segno* means to go back to the beginning and repeat to the sign 𝄋 (for *segno*). The abbreviation for *da capo* is *D.C.*

DA CAPO ARIA. A type of aria* used in operas, oratorios, and cantatas. It is in ternary* form, with the first and second sections completely written out, but with the direction *da capo al fine** given at the end of the second

74

section. The first section is repeated exactly, ending the aria. Notable examples of the *da capo* aria are found in Bach's cantatas and Passions and in Handel's oratorios.

DALLAPICCOLA (dah lah PICK oh lah), **Luigi.** Italian composer, born in Pisino, Istria, on February 3, 1904.

Dallapiccola studied at the Cherubini Conservatory in Florence, majoring in piano and composition. He graduated in 1924, and ten years later was appointed to the Conservatory's faculty. From the first, he was interested in atonal* music, and in 1930 he became associated with the violinist Materassi, with whom he gave performances of modern compositions for violin and piano. He became acquainted with Alban Berg* and studied his works as well as those of Webern* and Schoenberg,* and from that time on his own works became more and more based on the twelve-tone technique,* although they do not adhere to it completely. His works, which have been performed widely in Europe, and to some extent in the United States, include two operas, a ballet, choral works, orchestral works, compositions for voice and orchestra, piano pieces, and songs. His music for piano includes *Annalibera's Musical Notebook,* written for his daughter when she was eight years old.

DAL SEGNO (dahl SAYN yoh). An Italian term meaning "from the mark." It indicates that the performer is to go back to the sign 𝄋 and repeat. The abbreviation for *dal segno* is *D.S.*

DAMPERS. Small pieces of felt-covered wood that rest on the strings of pianos and harpsichords to keep the strings from vibrating. When a key is struck, the damper lifts and allows the string to sound. When the key is released, the damper covers the string again, and the sound stops. The pedal on the right (the *damper pedal*) lifts all the dampers when it is pressed. This allows all the strings to vibrate sympathetically with those being played, making the tones sound "louder" and fuller.

DEBUSSY (deh buh SEE), **Claude.** French composer, born in St. Germain-en-Laye on August 22, 1862; died in Paris on March 25, 1918.

It was not until Debussy was ten years old that he showed any unusual talent for music. At that time the mother-in-law of a famous poet, Verlaine, recognized that young Claude was gifted, and she herself prepared him to enter the Paris Conservatory. He began his studies there when he was eleven years old and continued for eleven years. During that time he won several prizes for piano playing and technical studies, and finally, when he was twenty-two he won the most sought-after prize of all, the *Prix de Rome** with his cantata, *L'Enfant prodigue.* The prize enabled him to study for two years in Rome, after which he settled down in Paris and devoted the rest of his life to composition.

Although Debussy did not "invent" the whole-tone* scale, it is employed in many of his works. His highly individual style, which is often compared with the "impressionistic" style of certain painters, is characterized by colorful harmonies and unusual tone colors.

Some of Debussy's most important works are his opera, *Pelléas et Mélisande*; his orchestral compositions, *Afternoon of a Faun, Nocturnes, Ibéria,* and *La Mer*; his string quartet, violin sonata, and cello sonata; his many songs; and his sets of piano pieces, *Suite bergamasque, Images, Preludes, Études,* and his famous *Children's Corner,* dedicated to his little daughter, Claude-Emma, when she was eight years old.

DECRESCENDO (deh cray SHEN doh). An Italian word meaning "to decrease." In music, it means to become gradually softer. The abbreviation for *decrescendo* is *decresc.* (See also *Diminuendo.*)

DE FALLA. (See *Falla.*)

DEGREE. A term used to name the place of a note in the scale. For example, in the scale of C major the first degree is C, the second degree is D, the third degree is E, and so on. There are seven degrees in a scale, the eighth note being again the first degree. Other names for the first through the seventh degrees of the major or minor scales are these:

1st degree	tonic	do
2nd degree	supertonic	re
3rd degree	mediant	me
4th degree	subdominant	fa
5th degree	dominant	so
6th degree	submediant	la
7th degree	leading tone	ti

DE KOVEN. (See *Koven.*)

DELIBES (deh LEEB), **Leo.** French composer and organist, born in St. Germain-du-Val on February 21, 1836; died in Paris on January 16, 1891.

Delibes was accepted as a student at the Paris Conservatory when he was just twelve years old. He first studied solfege,* and at the same time sang in the choirs of several churches, including the famous Madeleine. Two years later, having won a first prize in solfege, he began serious study of the organ and piano in addition to harmony and advanced composition. He was seventeen when he became the accompanist at the Lyric Theater.

From the beginning, Delibes' musical talent showed itself best in music for the theater. He wrote eighteen operas, the most popular of which was *Lakmé*. Among his other works, the most noteworthy were his four ballets, including the two which have become classics, *Coppélia* and *Sylvia*.

DELIUS, Frederick. English composer, born in Bradford on January 29, 1862; died in Grez-sur-Loing, France, on June 10, 1934.

Although Delius was born in England, his parents were German. His father, a wool merchant, wanted his son to become a businessman and he discouraged his study of music. The boy hated business, and when he was twenty he left home and came to the United States, where he became an orange grower in Florida. He continued his study of music by himself, and with the encouragement of friends who recognized his talent, gave up the orange-growing business after a few years and returned to Europe for study. He finally settled in France, where he remained for the rest of his life, teaching and composing until he became blind.

In addition to a great many charming songs and orchestral works, Delius wrote works for various solo instruments, several choral numbers, a few piano solos, and five operas that were published.

DELLO JOIO, Norman. American composer, pianist, and organist, born in New York City on January 24, 1913.

Dello Joio's family was a musical one. His first teacher was his father, an organist. He later studied with such eminent teachers as Bernard Wagenaar and Paul Hindemith.* At the age of twenty he had a jazz band of his own. Later he held positions as musical director of a ballet company and as teacher of composition at Sarah Lawrence College. He has won numerous awards, including a Juilliard Graduate Scholarship and two Guggenheim Fellowships.

Dello Joio is perhaps best known to American audiences for his opera,

The Trial at Rouen, based on the trial of Joan of Arc, which was produced on television by NBC in 1956. His other operas are *The Triumph of St. Joan,* an earlier work based on the story of Joan of Arc; *The Ruby*; and *Blood Moon.* In addition, Dello Joio has written a number of works for orchestra, several large choral works, chamber music, ballets, piano solos, and songs. Some of his songs for children have been published in school music textbooks.

DEMISEMIQUAVER. The English name for the thirty-second note: (𝅘𝅥𝅰). The demisemiquaver rest is the same as a thirty-second rest: (𝄿).

DESCANT. An added melody that is sung above another melody, as in this example:

Frequently a descant is sung by a group of sopranos while the congregation sings a familiar hymn. Descants are often added to folk or other songs in school music books, allowing the class to be divided into two groups of singers.

DÉTACHÉ (day tah SHAY). A French word meaning "detached." It is used to indicate a kind of bowing for stringed instruments in which single notes of the same value are given separate strokes. The strokes are rather broad and vigorous, not as short as *staccato.** Dashes below the notes are sometimes used to indicate *détaché.* (See also *Bowing.*)

DETT, Robert Nathaniel. American Negro composer, conductor, pianist, and writer, born in Drummondsville, Quebec, Canada, on October 11, 1882; died in Battle Creek, Michigan, on October 2, 1943.

Dett devoted much of his time to the advancement of musical education for Negroes. He received most of his own education at the Oberlin Conservatory, Columbia University, Harvard University, the Eastman School of Music, and Howard University. He studied also with the famous teacher, Nadia Boulanger,* in Paris. Both Harvard University and Oberlin Conservatory awarded him the honorary Doctor of Music degree.

Dett's music, which is strongly influenced by Negro folk tunes, includes two successful oratorios, *The Chariot Jubilee* and *The Ordering of Moses*; several suites for piano; many choruses and arrangements of Negro folk songs. His publications include *Religious Folk Songs of the Negro* and a four-volume collection of spirituals, *The Dett Collection of Negro Spirituals*.

DEVELOPMENT. (1) The means by which a composer extends and elaborates musical themes* in a composition. The original theme may be elaborated by varying its rhythm, by presenting it in a different key, by inversion* of the theme, and so on. (2) In a movement of a composition written in sonata form,* a *development section* follows the exposition.* (See also *Sonata Form.*)

DIAMOND, David. American composer, born in Rochester, New York, on July 9, 1915.

After receiving his basic musical education, chiefly at the Cleveland Institute of Music and the Eastman School of Music, where he studied intensively with Bernard Rogers,* Diamond took further work with Roger Sessions* in New York, then went to Paris for study with Nadia Boulanger.* He subsequently won enough grants and awards to enable him to work exclusively at composing. These awards included two Guggenheim Fellowships, the American Academy in Rome award, and a grant from the National Academy of Arts and Letters.

Diamond's early music was quite atonal,* but it has gradually become more clearly key centered. It is characterized by strong rhythmic patterns. His works include six symphonies, ballets, film music, choral works, chamber music, songs, and a number of pieces for piano.

D'INDY, Vincent. (See *Indy.*)

DIATONIC. A word used to describe the notes that are natural to a major or minor scale. For example, in the key of C major, the following notes are diatonic because they belong to the key of C. They form a diatonic scale.

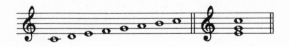

The chord E-G-C is *diatonic* because it is made up of notes that are natural to the Key of C major.

DIMINISHED. A term used to describe an interval that is a half step smaller than a perfect* or minor* interval. If, for example, the upper note of a perfect fifth is lowered a half step (or the lower note is raised a half step) the interval becomes a *diminished fifth*. The term *diminished* is also used to describe a chord in which two or more of the notes form diminished intervals with one another. (See also *Chords.*)

DIMINISHED SEVENTH CHORD. A diminished triad with a diminished seventh added at the top. The diminished seventh chords on B, C, and D look like this:

DIMINUENDO (dee mee noo END doh). An Italian word meaning "to get smaller." In music it means to gradually become softer. The abbreviation for *diminuendo* is *dim.* or *dimin.* (See also *Decrescendo.*)

DIMINUTION. A way of treating a theme* so that the time value of the notes is shortened; for example, quarter notes become eighth notes, half notes become quarter notes. Diminution is used occasionally in fugues and in the development* sections of sonatas, symphonies, and so on.

DISCORD. Any combination of notes that sounds harsh and unpleasant to the ear. Such a combination usually contains at least one dissonant interval. However, what seems like a discord to one person may not to another who is accustomed to a more dissonant type of music. (See also *Consonance.*)

DISSONANCE. (See *Consonance.*)

DIVERTIMENTO (dee vehr tee MEN toh). An Italian word meaning "amusement" or "recreation." A divertimento is a work of a rather light character in the form of a suite* of several movements, written for instrumental groups. It originated during the time of Mozart and Haydn and was popular as an entertainment feature. Examples are Haydn's *Divertimento* for horn, violin, and cello in E-flat major, and the well-known *Eine Kleine Nachtmusik* by Mozart.

DIVERTISSEMENT (dee vair tees maw). A French word meaning "entertainment." (1) A musical work based on familiar tunes, for example, Schubert's *Divertissement à la hongroise,* a duet for piano that is based on familiar Hungarian tunes. (2) A ballet inserted between the acts of an opera simply for variety.

DIVISI (dee VEE see). (Often abbreviated as *div.*) An Italian word meaning "divided." *Divisi* is used in music for stringed instruments to indicate that the instruments which have been playing the same part are now to play two or more separate parts. The end of the *divisi* is usually indicated by the term *unis.,* an abbrevation of the word that means "all together."

DO. The syllable name given one scale note in the system called solmization.* In this system the notes of the scale are called by the syllables *do, re, me, fa, sol, la, ti, do.* In the system called *fixed do, do* is always the note C. In the system called *movable do, do* is the first note of any major scale. In Europe the note *do* is sometimes called *ut.*

DODECAPHONIC (doh dek ah FON ick). A word derived from the Greek word *dodeka,* meaning twelve. The term *dodecaphonic* refers to the twelve-tone technique* or to twelve-tone compositions.

DOHNÁNYI (DOH nahn yee), **Ernö.** Hungarian composer and pianist, born in Pressburg (Bratislava) on July 27, 1877; died in Tallahassee, Florida, on February 9, 1960.

Dohnányi's first music lessons were with his father, a professor of mathematics and an amateur cellist. Later he studied both piano and composition at the Budapest Academy. He became a virtuoso pianist and toured widely in Europe and later, with great success, in the United States. At the same time, he continued to compose.

After holding positions at the Berlin *Hochschule* (high school for music) for ten years, and at the Budapest Conservatory (as Director) for three years, during which time he conducted the Budapest Philharmonic Orchestra, he left Europe and settled for a brief time in South America. In 1949 he became a professor of piano and composition at Florida State University in Tallahassee, where he remained until his death.

His works include three symphonies and other compositions for orchestra, three operas, several chamber music works, and a large number of pieces for piano.

DOLCE (DOHL chay). An Italian word meaning "sweet." Dolce is a direction to perform the music in a rather soft, sweet, and somewhat sentimental fashion.

DOLENTE (doh LEN tay). An Italian word meaning "sorrowful." It is a direction to perform the music rather slowly and sorrowfully.

DOMINANT. The fifth note in any major or minor scale. In the key of C the dominant is G, in the key of D it is A, and so on. The dominant triad is the triad whose lowest note is the dominant of a particular scale. For example, the dominant triad in the key of C is G-B-D. The *dominant seventh* is the same as the dominant triad with a minor third added above the fifth of the triad. (See also *Chords.*)

dominant   dominant   dominant
            triad   7th

DONIZETTI (don it TSET tee), **Gaetano.** Italian composer of opera, born in Bergamo on November 29, 1797; died there on April 8, 1848.

Donizetti's father, a weaver, wanted his son to become a lawyer. The boy, however, was devoted to music and finally convinced his father that he had enough talent to study at the Bergamo school of music. He did so well that his teachers recommended that he continue his studies in Bologna where there was an outstanding music school with fine teachers. Still not convinced that a career as a musician was right for his son, the father tried to persuade him to become a teacher. By that time, however, Donizetti knew that he wanted more than anything else to write for the theater, and for the rest of his life he devoted himself to writing operas. In his day, operas were written to suit the voices of "star" singers, and Donizetti was kept busy writing suitable works for this singer and that one. He turned out some seventy-five operas between 1816 and 1845, when his mind began to fail and he gradually became paralyzed.

He wrote very fast (he composed one opera in six days), and most of his works were too superficial to be of lasting value. A few, however, have survived and are still produced. They include *La Fille du régiment* (Daughter of the Regiment), *Don Pasquale, Lucia di Lammermoor,* and *L'elisir d'amore* (The Elixir of Love).

DORIAN MODE. A scale used in the music of the Middle Ages. It is represented by the white keys on the piano, beginning and ending with D. (See also *Modes.*)

DOT. A mark that looks like a period. A dot above or below a note indicates that the note should be as short as possible. (See also *Staccato.*)

A dot that follows a note indicates that the note should be held one and one-half times the note's normal length. For example, if a quarter note has the value of one beat, a dotted quarter note (♩.) is held for a beat and a half; a dotted half note (♩.) would be held for three beats, and so on.

A double dot after a note indicates that the note should be held one and one-half times the normal length plus one-fourth more. For example, a double-dotted quarter note (♩..) would be held for the length of a quarter note plus an eighth note plus a sixteenth note (♩ ♪ ♪).

DOUBLE. (1) Used in the same sense as the word *two,* as in *double bar** (two bars), *double dot** (two dots), *double flat** (two flats), *double concerto** (a concerto for two solo instruments), and so on. (2) Used to indicate that one part is given to two or more performers, or that one line or voice* is played by two or more instruments. (3) Used to indicate that one instrumentalist can play on more than one instrument; for example, a flute* player often *doubles* on the piccolo.* (4) Meaning "about an octave lower," as *double bassoon, double bass* (instruments that sound an octave lower than the music is written).

DOUBLE BAR. Two perpendicular lines on the staff that indicate the end of a section or the end of a piece. If the two lines are the same in width (‖) they indicate the end of a section; if one is wider than the other (‖) they indicate the end of a composition. If a double bar is preceded by dots (:‖) the preceding section is to be repeated; if it is followed by dots (‖:) the following section is to be repeated.

DOUBLE BASS. (Also called *string bass, contrabass,* or simply *bass.*) The largest and lowest-sounding of the bowed stringed instruments, its tone is deep and heavy, sounding one octave lower than the music is written. Its range is only about two and one-half octaves, but fine bass players can extend this considerably by the use of harmonics.* While the three smaller instruments of the violin family are tuned in fifths, the double bass is tuned in fourths:

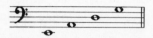

Some double basses have a fifth string that sounds the C below E. The bow used in playing the double bass is much shorter and heavier than the bow used for the smaller instruments.

The double bass is used most often in orchestras and dance bands, and very little solo music has been written especially for it. Only a few works for chamber groups have included the double bass, one example being Schubert's well-known *Trout Quintet* for violin, viola, cello, double bass, and piano. (See also *Violin Family*.)

DOUBLE COUNTERPOINT. A term used for invertible counterpoint* in two parts. It is so designed that two melodies, one above the other, can exchange positions. The intervals most often used are the octave,* the tenth,* and the twelfth.*

DOUBLE FLAT. A sign (♭♭) which indicates that a note is to be lowered two half steps. For example, on the piano keyboard E♭♭ is the same as D, C♭♭ is the same as B♭, and so on.

DOUBLE FUGUE. A fugue* in which two themes are introduced at the same time or one after the other and then are used throughout the piece in counterpoint* to each other. An example of a double fugue is J. S. Bach's Fugue No. 4 in C-sharp minor from the *Well-Tempered Clavier.**

DOUBLE SHARP. A sign (𝄪) which indicates that a note is to be raised two half steps. For example, on the piano keyboard C𝄪 is the same as D; E𝄪 is the same as F♯ , and so on.

DOUBLE STOP. A term used in playing a violin or any other bowed stringed instrument. It means that two or more notes are played at the same time by drawing the bow across two or more strings with one stroke.

DOWLAND, John. English composer and lutenist, born in 1563; died in 1626. (The exact dates and places of his birth and death are not known.)

Dowland was only seventeen years old when he went to Paris to serve the English Ambassador as a lutenist-composer. While there he became a Roman Catholic. He returned to England later, attended Oxford University, and in 1588 graduated with a Bachelor of Music degree. Because of his religion he was unable to secure a position at the English Court, and he returned to the Continent. He held a number of important positions and travelled extensively, then finally returned to England in 1612, where he became a Protestant again. He is famous mainly for his many songs with lute* accompaniment.

DOWN BEAT. The downward motion of the conductor's hand or baton to indicate the first beat* of a measure. (See also *Conducting*.)

DOWN BOW. The downward direction of the bow made when the player of a stringed instrument pulls rather than pushes the bow across the strings. The opposite of *down bow* is *up bow*.

DRONE. (1) The pipes on the bagpipe that do not change pitch. They supply the low, monotonous accompaniment to the melody. (2) Any sustained note, usually low in register,* that does not change pitch throughout a piece or a long portion of a piece.

DRUM. A percussion instrument which consists of a wood or metal cylinder with skin stretched tightly over one or both sides. It is played by striking the drum head with a stick or with the hands. Most drums have no definite pitch. (See also *Bass Drum, Bongo Drums, Side Drum, Snare Drum, Timpani*.)

DUET. A piece of music scored for two singers or two instruments, with or without accompaniment. A duet for piano is usually played by two performers on the same instrument. (See also *Duo*.)

DUFAY (duh fah ee), **Guillaume.** Flemish composer, born sometime before 1400 (the exact date and place are not known); died in Cambrai on November 27, 1474.

As a boy, Dufay sang in the chorus at Cambrai Cathedral; later he was a singer in the Papal Chapel in Rome. There he took the religious instruction that enabled him to hold the position of Canon (a kind of secular rank involving mainly the musical functions of a church or cathedral). Dufay, who is considered one of the two or three most important composers of his day, wrote many works for the church as well as secular works. They include Masses, two Magnificats, many motets* and chansons.*

DUKAS (duh KAH), **Paul.** French composer and music critic, born in Paris on October 1, 1865; died there on May 17, 1935.

Dukas entered the Paris Conservatory when he was seventeen years old. He did well in his studies, and some time later was given the responsibility of handling the orchestra class. He wrote music criticisms for several Paris newspapers, and he composed a large number of works. However, he was such a severe critic of his own works that he published very little.

Dukas' best-known work is *The Sorcerer's Apprentice,* one of the most popular scherzos ever written for orchestra. His opera *Ariadne and Blue-beard*; and a dance-poem, *La Péri* (The Persian Fairy) are also performed.

DULCIMER. An instrument popular in the Middle Ages. It consists of a number of strings stretched across a flat sounding board. It resembles the zither, but is played by striking the strings with small hammers held in the hands. It is actually a forerunner of the piano. A modern dulcimer, used mostly for folk music, is plucked with the fingers.

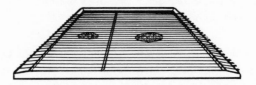

DUNSTABLE, John. English composer, died December 24, 1453. (The place and date of his birth are not known.)

Very little is known about Dunstable's life except that he was a mathematician and astrologer as well as a musician. He spent a great deal of time on the Continent, and most of his works have been found in old manuscripts there. Along with Dufay,* he is considered one of the most important composers of the fifteenth century. His works consist mainly of church music and secular songs.

DUO. A duet.* The term *duo* is more often used in reference to instrumental works, while *duet* is more common for vocal and piano music.

DUPLE TIME. Time in which the beats in a bar can be divided by two, as 2/4, 4/4, 2/2, and sometimes 6/8.

DUPLET. Two notes that are played in the length of time normally taken by three notes, as in this example:

DUPRÉ (dew PRAY), **Marcel.** Famous French organist and composer, born in Rouen on May 3, 1886.

Dupré was such a brilliant musician that at the age of ten he played in public all of Bach's Preludes and Fugues from memory. He was only twelve when he was appointed assistant organist at a church in Rouen, and only fifteen when an oratorio he had written was performed. He became the most outstanding pupil of his time at the Paris Conservatory, winning a number of prizes, including the *Prix de Rome** in 1914.

Between 1906 and 1934 Dupré was organist at two of the most famous churches in Paris, St. Sulpice and Notre Dame. He has toured widely in Europe and America as an organ recitalist, taught organ at the Paris Conservatory, acted as director of the American Conservatory in Fontaine-bleau, and since 1954 served as director of the Paris Conservatory.

In addition to his many works for organ, Dupré has written several songs, a cantata, much church music, music for instruments, and two orchestral works. He has also written a number of technical studies, including two on organ improvisation,* of which he is a master.

DVOŘÁK (DVORR zhahk), **Antonin.** Czech composer, born in a small village near Prague on September 8, 1841; died in Prague on May 1, 1904.

Dvořák, the son of an innkeeper and butcher, showed unusual musical talent at an early age. When he was only ten he played violin in his father's little band, which performed at fairs around the countryside. His school-master recognized his talent and gave him a good background in music theory, then encouraged him to go to Prague for further study. When he graduated from the Prague Organ School he accepted a position as violinist with a concert orchestra, but shortly afterwards transferred to the orchestra of the National Theater. He didn't earn enough money from that job to live on, so he gave music lessons on the side. At the same time he was busy composing, and ten years later he had his first big success when a composition of his called *Hymnus* was performed. From then on he devoted himself entirely to composing and teaching, and before long he gained recognition in Europe and in England as an outstanding composer.

In 1891 Dvořák came to America as director of the National Conservatory of Music in New York. During his stay here he became fascinated with the country, especially with the Negroes and their folk songs, the

Indians and their customs, and the country in general. He wrote several works that reflect this interest strongly, among them his best-known symphony, *From the New World*. In 1895 he returned to Prague, and six years later was made director of the Prague Conservatory. He held that position until his death.

Dvořák wrote nine symphonies in all, seven of them published. His other works include symphonic poems, overtures, and other pieces for orchestra; chamber music, choral music, many solos for piano and for voice; and ten operas.

DYNAMICS. Loudness and softness in music. Some of the more common words and abbreviations used to indicate dynamics are the following:

pianissimo	*pp*	very soft
piano	*p*	soft
mezzo piano	*mp*	moderately soft
mezzo forte	*mf*	moderately loud
forte	*f*	loud
fortissimo	*ff*	very loud
forzando	*fz*	accented heavily
sforzando	*sf, sfz*	accented heavily
crescendo	*cres.*	gradually louder
decrescendo	*decresc.*	gradually softer
diminuendo	*dim.*	gradually softer

Signs often used to show changes in dynamics are these:

gradually louder
gradually softer

E

E. The letter E has many uses in music: (1) E is the name given to one pitch in each octave throughout the musical range. (2) The name given to a scale* or key* whose first note is E. A composition may be written in the key of E major, E minor, E-flat major, or E-flat minor. (See also *Key Signatures.*) (3) On the piano keyboard E is the white key that lies just above each group of two black keys. (4) E-flat is used to identify instruments on which notes written as C actually sound E-flat. An example is the E-flat clarinet. (See also *Transposing Instruments.*)

ÉCOSSAISE (ay kaw SEZ). A French word meaning "Scottish." It is a lively dance in 2/4 time that was popular in France and England in the late eighteenth and nineteenth centuries. It is not a Scottish dance, but rather an English country dance. Beethoven was one of several composers who wrote pieces he called *Écossaise* for the piano.

EGK (ekk), **Werner.** German composer, born in Auchsesheim, a village near Augsburg, on May 17, 1901.

Egk, one of Germany's most popular composers, did not decide to make a career of music until he was a grown man. As a boy he studied music, at first almost by himself, and later with teachers in Munich. But he was equally attracted to literature and the fine arts. A visit to Italy, where he heard much good music, finally decided him to make composition his life's work.

Egk has written a good deal of music, including several works that were commissioned for radio broadcast. One of his ballets, *Abraxas,* caused a commotion when it was banned by some Bavarian authorities who considered it shocking. He has also written several works for orchestra, operas, piano pieces, and songs.

EIGHTH NOTE. The eighth note, which has half the value of a quarter note, one-fourth the value of a half note, and one-eighth the value of a whole note, is notated in two different ways: A single eighth note has a single "flag." When two or more eighth notes are grouped together they are joined by a cross bar called a *beam*: (♪♫ ♫♫).

EIGHTH REST. The eighth rest, which has half the value of a quarter rest, one-fourth the value of a half rest, and one-eighth the value of a whole rest, is notated this way: (ɣ).

EISTEDDFOD (ESS teth vod). A music festival held in Wales, and sometimes in other parts of the world. It originated in ancient times when the Bards* met together for music competition, and was revived in Wales in the nineteenth century. A Welsh *eisteddfod* is very colorful, with costumes and decorations copied after those of the original Bards.

ELECTRONIC INSTRUMENTS. Instruments in which electronic devices such as photo-cells, valves, vacuum tube oscillators, etc., are used to produce or amplify sound. An example of an instrument in which the sound is produced completely by electronic means is the electronic organ.* The sound on the electronic guitar, on the other hand, is produced naturally, but is made louder and more penetrating by electrical impulses. Some other electronic musical instruments are the Theremin,* the Novachord,* the Solovox,* and the Orgatron.*

ELECTRONIC MUSIC. Music that is constructed from sounds produced by electronic means in laboratories. These laboratory sounds are recorded on tape, and the work itself becomes a tape recording. Such electronic compositions can be played only from the tapes. Most of the experimentation with electronic music was pioneered in Germany in the 1950's. Karlheinz Stockhausen* was the first composer to publish a diagram, or "score," of an electronically produced composition.

ELECTRONIC ORGAN. A small organ, the tones of which are amplified by electricity, making them sound much like those of a pipe organ. It was invented in 1934 in Chicago by L. Hammond. The electronic organ has become a popular instrument for providing background music in restaurants and has been installed as a substitute for the regular pipe organ in many small churches. It has also become widely used as an instrument in the home.

ELEGY. A mournful type of song or instrumental piece, usually written as a memorial to someone who has died.

ELGAR, Edward William. British composer, born in Broadheath, England, on June 2, 1857; died in Worcester on February 23, 1934.

Elgar is considered one of the leading English composers of modern times. He was largely self-taught, although his father was a talented musician who ran a music store and acquainted his son at an early age with good music. Edward's father played the organ at a Catholic church in Worcester and the violin in a local orchestra. Young Edward himself played bassoon in the orchestra, and by the time he was fifteen had become an excellent musician; but he did not begin to write anything more than small pieces until he was in his thirties. From that time on he wrote a steady stream of works that were performed with great success in England and on the continent of Europe.

Elgar's best-known works include three oratorios, *The Dream of Gerontius* (considered his masterwork), *The Apostles,* and *The Kingdom*; two works for orchestra, the *Enigma Variations,* and a symphonic poem, *Falstaff*; a concerto for violin and one for cello; two cantatas, *The Black Knight* and *Caractacus*; three symphonies; and his often-played military marches, called *Pomp and Circumstance.*

EMBELLISHMENTS. (See *Ornaments*).

EMBOUCHURE (OM boo shoor). A French word meaning "mouth" or "mouthpiece." In the playing of wind instruments, the term *embouchure* refers to the position and shaping of the mouth, the lips, and the tongue. Good embouchure is an important part of good playing. With the oboe, French horn, and bassoon, the development of a good embouchure is especially difficult.

ENCORE (AHN core). A French word meaning "again." At musical performances, an encore is a number given after the regular program has been completed, usually on the request of the audience.

ENESCO, Georges. Rumanian composer, violinist, and conductor, born in Dorohoiû on August 19, 1881; died in Paris, France, on May 4, 1955.

Enesco was so gifted as a child that he was admitted to the Vienna Conservatory when he was just seven years old. He left that Conservatory at the age of twelve, already having won some of the highest awards for violin playing. He entered the Paris Conservatory for further study and when he was eighteen won the first prize there. From that time on he toured Europe and America as a virtuoso violinist and conductor. In his later years he became interested in teaching and many outstanding violinists studied with him, including the noted American, Yehudi Menuhin.

Enesco's compositions include a successful opera, *Oedipe,* first performed at the Paris Opera in 1936; two Rumanian rhapsodies for orchestra; chamber music; piano pieces; songs; and several sonatas for violin and piano.

ENGLISH HORN. (Sometimes called *cor anglais.*) A woodwind instrument that is actually an alto oboe,* pitched a fifth lower than the regular oboe. It is played with a double reed. Because of its length, the English horn has a curved piece of tubing attached to the upper end, and bent downward to reach the player's mouth. Its tone is softer and more mellow than the tone of the oboe. It is a transposing instrument* with a range of a little over two octaves, from the E below Middle C to the second A above Middle C. (See also *Woodwinds.*)

ENHARMONIC. A term used to describe different ways of notating the same tone. On a keyboard, for example, B double-sharp, C-sharp, and D-flat are the same; A double-flat, G, and F double-sharp are the same. The term is also used to describe chords that can be written in two different ways as:

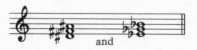

On keyboard instruments enharmonic notes and chords sound exactly the same. On wind and stringed instruments there is a very slight difference. An oboe player, for example, knows that G-sharp sounds a tiny bit higher than A-flat.

ENSEMBLE (ahn SAHM bl). (1) A group of performers, as a *vocal en-*

semble or an *instrumental ensemble.* (2) The term is sometimes used in describing the effectiveness of a particular performance. In speaking of a choral performance, a good ensemble might mean that the singers' voices were well matched, that the singing of the various parts was well balanced, and that the total effect was musically satisfying.

ENTR'ACTE (AHN trakt). A French word meaning "interval." An entr'acte is an intermission between the acts of a play, opera, or other stage work. Entr'acte music is music played during such an intermission.

EPISODE. A section in a piece of music that is less important than the main themes.* In a fugue* the episode occurs between entries of the main subject.* In the rondo* the episode occurs between recurrences of the main theme.

EQUAL TEMPERAMENT. The tuning of an instrument, especially a keyboard instrument, in such a way that all of the half-tones within each octave are equal. This system of tuning makes it possible to play in all keys because the intervals in any key have the same value. It is essential for performance of twelve-tone* music.

ESPRESSIVO (ess press EE voh). An Italian word meaning "with expression." It is used to tell performers to play or sing with feeling. It is often abbreviated as *espress.*

ÉTUDE (AY tude). A French word meaning "study." An Étude is a piece written primarily to give practice in finger technique—the playing of arpeggios, octaves, trills, and so on. Many Études are beautiful pieces at the same time, and are often included in the repertoire of concert artists. The Études of Chopin are examples of works that combine great artistry in composition and excellent material for study.

EUPHONIUM. A brass instrument used mainly in bands. It has four valves, and is similar to the tuba, but higher in pitch. Its normal range is from the second B-flat below Middle C to the B-flat above Middle C. Illustration on page 94.

EURYTHMICS. A system of expressing the different rhythms of music through bodily movements. It was invented by a Swiss named Jacques-Dalcroze who established a school for the teaching of eurythmics near

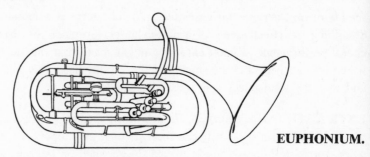

EUPHONIUM.

Dresden, Germany, in 1910. When the first World War broke out in 1914, he returned to his native Switzerland and founded the Jacques-Dalcroze Institute in Geneva. The system has had wide influence, especially on the modern dance, and has remained popular in Europe and America to this day.

EXPOSITION. The first statement of the main themes* in a musical composition, before they undergo development.* The term is usually applied to compositions written in sonata form* and to fugues.* In sonata form, the exposition usually includes the statements of two contrasting themes or groups of themes, the first in the tonic* key and the second in the dominant* key, connected by a modulating* bridge.* In fugues, the exposition is the first statement of the subject* (and answer*) in all voices.*

EXPRESSIONISM. (Also *Expressionistic.*) A term sometimes applied to the music of certain composers of the twentieth century. It was borrowed from painting and applied to music that expressed the composer's inner feelings as opposed to "impressions of the outer world" that dominated the music of such composers as Debussy, which preceded it. Expressionistic music is usually more harsh and discordant than impressionistic music. Examples may be found in the works of such composers as Schoenberg,* Berg,* and Webern.*

F

F. The letter F has many uses in music: (1) F is the name given to one pitch in each octave throughout the musical range. (2) The name given to a scale* or key* whose first note is F. A composition may be written in the key of F major, F minor, F-sharp major, or F-sharp minor. (See also *Key Signatures*.) (3) On the piano keyboard F is the white key that lies just below each group of three black keys. (4) The lower-case (small letter) *f* is used as an abbreviation for *forte* (loud); *ff* is the abbreviation for *fortissimo* (extremely loud); the abbreviation *fp* (for *forte-piano*) means loud followed immediately by soft. (5) When F is used before the name of an instrument, as "F-horn" it indicates a transposing instrument* on which the note written C sounds as F.

F-CLEF. (See *Clefs*.)

FA. In the system of *movable do*,* the syllable name given to the fourth note of the major scale. In the *fixed do** system, it is the note F.

FALLA (FAHL lyah), **Manuel de.** Spanish composer, born in Cadiz on November 23, 1876; died in Alta Gracia, Argentina, on November 14, 1946.

De Falla is considered by many to be the greatest Spanish composer of his time. He began his study of music with his mother, a talented pianist, and studied later in Madrid. There he won prizes for piano playing and for his opera, *La vida breve* (Life is Short). De Falla spent seven years in Paris and became a good friend of Debussy* and Ravel,* but his music does not resemble to any extent the "impressionism" of either of his friends. It is highly individual and very Spanish in character.

When the first World War broke out de Falla returned to Spain and remained there until 1940. Then, unhappy about the Spanish Civil War, he went to South America and lived for the rest of his life with a sister in Alta Gracia.

In addition to his opera *La vida breve,* de Falla's best known works are another opera, *El retablo de Mæse Pedro* (Master Peter's Puppet Show); two ballets, *El amor brujo* (Married by Witchcraft) and *El sombrero de tres picos* (The Three-cornered Hat); a work for piano and orchestra, *Noches en los jardines de España* (Nights in the Gardens of Spain); and a suite for piano, *Quatre pièces espagnoles* (Four Spanish Pieces).

FALSETTO. A kind of singing in which the male voice produces tones that are higher than the normal range. In earlier times, male voices were sometimes deliberately trained to sing falsetto in preparation for singing female roles in opera and for certain kinds of church music.

FANDANGO. A Spanish dance in 3/4 or 3/8 time. The dancers are usually accompanied by a guitar and castanets, sometimes with the added accompaniment of violins and other instruments.

FANFARE. A short "flourish" or tune for trumpets, usually played to announce the beginning of a ceremony, such as a royal procession or a military review.

FANTASY. A composition in which the composer writes according to his own fancy, rather than according to any particular form. Examples are Beethoven's *Fantasia in G minor* for piano, and Brahms' two sets of *Fantasien,* also for piano.

FARANDOLE. A very old dance in 6/8 time. It is danced by men and women in a long line, holding hands, and following a leader through intricate steps. It is accompanied by musicians who lead the procession as they play the traditional tunes on the pipe* and tabor.* The farandole is still popular in Provençe, a section of southern France where the dance originated.

FAURÉ (foh RAY), **Gabriel Urbain.** French composer and organist, born in Pamiers on May 12, 1845; died in Paris on November 4, 1924.

Fauré was the sixth child of a schoolmaster too poor to give his son musical training. But when the boy was eight years old a blind woman heard him play the village organ, and through her influence he was able to study music. A scholarship was offered him at the École Niedermeyer in Paris where he not only could study music but was given his board and room as well. During the ten years he stayed at the school he received an excellent education. He had become a fine organist, and after leaving school he made his living by playing at various churches. In 1896 he reached the "top rank" when he was appointed organist at the famous Madeleine in Paris. For eight years he taught composition at the Paris Conservatory, then was appointed Director of the Conservatory in 1905, a position he held until increasing deafness forced him to retire.

In addition to many beautiful songs, Fauré wrote a number of orchestral and chamber music works; two operas, *Prométhée* and *Pénélope*; incidental music for the theater; numerous compositions for piano; and a Requiem Mass.

FERMATA (fair MAH tah). An Italian word meaning "stop." The fermata is represented by the sign ⌒ , and indicates that the note or notes under the sign are to be held longer than their written duration. A fermata over a barline indicates a pause.

FIDDLE. A violin. Although the term "fiddle" is used most often in referring to such "unserious" music as accompaniment for "square" or other types of country dances, it is a correct synonym for *violin*. *Fiddle* derives from the Latin word *fides*; *fiddler* from *fidicen*.

FIELD, John. Irish pianist and composer, born in Dublin on July 26, 1782; died in Moscow, Russia, on January 23, 1837.

Field was the son of a violinist and the grandson of an organist. He studied first with his grandfather, with whom he made such progress on the piano that he gave a highly successful public concert when he was ten years old. Two years later he made his debut as a concert pianist in London. Field's father apprenticed the talented boy to the famous pianist and teacher, Clementi,* who was then in England. Clementi manufactured pianos on the side, and in exchange for lessons, young Field served as a kind of "demonstrator" for his master's instruments. He traveled widely with Clementi, leading a hard and poorly-paid existence, but continuing to develop as a pianist. He completed his apprenticeship with Clementi while they were in Russia, and there he decided to stay. And although he was still in his early twenties he was so greatly admired as a pianist and teacher, he was able for the first time in his life to earn enough money to live comfortably. He made a number of concert tours in Europe, but most of his time was spent in Russia. Field wrote seven piano concertos, four sonatas, and other works for piano, including eighteen nocturnes. He invented the name *Nocturne* as well as the characteristic style of the nocturne,* and for that more than anything else he is noted. Chopin* especially admired Field's Nocturnes, and he as well as others more or less adapted the style, and frequently the name, in their own compositions.

FIFE. A small flute used in military bands and in fife and drum corps. It is pitched slightly lower than the piccolo* and is played by blowing into an opening in the side of the instrument. It has five or six fingerholes and sometimes several keys.

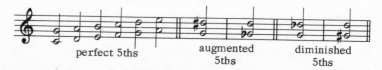

FIFTH. An interval* that covers four ascending steps in the major or minor scale. The *perfect fifth* consists of three whole steps and one half step. In the key of C-major, for example, C to G is a perfect fifth. Other perfect fifths in the key of C-major are D to A, E to B, F to C, G to D, and A to E. The *augmented fifth* is a fifth with the upper note raised a half step or the lower note lowered a half step. A *diminished fifth* is a fifth with the upper note lowered a half step or the lower note raised a half step. (See also *Intervals.*)

perfect 5ths   augmented   diminished
                          5ths   5ths

FIGURED BASS. (Also called *Continuo* or *Thorough Bass.*) A bass part for a keyboard instrument, with figures to indicate the harmonies to be played above the single bass notes. The example below, from a trio sonata* by Corelli,* shows the figured bass to be used as an organ accompaniment. The figures under the notes indicate the other notes to be played with the bass note. For example, the 5 indicates the interval of the fifth, or E and B; the figure 6 by itself implies a 3 also, so the chord would consist of the notes E, C, and G; the figures $\frac{6}{5}$ indicate a chord made up of F♯ ,

C, and D; the bass note G with no figures under it implies the intervals 5 and 3 above, so the chord would consist of G, B, and D. Accidentals are indicated by their signs placed under or after the figures. An example is the 7 in the above figured bass, which indicates the interval of B to A.

The figured bass, or continuo, widely used during the Baroque* period, allowed the accompanist to improvise as he wished, just so long as he employed the harmonies indicated by the figures.

FINALE (fee NAHL lay). An Italian word meaning "final." (1) *Finale* is used as a title for the last movement of a work such as a sonata* or a symphony;* and (2) the last part of an act, often at the very end, of an opera, operetta, or musical comedy, when the entire cast performs on the stage together.

FINE (FEE nay). An Italian word meaning "the end." *Fine* is used when the end of a composition is not the same as the last written notation. A sign or direction tells the performer to go back and repeat a certain part and end the piece where the word *fine* occurs. (See also *Da Capo*.)

FINE, Irving. American composer, born in Boston on December 3, 1914.

Fine studied music at Harvard University, where he earned a Bachelor's degree in 1937 and a Master's degree in 1938. He later studied composition with the noted French teacher, Nadia Boulanger.* He has taught at Harvard and Brandeis Universities and at the Berkshire Music Center in Tanglewood, Massachusetts. In addition to a number of piano pieces and songs, Fine's works include a cantata, *The Choral New Yorker*; a violin sonata; a *Cantata Concertante* for orchestra; a *Partita* for wind quintet; a string quartet; and a choral cycle called *The Hour Glass*.

FINGER BOARD. The part of a stringed instrument against which the fingers press the strings to shorten their vibrating length and thus produce higher pitches. It usually consists of a long piece of black wood attached to the neck of the instrument. On some instruments, as the guitar and the banjo, the fingerboard is fretted. That is, it has thin lines of metal or wood set in at intervals to indicate the position of notes in the scale. The members of the violin family are not fretted; the player learns through practice the exact place on each string that must be pressed to play the correct pitch.

FINGER HOLES. Holes bored in the side of a woodwind* instrument to produce different tones when covered or uncovered. Originally, the fingers were used to cover the holes on all woodwind instruments. Most woodwinds today are equipped with keys and levers that are manipulated by the fingers to cover the holes. The recorder* is one of a very few instruments with holes that are covered by the fingers.

FINGERING. Small figures supplied by a composer or music editor to indicate the correct fingers to use in playing a piece of music. In music for keyboard instruments the figure 1 refers to the thumb, and the figure 5 to the little finger. The figures 2, 3, and 4 refer to the fingers in between. In most piano music fingering is indicated for only those notes where certain fingers best fit the passage, as in the following excerpt from Bach's Two-Part Invention No. 4:

Allegro deciso

This passage begins with six notes that follow each other in rapid succession. By starting with the second finger, the player can play the second note with his thumb and finish comfortably with the little finger and be ready immediately to attack the first note of the second measure with his thumb.

The thumb is not used in playing the violin and viola, so the figures 1, 2, 3, and 4 refer to the fingers alone, the little finger being indicated by the figure 4. In playing the cello, the thumb is used in the higher position and is indicated by this symbol: (ϙ).

FINNEY, Ross Lee. American composer, born in Wells, Minnesota, on December 23, 1906.

Finney studied music at the University of Minnesota and at Harvard University. He later studied privately with Rogers Sessions,* Alban Berg,* and Nadia Boulanger.* He has won a number of prizes for composition, including a Guggenheim Fellowship and a Pulitzer Scholarship, and has taught at Smith College, Mt. Holyoke College, and the University of Michigan. His works include chamber music, piano sonatas, choral compositions, concertos, two symphonies, and several other compositions for orchestra.

FIRST. A term used in reference to orchestras that indicates a position of leadership, as *first violins, first trombone,* etc.

FIVE, THE. A name sometimes used to identify five Russian composers—Balakirev*, Borodin,* Cui,* Mussorgsky,* and Rimsky-Korsakov*—who were friends and who did much to develop a national style of music in Russia during the nineteenth century.

FIXED DO. See *Solmization.*

FLAGEOLET (flaj oh LETT). A small, flute-like instrument that was popular in the seventeenth century. It had six fingerholes, four on the top and two on the underside for the thumbs, and was played by blowing through a kind of whistle mouthpiece.

FLAM. A short stroke on the snare drum,* consisting usually of two quick beats. If the first beat is accented, it is an *open flam*; if the second beat is accented, it is a *closed flam.*

FLAMENCO. A Spanish dance, especially popular among the Gypsies, that originated in Andalusia, a province of Spain. It is usually accompanied by the guitar. The flamenco is danced by a man and a woman who circle around each other, holding their upper bodies in a rigid position, stamping their feet furiously, and executing some intricate arm movements, all the while playing castanets with great skill.

FLAT. (1) The sign (♭) placed before a note to indicate that the note is to be lowered a half step. If the sign is in the key signature,* every note on that pitch in any octave throughout the piece is to be lowered a half step, unless another sign cancels or changes it. If the sign is before a single note, only that note and repetitions of the note (on the same line or space) within the measure are to be lowered a half step. (See also *Accidentals.*) (2) The term *flat* is used also to describe a tone that is below its correct pitch, or a kind of singing or playing of an instrument that is consistently below normal pitch.

FLAUTANDO (flou TAHN doh). A direction to violin players to bow close to the end of the fingerboard in order to get a flute-like tone. It is sometimes used also to indicate the use of *harmonics.**

FLOTOW (FLOH toh), **Friedrich von.** German composer, born in Teutendorf on April 26, 1812; died in Darmstadt on January 24, 1883.

Flotow was the son of a nobleman who wanted his son to be educated for the diplomatic service. When the boy was fifteen he was sent to Paris for further study. There, however, he became acquainted with artists and musicians and discovered his own talent for music. He studied composition and theory, and by the time he was twenty-five he had written a short lyric piece, *Alessandro Stradella,* which was performed in Paris. He enjoyed composition and wrote a number of ballets, some incidental music for the theater, and some twenty-five operas. For a while Flotow's music enjoyed a good deal of popularity in France, but today he is known best for his opera *Martha,* one of the favorites in both Europe and America.

FLÜGELHORN (FLEE gel horn). A brass instrument similar in size and shape to the cornet,* but with a fuller tone. Its range is from the E below Middle C to the second B-flat above Middle C. It is a transposing instrument* and, like the cornet, has three pistons and a cup-shaped mouthpiece. The flügelhorn, a member of the saxhorn* family, is used most often in bands.

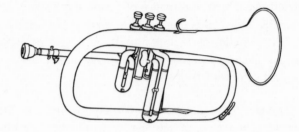

FLUTE. One of the oldest wind instruments. In former times it was made of wood, but modern flutes are made of metal. It is played by blowing across a mouth hole placed on the side of the instrument near the closed end of the tube. The modern flute usually has fifteen holes and twenty-three keys and levers. The tone quality of the flute varies considerably from low to high. The low notes sound rather breathy, while the high notes are bright and penetrating. Although there is a flute in D, used sometimes in bands, the orchestral flute is in C. It has a range of three octaves, from Middle C upward, the second and third octaves being played by a method called *overblowing,** and by alternate fingerings. (See also *Flageolet, Fife, Piccolo,* and *Recorder,* other members of the flute family.)

FOLK SONG. In general, a folk song may be thought of as the musical expression of a group of people rather than of a single composer. From earliest times people have expressed themselves in songs—lullabies, battle songs, love songs, songs to accompany dancing, and so on. In the beginning these songs were not written down. They were sung by the older people to the younger, and were passed down from generation to generation, in this manner, to the present time. Every country in the world has its own characteristic folk songs. Many of those heard in rural sections of America —and often sung by professional "folk singers" on radio and television— are variants of ancient folk songs that stemmed from the English, Scotch, German, and other nationalities who settled in this country.

Folk songs such as *Lord Russell* and *Barbara Allen* are inherited from England; *Alouette* from Canada, originally from France; *Cockles and Mussels* from Ireland, and so on. Others, not nearly so old, originated in this country. Such songs as *The Erie Canal, On Top of Old Smoky, Sweet Betsy from Pike,* and *Frankie and Johnny* are examples of folk songs that reflect the experiences and feelings of people in different sections of the United States.

Folk songs are valuable to historians, anthropologists, and sociologists because they tell much about the customs and beliefs of the ordinary people of the past. For this reason great efforts are made to write down or to record as many as possible of the surviving folk songs before they are lost forever. Such men as Bartók* and Kodály* have recorded thousands of folk songs of the Hungarians and other Middle European peoples. Other collectors have been busy doing the same thing all over the world.

FORLANA (for LAHN nah). A dance that originated in northeastern Italy. It is usually played in a fast 6/8 or 6/4 time. A number of composers have used the *Forlana,* among them Bach in his Suite No. 1 in C major for orchestra; Campra in *Les Fêtes Vénitiennes*; Ravel in *Le Tombeau de Couperin.*

FORM. Form has to do with the organization of music. All music, from the simplest folk song to the most complex symphony, has form. And with music, as with other arts and crafts, form is produced by the overall organizing principles of repetition, contrast, and variation. Without repetition, music would lack unity; without contrast, it would lack variety and be monotonous; without variation, which, in a way, is a combination of repetition and contrast, music would be primitive and lack sophistication.

A useful distinction is sometimes made between form *in* or *within* music and form *of* music.

Form *in* music involves its internal organization—the interrelationships of its various elements, the operation of the three organizing principles (repetition, contrast, variation) on the elements of melody,* harmony,* rhythm,* texture, tone quality. Within a composition the principles operate in various combinations. For example, a melody or melodic fragment may be repeated and the harmony changed; a rhythmic pattern repeated and the melodic line varied; melody, harmony, rhythm, texture, repeated with contrasting tone quality; and so on.

Throughout the history of music, composers, through the application of these principles, have evolved elaborate techniques of musical composition—canon,* stretto,* augmentation,* diminution,* inversion,* retrograde,* ostinato,* and so on. In various styles and period of music, they have used these techniques as well as more elementary applications of repetition, contrast, and variation, to create the internal organization of their compositions.

Form *of* music concerns the external organization or overall patterns of music, and this is the sense in which the term *musical form* is most often used. In the history of music a considerable number of musical forms have emerged. Some of the more familiar forms (or structural patterns) are: strophic form,* variation form,* binary form,* ternary form,* sonata or sonata-allegro form* (exposition, development, recapitulation), four-part form, five-part form, rondo form.* There is also what is called through-composed form,* and there are the imitative forms (fugue,* ricercar,* and so on). The term *form* is also used to designate composite forms (sonata,* symphony,* concerto,* suite,* cantata,* opera,* oratorio,* Mass,* and so on).

FORTE (FOHR tay). An Italian word meaning "strong." In music it means "loud." It is usually abbreviated as *f*. (See also *Dynamics.*)

FORTISSIMO (fohr TEE see moh). An Italian word meaning "very strong." In music it means "very loud," and is usually abbreviated as *ff* or *fff*. (See also *Dynamics.*)

FORZANDO (fort ZAHN doh). An Italian word meaning "with force." In music it usually means "to play forcefully," and is often abbreviated as *fz*. (See also *Dynamics.*)

FOSS, Lucas. American composer, born in Berlin, Germany, on August 15, 1922.

Although Foss was born in Berlin, he is considered an American composer because he has lived in the United States since he was fifteen. He began his study of music in Berlin when he was very young. By the time he was eleven he had shown such talent that he was sent to Paris to study piano and composition. After his parents brought him to the United States he continued to study piano and composition, and he added conducting to his other accomplishments. He was only twenty-two when he was made the official pianist with the Boston Symphony Orchestra. A year later he won a Guggenheim Fellowship, the youngest ever to be awarded that honor in composition.

Foss has appeared as piano soloist with many symphony orchestras, conducted in cities all over the country, and in addition has composed a large number of works—many of them in twelve-tone idiom. Two of his best known works are the folk opera, *The Jumping Frog of Calaveras County* (based on a story by Mark Twain) and the opera *Griffelkin,* which was produced on television in 1955. In 1963 Foss was appointed conductor of the Buffalo Symphony Orchestra.

FOSTER, Stephen Collins. American composer, born in Pittsburgh on July 4, 1826; died in New York City on January 13, 1864.

Although Stephen Foster was almost completely self-taught, he wrote some of the most popular songs the world has ever known. As a child he studied the flute, but he had no lessons in formal composition or theory.

Nevertheless, he wrote songs that were enormously appealing, and became popular at once. Most of his life was spent in the Middle West, where he had very little contact with musicians of the European school, and his songs are thoroughly American. His first song was published when he was eighteen.

Foster's father and brothers were business men and they could not understand the boy's dreamy nature and his desire to spend his time writing songs. They persuaded him to go to Cincinnati as an accountant in his brother's firm. He continued to write songs, however, and eventually was able to devote all of his time to music. In all, he wrote more than 180 songs, most of them to his own words. The best known are *Oh, Susanna! My Old Kentucky Home, Massa's in de Cold, Cold Ground, Jeanie with the Light Brown Hair, Old Black Joe,* and *Beautiful Dreamer.*

FOURTH. An interval that covers three ascending steps in the major or minor scale. The perfect fourth is made up of two whole steps and one half step. In the key of C major, C-F is a perfect fourth. Other perfect fourths in the key of C major are D-G, E-A, G-C, A-D, and B-E. The *augmented fourth* is a fourth with the upper note raised a half step or the lower note lowered a half step. The *diminished fourth* is a fourth with the upper note lowered a half step or the lower note raised a half step.

perfect fourths   augmented   diminished
                          fourths   fourths

FOX TROT. A ballroom dance, usually in 2/2 or 2/4 rhythm, that originated in America about 1912. Other dances in duple* rhythm, such as the turkey trot and the two-step, evolved from it. Examples of popular music to which the fox-trot was danced are *Alexander's Ragtime Band* and *Everybody's Doing It,* both by Irving Berlin.*

FRANCK (FRAHNK), **César Auguste.** Belgian composer and organist, born in Liége on December 10, 1822; died in Paris on November 8, 1890.

Although Franck was born a Belgian, he spent the greater part of his life in France. In 1873 he became a naturalized French citizen.

Franck first studied music in his home town of Liége. He made such remarkable progress that he went on tour as a concert pianist when he was only eleven years old. His parents not only approved of his musical career, they actually pushed the boy. In fact, they moved to Paris so he could have the advantage of the best musical training. He was accepted as a pupil at the Paris Conservatory when he was fifteen. After his graduation in 1842 he taught privately, then in 1872 returned to the Conservatory as a professor of organ. Although Franck taught organ and was organist in two Paris churches, he was more deeply interested in composing, and he soon developed an individual style.

Today Franck is recognized as one of the great composers, his Symphony in D minor being one of the most frequently played of all symphonies. But in his own day he was not given the recognition he deserved except by his pupils, a number of whom became famous composers themselves.

In addition to his Symphony, Franck wrote several symphonic poems; works for piano and orchestra and for chorus and orchestra; chamber music; organ works; three operas; choral works; a large number of pieces for piano; and many songs.

FRANZ, Robert. German composer, born in Halle on June 28, 1815; died there on October 24, 1892.

Franz's family name was Knauth, but the father adopted legally the name Franz when Robert was thirty-two years old. The parents were not in favor of a musical career for their son, but he managed to learn to play the organ, and later to study further in Dessau. His first set of songs, published in 1843, was warmly received. At various times he held posts as organist in a Halle church, conductor of the Halle *Singakademie,* and director of music at Halle University. His career as a musician was cut short in 1868 when deafness and a nervous disorder forced him to retire. Money for his support was raised by admirers both in Europe and America through benefit concerts and donations. Franz wrote a quantity of church music, including additional accompaniments to oratorios of both Bach* and Handel,* but he is best known for the more than 250 songs he wrote.

FRENCH HORN. A name given to the orchestral horn to distinguish it from the English horn.* (For a description of the instrument, see *Horn.*)

FRESCOBALDI (fress coh BAHL dee), **Girolamo.** Italian composer and organist, born in Ferrara in 1583 (the exact date is not known; he was baptized on September 9); died in Rome on March 1, 1643.

Frescobaldi studied organ in his home town, and in January, 1607, was appointed organist at the church of Santa Maria in Rome. In June of that year he went to the Netherlands, where he stayed for a year. On his return to Italy he was appointed organist of St. Peter's in Rome. By that time he had already become so famous that 30,000 people are said to have attended his first performance. Except for five years, when he served as court organist in Florence, he remained at St. Peter's until his death. In addition to a great many compositions for keyboard instruments, his works include pieces for instrumental ensembles, arias for one or more voices, and a set of madrigals.

FRETS. Thin pieces of wood or metal set crosswise at intervals on the fingerboards of certain stringed instruments such as the guitar, the banjo, and the ukelele. Each fret indicates the place where the fingers press a string to play a certain note of the scale. Frets are not used on violins, violas, cellos, or double basses.

FRIML, Rudolf. Czech (later a naturalized American) composer and pianist, born in Prague on December 7, 1879.

As a young man, Friml studied at the Prague Conservatory. In 1901 he visited the United States as accompanist to the famous violinist Kubelik. In 1906 he returned and from then on made his home mainly in New York and Hollywood.

Although Friml wrote a great many works for piano, including a concerto that he performed with the New York Symphony Orchestra, he is best known for his operettas, *Katinka, The Firefly, Rose Marie,* and *You're in Love.*

FROG. A name sometimes used for the part of a violin bow (or the bows of other stringed instruments) held in the hand. (See also *Nut (2).*)

FUGATO (foo GAH toh). A section of a composition that is written in the style of a fugue,* although the composition itself is not a fugue. Examples of *fugato* are found in the first and fourth movements of Beethoven's Symphony No. 3.

FUGHETTA (foo GET tah). A miniature fugue.* That is, a fugue in which all the rules of fugal composition are followed, but in a condensed form. Bach's *Goldberg Variation* No. 10 is an example of a fughetta.

FUGUE. A composition in which two, three, four, or even five parts are woven together according to certain principles of imitative counterpoint.*

The first statement of the subject* by all voices is called the exposition.* In the exposition, the subject or theme* is first stated alone by one voice.* A second voice then restates the theme in the dominant* (this is called the answer*) while the first voice continues on to other melodic material. If there are other voices, they enter in succession, stating the subject or the answer alternately. If the same melodic material is used against each statement of the subject or answer, it is called a *countersubject*. After the exposition, a fugue is completely free in form, though new statements of the subject are usually alternated with sections in which the subject is not stated, called *episodes*. Most fugues end with a coda.* Among the devices used in fugues are augmentation,* diminution,* inversion,* and stretto.*

FUGUING TUNE. A kind of hymn tune that became popular in the eighteenth century, especially in America. It is called a fuguing tune because the parts, or voices,* imitate each other somewhat as they do in a real fugue,* but in a very simple way. William Billings,* one of America's first composers, wrote many fuguing tunes.

FUOCO (foo OH koh). An Italian word meaning "fire." It indicates that the passage is to be played in a lively and flashy way.

FURIANT (foo ree AHNT). A lively Bohemian dance in 3/4 time, with a syncopated* rhythm. Smetana,* Dvořák,* and other Czech composers have used the furiant in their works, sometimes in place of the scherzo.* Dvořák wrote a piece called *Two Furiants*, Op. 42, for piano.

G

G. The letter G has many uses in music: (1) G is the name given to one pitch in each octave throughout the musical range. (2) The name given to a scale* or key* whose first note is G. A composition may be written in the key of G major, G minor, G-flat major, or G-sharp minor. (See also *Key Signatures.*) (3) On the piano keyboard G is the white key that lies just above the first black key in each group of three black keys. (4) When G is used with the name of an instrument, as the alto flute in G, it indicates a transposing instrument* on which the note written C sounds as G.

G-CLEF. (See *Clefs.*)

GABRIELI (gahb ree YELL ee), **Andrea.** Italian composer and organist, born in Venice about 1520; died there in 1586. (The exact dates are not known.)

Andrea Gabrieli studied organ with Willaert* at St. Mark's in Venice. In 1566 he was appointed second organist there, and eighteen years later became first organist. He was a prolific composer, and the originality of his works brought him fame throughout Europe. Pupils came to study with him from many parts of the Continent. One of his most talented pupils was his nephew, Giovanni Gabrieli.* His compositions include Masses,* a number of instrumental works, madrigals,* and motets.*

GABRIELI (gahb ree YELL ee), **Giovanni.** Italian composer and organist, born in Venice in 1555 (the exact date is not known); died there on August 12, 1612.

Little is known about Giovanni's early life except that he studied music with his famous uncle, Andrea Gabrieli.* When he was eighteen he went to Munich, Germany (then Bavaria), where he served for several years

110

as musical assistant in the Court Chapel. In 1584 he was appointed second organist at St. Mark's in Venice, and when his uncle Andrea died in 1586 Giovanni succeeded him as first organist. Among the many pupils who came from all parts of Europe to study with him, his favorite was Heinrich Schutz* who stayed close to him for the three years before his death. His many works include organ compositions, motets* with orchestral accompaniments, several "Sacred Symphonies" for voices and instruments, and music for brass ensembles.

GALLIARD (GAL yard). A lively dance with great leaps, usually in 3/2 time, dating from the fifteenth century. It was often paired with a more dignified dance, the pavane,* which was in slow 2/2 or 2/4 time.

GALOP. A round dance in 2/4 time that was popular as a ballroom dance in the nineteenth century. The steps are performed in a kind of hop-glide, hop-glide fashion.

GAVOTTE (gah VOT). An old dance that originated in France among a mountain people called Gavots. It became popular with the people of the French court in the seventeenth century, then spread to other European countries. It is a rather gay and lively dance in 4/4 time. Many of the classical suites* contain a gavotte, often following another type of dance called the sarabande.* An example is Bach's Suite No. 3 for Orchestra in D major.

GEBRAUCHSMUSIK (ger BROWCHS moo zeek). A German word meaning "music for ordinary use." Music that is composed for practical purposes rather than for artistic performance, and that is easy enough to be played by amateurs came to be called *Gebrauchsmusic* in the 1920's. Paul Hindemith* and Kurt Weill* are examples of two "serious" musicians who have written a good deal of *Gebrauschsmusic.*

GEMINIANI (jeh meen YAHN ee), **Francesco.** Italian composer and violinist, born in Lucca in 1687 (the exact date is not known); died in Dublin, Ireland, on September 17, 1762.

Geminiani studied violin with the great teacher and violinist Corelli.* In 1714 he went to England, where he enjoyed a great success as a violin soloist. In 1733 he went to live in Dublin, where he stayed for seven years teaching, writing, and giving concerts. He returned again to Dublin in

1759 and remained until his death. His works include numerous violin sonatas, trios, and concertos and some harpsichord solos, but his fame rests largely on a treatise he wrote on violin playing, *The Art of Playing on the Violin.*

GERSHWIN, George. American pianist and composer, born in Brooklyn, New York, on September 28, 1898; died in Beverly Hills, California, on July 11, 1937.

Gershwin, who came of a poor family, did not become interested in music until he was in his teens. Then he managed to take piano lessons. He did so well that a "Tin Pan Alley" music firm hired him to "plug" their songs—that is, to get well-known musicians to play or sing them professionally. He studied composition with Rubin Goldmark,* an excellent teacher, and soon was composing songs of his own. His first "hit" song was *Swannee,* a number that sold millions of copies. He became interested in jazz, and Paul Whiteman, a successful dance band leader, commissioned him to write *Rhapsody in Blue,* a kind of jazz concerto. That, too, became widely popular. Soon afterwards he wrote *Piano Concerto in F,* and then a clever orchestral work, *An American in Paris.* He wrote the music for a number of highly successful musicals, among them *Lady Be Good, Strike Up the Band, Show Girl,* and *Of Thee I Sing.* He also wrote the music for the highly successful American opera, *Porgy and Bess.*

GESUALDO (jeh soo AHL doh), **Carlo.** Italian composer, born in Naples about 1560 (the exact date is not known); died there on September 8, 1613.

Gesualdo was of noble birth. His father was the Prince of Venosa, and he himself succeeded to the title in 1591. He was intensely interested in poetry and music and became a skillful lute* player. He published six books of madrigals* during his lifetime (a seventh was published after his death), two books of motets,* and other works.

GIBBONS, Orlando. English composer and organist, born in Oxford in 1583 (the exact date is not known); died in Canterbury on June 5, 1625.

Orlando came from a musical family: his father and three brothers were all musicians. Orlando sang in the King's College Choir, Cambridge, from his twelfth to his fourteenth year, and later received the B.Mus.* and M.Mus.* degrees from the same university. When he was only twenty-one years old he was appointed organist of the Royal Chapel, a position he held for the rest of his life. During the two years before his death he served also as organist at Westminster Abbey. His works include about forty anthems* and other church music, madrigals* and motets,* chamber music, more than forty pieces for keyboard instruments, and several masques.*

GIGUE (zheeg). A French word meaning "jig." The gigue is a rather lively dance form, usually in 6/8 or 12/8 time. In suites, as those of Bach, the gigue is usually the last of the four dances, following the allemande,* courante,* and the sarabande.* It developed from the earlier jig of Ireland, Scotland, and England, that first became popular in the early seventeenth century and is still popular today at country dances, especially in Ireland.

GIORDANO (zhor DAH noh), **Umberto.** Italian composer, born in Foggia on August 27, 1867; died in Milan on November 12, 1948.

Giordano's mother and father were not enthusiastic about having their son study music. The boy showed such talent, however, that friends prevailed upon the family to let him try to make a career of music. He graduated from the Naples Conservatory, and by the time he was thirty had already made a name for himself as an opera composer.

Giordano is best known in this country for his opera *Andrea Cheniér,* which is produced frequently. Another of his operas, *Madame Sans-Geñe,* was first produced at the Metropolitan Opera House in New York in 1915.

GIUSTO (JOO stoh). An Italian word meaning "proper" or "right." It is usually used with the word *tempo* (time), as *tempo giusto,* to indicate that strict time should be followed.

GLASS HARMONICA. (The correct name is *armonica.*) Benjamin Franklin invented the glass harmonica after hearing a performer in England play a concert on a set of tuned glasses. Franklin's instrument consisted of glass bowls fitted on a horizontal rod. The bowls were graded as to size so the entire scale could be played quite accurately. The rims of the bowls were kept wet, and the performer played by touching the wet rims with his fingers. At one time the instrument was quite popular both in America and in Europe. The delicate quality of the tone appealed to a number of composers who wrote compositions especially for it. Mozart wrote a lovely quintet for armonica, flute, oboe, viola, and cello in 1791 for a blind girl who was a talented armonica player.

GLAZOUNOV (GLAHZ oo noff), **Alexander.** Russian composer, born in St. Petersburg (now Leningrad) on August 10, 1865; died in Paris on March 21, 1936.

Glazounov, whose father was a well-known publisher and book seller, showed great talent for music while he was still quite young. He began the study of piano when he was nine, and shortly afterwards became interested in theory. In no time at all he was composing music of his own, and while still in his mid-teens showed such promise that the great composer Rimsky-Korsakov* accepted him as a pupil. Glazounov was only sixteen when his first symphony was played in St. Petersburg. He had an amazing musical memory and could write down or play almost any composition after hearing it just once. In later years he helped Rimsky-Korsakoff finish the opera *Prince Igor* which Borodin* had not completed at the time of his death.

Most of Glazounov's works were instrumental. They include eight symphonies, two piano concertos, concertos for other instruments, seven string quartets, seven choral works, three ballets, and a number of works for piano.

GLEE. A fairly simple song in three or more parts, usually for male voices, and sung without any accompaniment. The glee became popular in England in the eighteenth and early nineteenth centuries, and many glees written during that period are performed by glee clubs* today.

GLEE CLUB. A group of singers who sing not only glees but other fairly short classical and popular numbers. In America today many high schools and colleges have glee clubs. Most of them are made up of male singers, although in some high schools there are girls' glee clubs and mixed glee clubs as well. The name stems from the famous Glee Club that was founded in London in 1787 for the purpose of singing glees,* madrigals,* canons,* and motets.*

GLINKA, Mikhail Ivanovich. Russian composer, born in Novospasskoe, Government of Smolensk, on June 1, 1804; died in Berlin, Germany, on February 15, 1857.

Glinka was the son of a wealthy landowner and spent most of his boyhood in the country. He enjoyed listening to the songs of the peasants and to the music of native musicians hired by his father. He studied piano with his governess and later with several teachers in St. Petersburg (now Leningrad). Although he was exceptionally talented and began composing at quite an early age, he did not study theory and composition until some time later.

Glinka enjoyed French and Italian opera, but he was determined to write a really Russian opera—one that was based on Russian history and that utilized native Russian musical ideas. He set to work and in 1836 completed an opera, *A Life for the Czar,* that was based on the story of the Polish invasion of Russia in the seventeenth century. It was produced in St. Petersburg with great success. This was followed by another famous opera, *Russlan and Ludmila,* produced in 1842.

These two operas were the first Russian operas to gain recognition outside the country, and the first to employ a characteristic Russian style. Because of their influence in developing a national school of music in Russia, Glinka is sometimes considered to be the "father" of Russian music.

Glinka also wrote a number of works for orchestra, several choral works, a large number of songs, and many pieces for piano.

GLISSANDO (glee SAHN doh). A word taken from the French *glisser,* which means "to slide." In music, a glissando is a scale-wise series of notes, up or down, played so rapidly that individual notes do not sound. On different instruments the glissando is played differently: (1) On the piano the glissando is played with the nails of the fingers—usually with the nail of the middle finger for an ascending glissando; with the thumb nail for a descending glissando. (2) On stringed instruments of the violin family the glissando is played by sliding the finger up or down the string very rapidly. (3) On most wind instruments a kind of glissando effect is made by increasing the pressure of the lips enough to raise the pitch of each individual note in rapid succession. On the trombone,* of course, a glissando is played with the slide. (4) On the harp* the glissando is played by brushing the fingers across the strings. (5) On the timpani* a glissando can be played by moving the foot pedal while executing a roll* with the sticks.

The abbreviation for glissando is *gliss.* It is often indicated by a straight or wavy line between the two notes that show where the glissando begins and ends, like this:

GLOCKENSPIEL (GLOCK en shpeel). A German word meaning "Chimes." The glockenspiel is a percussion instrument consisting of steel bars of different lengths attached to a frame, rather like a piano keyboard. It is played by striking the bars with wooden hammers, one held in each hand.

The glockenspiel has a light "tinkling" sound that makes it an important instrument in the orchestra for certain effects. Some examples are: Papageno's music in Mozart's *The Magic Flute*; "Dance of the Hours" from Ponchielli's opera *La Gioconda*; and "Magic Fire Music" from *Die Walküre* by Richard Wagner.*

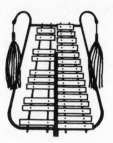

GLORIA. A Latin word meaning "glory." It is the first word in the phrase *Gloria in excelsis Deo* (Glory to God in the highest), which is the second part of the Ordinary of the Mass* sung in Roman Catholic churches. It is also the first word of *Gloria Patri* (Glory to God), the familiar Doxology which begins "Praise God from Whom All Blessings Flow," sung in some Protestant churches, usually after a psalm or canticle.

GLUCK (GLOOK), **Christoph Willibald.** German composer, born in Erasbach on July 2, 1714; died in Vienna, Austria, on November 15, 1787.

Gluck was given a good general education, but he was eighteen years old before he began the serious study of music. He was sent to Prague to complete his education, and soon became a good enough cellist to make a living by giving lessons. He also played organ in church. He was hired by Prince Melzi as a musician in Vienna, and later went with him to Italy. There he became interested in opera. By this time he had become such a skillful composer that he could quickly turn out operas of the kind that were popular then in Italy. Between 1741 and 1744 nine of his operas were performed in various Italian cities. In 1746 he went to London, but the two operas he presented there were not successful and he returned to

Vienna. Up to about this time Gluck has been happy to compose operas in the Italian style, that is, operas with music that tended to show off the voices of the "star" singers without much regard for the story the opera was supposed to tell. Now, Gluck decided, he would write only operas that expressed the true feeling of the story itself. This change in style was an important reform that influenced later Italian, German, and French operas very greatly.

In all, Gluck wrote some 100 operas, many of which have been lost. Today, only one of his operas, *Orpheus and Euridice,* is still widely produced. It was first performed in Vienna more than 200 years ago, and is one of the earliest operas performed today.

GOLDMARK, Rubin. American composer, born in New York on August 15, 1872; died there on March 6, 1936.

Goldmark was sent to Vienna when he was seventeen to study piano and composition at the famous Vienna Conservatory. Three years later he returned to the United States for further study at the National Conservatory in New York. Except for seven years spent in Colorado for reasons of health, Goldmark spent most of the remainder of his life in New York. He made a number of concert-lecture tours throughout the United States, and from 1924 until his death served as head of the composition department of the Juilliard School of Music. Two of his pupils who became famous composers themselves were George Gershwin* and Aaron Copland.* His compositions include a number of works for orchestra, chamber music, piano pieces, songs, and choruses.

GONG. A percussion* instrument consisting of a flat metal plate (usually bronze) about three feet in diameter with the edges turned over. The gong swings from a wooden frame and is played by being struck with a heavy beater that looks like a bass drumstick. Its tone ranges all the way from a soft, muffled sound to a loud, crashing effect.

GOOSENS, Eugene. English composer and conductor, born in London on May 26, 1893, died there on June 13, 1962.

Both Goosens' grandfather and father were named Eugene, and both were well-known opera conductors. So it was not surprising that Eugene the Third should exhibit musical talent at an early age. When he was ten years old he was sent to Belgium to study at the Conservatory of Bruges. Three years later he returned to England and completed his musical education, first in Liverpool and later at the Royal Conservatory in London. Soon after graduation he began to build a reputation as a conductor of symphony orchestras. In 1923 he accepted an offer to become permanent conductor of the Rochester Philharmonic Orchestra in New York State, a position he held until 1931 when he became conductor of the Cincinnati Symphony Orchestra. In 1947 he left the United States for an important double post in Australia: conductor of the Sydney Symphony Orchestra, and Director of the New South Wales Conservatory of Music.

Goosens' many compositions include orchestral works, chamber music, pieces for piano and for other instruments, songs, incidental music for several plays, a ballet, and two operas.

GOPAK. (See *Hopak.*)

GOULD, Morton. American composer, born in New York City on December 10, 1913.

Morton Gould, one of America's best known young composers, studied at the Institute of Musical Art in New York and later became a pianist on radio and a conductor of rather light music. He has written both classical and popular music, including music for films and musical comedies. His serious music contains a good deal of jazz rhythm and at the same time some advanced harmonic ideas. His compositions include several symphonies, a piano concerto, a violin concerto, ballets, assorted works for orchestra, and three sonatas for piano.

GOUNOD (goo NOH), **Charles François.** French composer, born in Paris on June 17, 1818; died in Saint-Cloud on October 18, 1893.

Gounod was only five when his father, a well-known painter, died. His mother, a talented musician, was able to give the boy piano lessons and to see that he received a good primary education. He entered the Paris Conservatory when he was eighteen, and did so well that he won the *Prix de Rome** in composition when he was twenty-one. This gave him an opportunity to study and compose in Rome for several years. When he returned to Paris he obtained a job as a church organist. At the same time, he studied theology with the idea of becoming a priest. He changed his mind, however, and decided to devote himself to composition.

Gounod wrote twelve operas, including *Faust,* one of the most popular operas ever written. He also wrote a great deal of church music, choral works, two symphonies, chamber music, and many compositions for piano and for organ. One of his well-known pieces is the *Meditation* (usually called *Ave Maria*) for which he used Prelude No. 1 from J. S. Bach's *Well-Tempered Clavier* as a harmonic background. Another is the humorous little piece for orchestra called *Funeral March of a Marionette.*

GRACE NOTE. An ornament,* played quickly, which has no time value of its own, but takes its value either from the note it precedes or from the note it follows. In notation the grace note is a smaller size than the regular notes. (See also *Appoggiatura.*)

GRADUAL. (1) The second part of the Proper of the Roman Catholic Mass.* It consists of a responsorial chant* sung between the Epistle and the Gospel. (2) A book containing all the music of the Mass that is sung by the choir.

GRAINGER, Percy. Australian-born pianist and composer (naturalized U.S. citizen), born in Melbourne on July 8, 1882; died in White Plains, New York, on February 20, 1961.

As a young child, Grainger was taught piano by his mother, and when he was about twelve she took him to Germany for further study. Not long afterwards he began his long career as a concert pianist. The composer Grieg became interested in the young pianist and the two became great friends. Grainger became famous for his playing of Grieg's popular piano concerto, and it was through Grieg's influence that Grainger became interested in collecting and recording folk songs in the British Isles. Many of his own compositions show the effects of his interest in folk material. In 1914 Grainger settled in the United States and soon became celebrated as a pianist, composer, and conductor. He was married in an elaborate ceremony in the Hollywood Bowl, during which he conducted a piece he had composed in honor of his bride, *To a Nordic Princess.*

In addition to many choral and orchestral works, Grainger wrote much chamber music, several compositions for military band, a large number of settings of British folk music, more than thirty settings of Rudyard Kipling's poems, including a "Jungle Book" cycle, and several two-piano numbers.

One of his piano pieces, *Zanzibar Boat-Song,* calls for three players at one instrument.

GRANADOS (grah NAH dohs), **Enrique.** Spanish pianist and composer, born in Lérida on July 27, 1867; died at sea on March 24, 1916.

Granados' father, an officer in the Spanish Army, wanted his small son to study music and made arrangements to have a fellow officer give the child piano lessons. Later, when the family settled in Barcelona, Enrique studied with two well-known teachers. When he was sixteen he won the first prize in a piano contest, and soon afterward was earning his living by playing in a cafe. In 1887 he went to Paris for further study. Two years later he returned to Barcelona and gave a highly successful recital, shortly after which a well-known orchestra played several of his compositions.

Granados was best known as a concert pianist, but he also did a great deal of teaching and composing. He wrote a number of orchestral works, chamber music, songs, six operas, and many pieces for piano. One of his greatest works was the two-volume collection of piano pieces called *Goyescas.* Each piece in the collection is based on one of the paintings or tapestries of the great Spanish artist, Goya. Later, he expanded *Goyescas* into an opera. (A libretto was written for it by Ferando Periquet.) The opera was performed by the Metropolitan Opera Company in New York in 1916. While returning to Europe from that occasion his ship was torpedoed by a German submarine, and both Granados and his wife lost their lives.

GRAND OPERA. The word *grand* is applied to an elaborate type of opera to distinguish it from *comic* or *light* opera. A grand opera consists of music throughout, with no spoken dialogue, and its plot is serious, often tragic. In addition to individual singers, it usually calls for a large chorus, a ballet, lavish sets, and a full orchestra. Because of its large cast and complicated staging, a grand opera is most often performed in an opera house or amphitheater.

GRAVE (GRAH vay). An Italian word meaning "serious." It indicates that the music should be performed rather slowly and solemnly.

GRECHANINOV (grah CHAHN ee noff), **Alexander.** Russian composer, born in Moscow on October 25, 1864; died in New York City on January 3, 1956.

Grechaninov's father did not want his son to become a musician, and it was not until the boy was seventeen that he was allowed to study music seriously. He was sent then to the Conservatory in Moscow, but there one of his teachers said he had no talent and he went to St. Petersburg (now Leningrad) and entered the Conservatory. There, under the famous Rimsky-Korsakov* he made rapid progress. After graduating from the Conservatory he taught for several years, then returned to Moscow where he completed the opera *Dobrina Nikitch,* which was performed with great success. In spite of this, Grechaninov devoted himself mainly to composing church music and songs. In all, he wrote some 250 songs, including a number of children's songs and an opera for children.

The Soviet government, which had come into power, did not approve of the kind of music Grechaninov wrote, so in 1924 he left Russia and went to live in Paris. The Nazi occupation of France found him on a concert tour of the United States, and he decided to stay. He became a naturalized citizen in 1946.

GREGORIAN CHANT. (Sometimes called *plainsong.*) This kind of chant is used for liturgical purposes in the Roman Catholic church. It was named for Pope Gregory I, although some present-day scholars think it may have been of later origin.

A Gregorian chant consists of a single unison melody, sung without countermelodies or accompaniment. It is not divided into bars, and it has no set time, such as 3/4 or 4/4, but the music follows the rhythm of the words. The words are usually taken from the Bible, and usually sung in Latin. Instead of being in a key,* as is most music of our time, a Gregorian chant may be in any one of eight church *modes,** a system of scales used in Medieval times.

GRIEG (greeg), **Edvard.** Norwegian composer, born in Bergen on June 15, 1843; died there on September 4, 1907.

Grieg began to study piano when he was six years old with his mother as teacher. When he was nine he was already composing, and by the time he was fifteen he showed so much talent that a great Norwegian violinist, Ole Bull, persuaded his parents to send him to Leipzig, Germany, to study. After four years in Leipzig and another period of study in Copenhagen, Denmark, he returned to Norway and settled in Christiania. There he gave music lessons and continued to compose. One of his compositions was the incidental music to a play, *Peer Gynt* written by the famous Norwegian dramatist and poet, Henrik Ibsen. This music became so popular in Norway that the Norwegian Government gave Grieg a pension for life. Although not large, the pension made it possible to him to give up teaching and devote his time to composing.

Grieg tried in his music to express the Norwegian character, and he succeeded so well that he became one of the most popular of all composers. He wrote many beautiful songs and a large number of piano pieces. Among his works for orchestra, his two suites from *Peer Gynt* are favorites of audiences throughout the world. His *Piano Concerto in A Minor* is one of the best known of all concertos.*

GRIFFES, Charles Tomlinson. American composer, born in Elmira, New York, on September 17, 1884; died in New York City on April 8, 1920.

Although Charles Griffes died when he was still a young man, he is recognized as one of America's outstanding composers. He started out to be a pianist and went to Berlin, Germany, to study. There, however, one of his teachers, the famous composer Humperdinck,* recognized the boy's talent for composition and encouraged him to concentrate on writing music. When he returned to America, Griffes was forced to make a living by teaching music in a boys' school, but he continued to compose on the side, and before long had achieved recognition for such compositions as *The White Peacock* for piano (also scored for orchestra) and his tone poem for orchestra, *The Pleasure Dome of Kubla Khan*. Griffes' other works consist mainly of piano music, songs, chamber music, several stage works, and compositions for orchestra.

GROUND BASS. A short melody in the bass* that is played over and over again while the upper parts change. Compositions with this kind of bass part were popular in the seventeenth and eighteenth centuries, and sometimes were called *grounds*. (See also *Chaconne* and *Passacaglia*.)

GUARNERI (gwahr NEHR ee). The name of a famous family of violin makers of Cremona, Italy. The first was Andrea, who died in 1698, and who was a fellow-pupil with Stradivari* of the great violin maker Amati.* The most celebrated member of the family was Giuseppe, a grandson of Andrea, who died in 1744. Giuseppe became known as Giuseppe del Gesù to distinguish him from his father, also a violin maker, who had the same name. Guarneri violins, like Stradivari and Amati instruments, are highly prized for their fine workmanship and beautiful tone quality.

GUIDO d'AREZZO (GWEE doh dah RED zoh). Italian theorist and teacher, born about 990; died in Pomposa about 1050 (the exact places and dates are not known).

Guido was a Benedictine monk and for some time was in charge of the choir school at Arezzo, the town from which he took his name. While there he devised a system to help the choirboys learn to read music more easily. This system, for which he is famous, consisted of associating each note of a hexachord* with a particular syllable. Known as solmization,* it assigned to each note the syllables *ut, re, mi, fa, sol, la.* Another innovation of his was the music staff of four lines, which eventually evolved into our present-day five-line staff.* The use of the lined staff did away with all uncertainty as to pitch, and proved invaluable to composers and performers.

GUITAR. A stringed instrument with a fretted fingerboard. The six strings of the guitar are played by being plucked with the fingers or with a plectrum.* The guitar was introduced into Spain by the Moors during the Middle Ages, and it is still a popular instrument there. In fact, most of the classical guitar players today are Spanish, Andres Segovia being perhaps the greatest of all. In the United States the guitar has become popular as a jazz instrument in dance bands, and for accompanying folk and "hillbilly" songs.

The Hawaiian guitar, which is similar in appearance to the normal guitar, is equipped with a movable metal bar that runs across all the strings. This bar, instead of the fingers, is used to "stop" the strings. By sliding the steel bar up or down, particular intervals can be reproduced at any pitch. The sound produced by the sliding gives the instrument its characteristic "Hawaiian" sound.

The steel guitar is an electronic instrument* used mainly in dance orchestras. The body, which supports the strings, is shaped like a box. A separate cabinet contains an amplifier connected by a cable to an electric pickup system that produces the sound.

H

H. The letter H (pronounced "ha") is the German symbol for the note (or key) that we call B-natural. The German B is the same as our B-flat.

HABANERA (ah bah NAY rah). A dance that originated in Cuba and is named for Cuba's largest city, Havana. The dance became very popular in Spain. The music is in 2/4 time and has a characteristic syncopated rhythm that goes like this: (♪♩♪♪♩). A famous habanera occurs in the first act of Bizet's opera *Carmen*. Bizet adapted it from a song, *El Arreglito*, by the Spanish song writer Sebastian Yradier. Another famous habanera is the familiar *La Paloma,* also by Yradier.

HADLEY, Henry Kimball. American composer and conductor, born in Somerville, Massachusetts, on December 20, 1871; died in New York City on September 6, 1937.

Hadley studied music first with his father, then at the New England Conservatory in Boston. He began his conducting career with a small Boston opera company, but wanting to learn more about composing he left a year later to study in Vienna. From then on he did a great deal of composing and enjoyed an outstanding career as a conductor. His conducting appointments included the Mainz Municipal Opera in Germany, the Seattle Symphony Orchestra, the San Francisco Symphony, and the New York Philharmonic (as associate conductor). Although his own works were performed frequently, Hadley felt that American composers in general were neglected by the major symphony orchestras, and he formed the Manhattan Symphony Orchestra for the purpose of performing their works.

Among Hadley's more important compositions are a one-act opera,

Safié, first produced in Mainz, Germany, while he was conducting there; the operas *A Night in Old Paris, Nancy Brown* (a comic opera), *The Garden of Allah,* and *Cleopatra's Night.* He also wrote four symphonies and other works for orchestra, chamber music, a number of choral works, and about 100 songs.

HALF NOTE. (See *Notes and Rests.*)

HALF REST. (See *Notes and Rests.*)

HALF STEP. The smallest interval or distance between notes that is used in our Western type of music. On the piano, this is the distance between any two adjacent keys, as between B and C or between C and C-sharp (the black key immediately above C).

HALF TONE. Same as *Half Step.**

HALLELUJAH (hah lay LOO ya). A word taken from the Hebrew that means "Praise the Lord." It has been used in many cantatas and oratorios. The most famous example is probably the Hallelujah Chorus in Handel's great oratorio *The Messiah.*

HAMMOND ORGAN. (See *Electronic Organ.*)

HANDEL, George Frideric. English (naturalized) composer, born in Halle, Germany, on February 23, 1685; died in London, England, on April 14, 1759.

When Handel was a small child he showed a great love for music, but his father, a barber-surgeon, was a business man with a great respect for money and did not want his son to be a musician. The father, however, was employed as court surgeon by the Duke of Saxe-Weissenfels, and frequently took young George with him on his visits to the court. There the Duke heard the child perform. So impressed was he with the lad's talent that he insisted on his having musical training. The father enrolled George in the Grammar School where he would get a good education in Latin and other non-musical studies, but he allowed him to take lessons with the organist at one of the Halle churches. From the organist George learned a great deal about counterpoint and harmony and became a proficient performer on the harpsichord, organ, violin, and oboe.

Handel was only twelve years old when he was appointed assistant organist at the *Domkirche* (Cathedral Church) in Halle. Four years later he was made organist, a position that paid fairly well and provided lodging. In the meantime he entered the University to study law, which had been his father's wish. He stayed for only a year, and shortly after his father died he left Halle for the large city of Hamburg. There he was hired by the Hamburg Opera as a violinist, and later as harpsichordist. All the while he was busy composing, and shortly before his twentieth birthday his opera *Almira* was performed by the Hamburg Opera. His second opera, *Nero,* was given a short time later.

In 1706 Handel went to Italy, where he stayed for three years, meeting many musicians, hearing music, and becoming acquainted with Italian music in general. One of his own operas, *Rodrigo,* was performed with great success in Florence, and another, *Agrippina,* in Venice.

In 1710, when he was just twenty-five years old, Handel accepted the job of *Kapellmeister* (head musician) to the Elector of Hanover, Germany. That same year he visited London, and while there wrote an entire opera, *Rinaldo,* in fourteen days, which made a great hit in London. After a short return to his position in Hanover, Handel returned to London, where he remained for the rest of his life. Queen Anne granted him a life pension and sometime after her death the new king, George I, increased it.

Most of Handel's earlier works were opera, and most were written in the Italian style. When Italian opera went out of favor in London, Handel turned to oratorio. Today, Handel's operas are not often performed, but his oratorios are heard frequently. His most famous oratorio, *The Messiah,* is performed more often now than it was in Handel's time.

In all, Handel wrote an enormous number of works: forty-six operas; thirty-two oratorios; over one hundred cantatas; many works for orchestra, including his famous *Water Music* and *Fireworks Music*; and harpsichord pieces.

In 1727 Handel became a naturalized citizen of England; in 1750, while working on his last oratorio, *Jephtha,* he became partially blind; and in 1751, eight years before his death, he became totally blind.

HANSON, Howard. American composer and teacher, born in Wahoo, Nebraska, on October 28, 1896.

Hanson's first musical training was in his home town. Later he studied at the Institute of Musical Art in New York, and then at Northwestern University in Evanston, Illinois. His first position after graduation was

Instructor in Music at the College of the Pacific in California. Three years later he was made Dean, a position he held until he won the American *Prix de Rome* in 1921. That prize made it possible for him to spend three years at the American Academy in Rome, during which time he composed several important works.

In 1924 Hanson became Director of the Eastman School of Music in Rochester, New York. His compositions include four symphonies, several symphonic poems, chamber music, songs, piano pieces, and an opera, *Merry Mount.* The opera was commissioned by the Metropolitan Opera and produced there in 1933. Besides the American *Prix de Rome,* Hanson has won several important prizes. One of the most distinguished was the 1944 Pulitzer Prize for his Symphony No. 4.

HARMONICA. A small wind instrument, sometimes called a "mouth organ." It is shaped like a narrow rectangular box and is equipped with one or two rows of small square holes, one hole for each pitch. The holes lead to metal reeds. The player changes pitch by moving the harmonica from side to side so that air is forced through his lips into the various pitch channels, both as he exhales and inhales. Although the harmonica is most often used as a "folk" instrument and by children, it has been used as a solo recital instrument. Both Milhaud* and Vaughan Williams* have written harmonica compositions for Larry Adler, who is probably the world's greatest harmonica player. (See also *Glass Harmonica.*)

HARMONIC MINOR. (See *Minor.*)

HARMONICS. Soft, flute-like sounds produced on a stringed instrument by touching a string lightly instead of pressing it down. Different pitches are obtained by touching the string at different points. The G string on the violin, for example, when touched at the half-way point will produce a G an octave higher. Harmonics are indicated by small circles above the notes to be played: (𝅘𝅥𝅮𝅘𝅥𝅮𝅘𝅥). (See also *Harmonic Series.*)

HARMONIC SERIES. The upper partials or overtones (sometimes called *harmonics*) that vibrate sympathetically with a fundamental tone. For every tone there is a series of these overtones that has a certain mathematical ratio to the fundamental. For example, the first overtone that vibrates with Middle C is the C an octave above; the second overtone is the G above that (a twelfth above the fundamental tone), the third overtone is the next C (a sixteenth, or two octaves above the fundamental tone), and so on. Overtones, or partials, are not audible because they are much softer than the fundamental tone. But they are very important because they determine the quality or *timbre** of a tone. (See also *Acoustics.*)

HARMONIUM. A reed organ, about the size of a small upright piano, with a piano-like keyboard. Two pedals that are worked with the feet blow air through sets of reeds. When the keys are struck at the same time that the pedals are worked, sound comes out. A set of buttons just above the keyboard can be pushed in or pulled out to get different sound effects, somewhat like the effects obtained on a pipe organ by using the stop.*

HARMONY. The composition, relationship, and sequence of chords in a piece. While a melody* (or counterpoint*) consists of single tones following each other, harmony involves two or more tones that are sounded together according to certain rules. Some people refer to harmony as the *vertical* aspect of music and melody as the *horizontal*. The study of harmony involves the various chords in the different keys, the ways in which they are related to each other, and the ways in which they can progress from one to another in a musical composition. (See also *Chords.*)

HARP. A large, triangular shaped stringed instrument whose strings are played by being plucked with the fingers of both hands. The modern harp has forty-six strings stretched between two sides of the frame. The strings are tuned diatonically (according to the whole and half steps in the major scale) in the key of C-flat, with seven strings for each octave. At the base of the harp there are seven pedals (one pedal for each note) that are used to raise the pitch of the strings. One pedal, for example, if pressed down one notch will raise the pitch of all the C-flats to C-natural. If pressed all the way down, it will raise the pitch one whole step to C-sharp. Another pedal does the same for the D-flat strings, another for the E-flat strings, and so on. This makes it possible to play in every major and minor key, just as on the piano.

The compass of the harp is almost equal to that of the piano. Its lowest note is the C-flat three octaves below Middle C; its highest note is the C-flat three and a half octaves above Middle C.

HARPSICHORD. A keyboard instrument that looks something like a small grand piano. It was widely used from the sixteenth century until about the middle of the eighteenth century when the piano took its place. The harpsichord is now used mainly for playing music that was written for keyboard instruments of the period, although some present-day composers are writing music for it.

The strings of the harpsichord are plucked mechanically rather than being struck by hammers. The plucking is done by tongues (called *plectrums**) made of strips of leather or quills that are attached to the tops of narrow pieces of wood called *jacks.** A jack lies below each string, and when a key is pressed the jack flies up and the plectrum attached to it plucks the string. Some of the larger harpsichords have two separate keyboards and two sets of strings.

The tone of the harpsichord is somewhat metallic, but its effect is charming, especially when the instrument is used to play works of such composers as Bach and Haydn who wrote much lovely keyboard music.

HARRIS, Roy Ellsworth. American composer, born in Lincoln County, Oklahoma, on February 12, 1898.

When he was a small child, Harris moved to California, where he attended school and studied music. Later he went to France and studied with the noted teacher Nadia Boulanger.* On his return to the United States he settled for a while in California, then in 1934 accepted a position as head of the composition department at the Westminster Choir School in Princeton, New Jersey. Since then he has taught at a number of schools, including Cornell University, Colorado College in Colorado Springs, Pennsylvania College for Women in Pittsburgh, Indiana University, the University of California at Los Angeles, and the University of the Pacific.

Since 1926, when his suite for string quartet, *Impressions of a Rainy Day,* was first performed, Roy Harris has written a great many works. They include three ballets; more than twenty choral works; seven symphonies plus some twenty other compositions for orchestra; chamber music; piano pieces, songs, band music, and a number of works for solo instruments.

HAYDN (HIGH dn), **Franz Joseph.** Austrian composer, born March 31, 1732, in Rohrau; died May 31, 1809, in Vienna.

By the time Joseph Haydn was eight years old he was already such a good musician that he was invited to become a choir boy at St. Stephen's Cathedral in Vienna, where he studied the clavier* and the violin as well as voice. Haydn stayed at St. Stephens until 1749. Then, because his voice broke and he was no longer able to sing in a boys' choir, he was dismissed. He was only seventeen, and penniless, but for the next ten years he managed to make a living by giving music lessons and playing accompaniments for the composer and voice teacher, Niccolo Porpora. Porpora taught him a little about composition, all the formal training Haydn ever had. He was so talented, however, and his compositions were so interesting, that he managed to make a name for himself. In 1761 Prince Esterházy, a wealthy Hungarian nobleman, hired him as assistant musical director at his elaborate palace in Esterház. He became *Kapellmeister* * six years later and remained for many years with the Esterházy family. He was provided with an orchestra of his own, and he had sufficient time to write a great deal of music. He was able to experiment with different ways of using the instruments of the orchestra, and he worked out so many new orchestral ideas that he is often called "the father of the symphony."

Haydn made two visits to England; once for six months and once for an entire year. During those visits he made many English friends and composed a number of works: an opera, twelve symphonies (known as the London symphonies), and some twenty other pieces. Oxford University gave him an honorary Doctor of Music degree.

Haydn was a rather gay and lighthearted person, and much of his music is of a gay and lighthearted nature. Altogether he wrote more than a hundred symphonies, an enormous number of string quartets and other chamber works, eight oratorios, twelve Masses and other church music, concertos for various instruments, several operas, works for keyboard instruments, and about forty songs.

HEAD VOICE. The upper range of the voice. A singer is said to be using his head voice when the resonance is thought to come largely from the cavities in the head. The lower range, when the resonance is believed to come more from the chest, is called the "chest voice."

HELDENTENOR. A "heroic" tenor; that is, a tenor voice of great power, capable of singing such roles as Lohengrin, Tristan, and Tannhäuser in operas by Richard Wagner.*

HELICON. A kind of tuba* that encircles the player's body. The helicon is used most frequently in marching bands. It is sometimes called a *Sousaphone*.

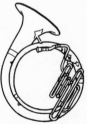

HELLER, Stephen. Hungarian pianist and composer, born in Pest on May 15, 1814; died in Paris on January 14, 1888.

When Heller was nine years old he played a concerto with his teacher, and did so well that his father was convinced that his son would have a great career as a concert pianist. He sent the boy to Vienna to study with the great teacher Czerny,* but he could not afford the high fees and had to be content with less well-known teachers. Even so, by the time he was fourteen he was ready to start on a long concert tour. He traveled for two years, giving concerts in many parts of Europe, before the strain became so great that he was forced to cut short the tour. In Augsburg, Germany, he found a position as music master to the children of a noble family. This allowed him enough time to do some serious study of composition. Eight years later he went to Paris for further study, and there he remained for the rest of his life, teaching and composing.

Heller is well known to piano students for the many sonatas, fantasias, etudes, and "romantic" pieces he wrote—about 150 compositions in all.

HEMIDEMISEMIQUAVER. The English name for the sixty-fourth note:

(♬). The hemidemisemiquaver rest is the same as a sixty-fourth rest:

(♬).

HERBERT, Victor. Irish-born composer, conductor, and cellist, born in Dublin on February 1, 1859; died in New York City on May 26, 1924.

Herbert was just seven years old when he was sent to the Stuttgart Conservatory in Germany to study music. He became a fine cellist and later toured Germany, France, and Italy as a cello soloist. In 1886 he married a German opera singer, and when she was engaged by the Metropolitan Opera Company the same year, he accompanied her to New York. From that time on he spent most of his life in America, playing cello in the Metropolitan Opera and other orchestras, composing, occasionally conducting, and for eight years acting as bandmaster of the 22nd Regiment of the New York State National Guard.

Herbert wrote a number of works for cello, but he is best known as a writer of operettas. Altogether he wrote thirty-five operettas, among them the very popular *Babes in Toyland, Mlle. Modiste, The Red Mill,* and *Naughty Marietta.*

HEXACHORD. A scale of six notes adopted by Guido d'Arezzo* and used in a system of Medieval theory. Each of the three hexachords consisted of two whole steps, a half step, and two whole steps: C-D-E-F-G-A, G-A-B-C-D-E, and F-G-A-Bb-C-D.

HIGH FIDELITY. (Often abbreviated HI-FI.) The recording of music on records, tape, wire, and film in such a way as to make the recorded music sound as much as possible like the actual performance when heard "live" in the concert hall.

HINDEMITH (HIN deh mit), **Paul.** German composer, born in Hanau on November 16, 1895; died in Frankfurt on December 29, 1963.

Paul Hindemith left home at the age of eleven because his parents were opposed to his studying music seriously. By the time he was thirteen he had become a professional violinist and managed to make his living by playing in cafes, theaters, and movie houses. At the same time he continued to study music at the *Hoch Conservatorium* in Frankfurt. He was twenty years old when he was appointed concertmaster at the Frankfurt Opera, and some time later became its conductor. He remained with the Frankfurt Opera until 1923. In the meantime he had organized with Licco Amar, a Hungarian violinist, the famous Amar-Hindemith Quartet, an organization that toured Europe with great success. Between 1923 and 1927, when he accepted a position at the Berlin *Hochschule,* he composed a great many quartets and became better known internationally. He remained in Berlin until 1934, when the Nazis banned his music because of its ultra-modern style. Then, after a stay in Turkey, where he acted as musical advisor to the Turkish government, he came to the United States. In 1942 he became a professor of music theory at Yale University. Ten years later he returned to Europe and settled in Switzerland where he has taught courses in composition at the University of Zurich.

Hindemith, who is considered one of the world's foremost composers, has written a great many works for orchestra, for solo instruments and orchestra, for voice and orchestra, for chamber music groups, for solo instruments, and for voice. Perhaps his best-known work is the symphonic piece he made from his opera, *Mathis der Maler* (Matthias the Painter).

HOLST, Gustav. English composer, born in Cheltenham on September 21, 1874; died in London on May 25, 1934.

From the time Holst first learned to write he was composing music and playing the violin, the piano, and the organ. His father wanted him to become a concert pianist, but Gustav was much more interested in composition. He was still in his teens when he was given the post of village organist, a position that gave him an understanding of choral singing that was valuable to him later. When he was nineteen he entered the Royal College of Music, where he studied piano, organ, trombone, and theory. When he left the College five years later he accepted a position as trombonist with an opera orchestra. Then for a good many years he played in various orchestras, and for some time was organist with the Royal Opera in London.

In 1903 Holst began his remarkably successful career as a teacher. From that time to the end of his life he devoted his time to teaching and composing. His works include several operas, a great many choral and orchestral works, chamber music, songs, piano solos, and three numbers for military band. His best known work is a suite for large orchestra called *The Planets*.

HOMOPHONIC. A word used to describe music that consists of a single melody supported by chords. The melody may be a single line of notes in the treble, with chords in the bass. Or the melody may be in the bass, with the supporting chords above.

HONEGGER (ON egg air), **Arthur.** Swiss composer, born in LeHavre, France, on March 10, 1892; died in Paris on November 27, 1955.

Honegger studied music for a time in Switzerland, but most of his student days were spent in Paris. He wrote a great many works, including operas, ballets, chamber music, piano music, and songs. Some of his best known works are the oratorios *King David* and *Judith*; his setting of *Joan of Arc at the Stake,* a kind of concert opera with libretto by Paul Claudel; and his orchestral piece *Pacific 231*. In *Pacific 231* Honegger used the instruments of the orchestra in such a way as to imitate the sounds of a steam locomotive.

Honegger was one of a group of influential composers who became known as *Les Six** (the six).

HOPAK. (Sometimes spelled *Gopak.*) A Russian folk dance in fast 2/4 time. Russian composers sometimes used the hopak in their operas and orchestral music. Moussorgsky, for example, included a lively hopak in his opera, *The Fair of Sorotchinsk.*

HOPKINSON, Francis. Generally considered the first American composer, he was born in Philadelphia on September 21, 1737, and died there on May 9, 1791.

Hopkinson, a lawyer and statesman, was one of the signers of the Declaration of Independence. He learned to play the harpsichord, and enjoyed getting together with other amateur musicians to play and listen to music. His first composition, written when he was seventeen, was called *Ode on Music*. Unfortunately, no copies of that piece have survived. He also wrote what is considered to be the first original song by an American composer, *My Days Have Been So Wondrous Free*. Among his other works was "an oratorical entertainment" called *The Temple of Minerva*, performed in 1781, and a collection of eight songs which he dedicated to George Washington.

HORN. Originally the horn was a simple kind of instrument made from the horn of an animal, such as the ox. Toy horns and hunting horns are still of that simple type. The orchestral horn, however, is a much more complicated instrument. It is called the French horn to differentiate it from the English horn* (which is a member of the woodwind family) and also because its modern form was developed in France.

The modern French horn has a tube about eleven feet long with a funnel-shaped mouthpiece at one end and a large flaring bell at the other end. Because the tube is so long, it is curled into two circles to make it easier for the player to handle. Inside the two curls are three valves and the extra tubing needed for them. It is a transposing instrument* with a range from the third B below Middle C to the second F above Middle C.

The French horn is a difficult instrument to play, but it is one of the most important instruments of the orchestra. It has a mellow tone that can be changed in several ways by the player: By inserting his hand in the bell (called *stopping*) he can change the pitch as well as the quality of the tone. By inserting a pear-shaped object (called a *mute*) into the bell he can get a muffled tone. By increasing the pressure of his lips he can get a kind of "brassy" tone.

HORNPIPE. An old English dance that was originally written in quick 3/4 time and danced to music of a pipe made of horn. Both Purcell* and Handel* wrote hornpipes in 3/4 time. Later the hornpipe was written in 4/4 time and became popular with British sailors.

HOVHANESS, Alan. American composer, born in Somerville, Massachusetts, on March 8, 1911.

Hovhaness studied music at the New England Conservatory, where his composition teacher was Frederick Converse. During the time he was learning the techniques of composition he became interested in the music of his father's native country, Armenia, and the music of other Middle Eastern countries. As a consequence, his own compositions reflect strongly some of the exotic characteristics of that kind of music. In spite of the fact that in 1940 he destroyed about a thousand of his compositions because he felt they were not up to his own later standards, his published works are numerous. They include about twenty works for orchestra, usually with a solo instrument or voice; chamber music; pieces for violin and piano; piano solos; pieces for two pianos; and several songs.

HUMORESQUE. A title given to pieces of a rather light, romantic nature by some composers of the nineteenth century. The most familiar one is probably Dvořák's *Humoresque in G-flat major,* Op. 101, for piano. Other composers who have written Humoresques are Grieg, Heller, and Schumann.

HUMPERDINCK (HOOM per dink), **Engelbert.** German composer, born in Siegburg on September 1, 1854; died in Neustrelitz on September 27, 1921.

While he was still a young man, Humperdinck won several prizes that made it possible for him to study at the Royal Music School in Munich, and later to travel in Italy. In Naples he met Richard Wagner,* and the two became great friends. Wagner invited Humperdinck to go with him to Bayreuth and to assist him with the first performance of *Parsifal* there. Humperdinck taught for many years in Germany, and for two years in Spain. He wrote seven operas, but only one, his masterpiece, *Hansel and Gretel,* with libretto by his sister, has enjoyed much success. His other works include music for two festivals, incidental music for a number of plays, several choral works, songs, chamber music, and two orchestral works.

HURDY-GURDY. (Also called *Vielle.*) A mechanical stringed instrument that was popular during Medieval times in Europe. The strings were sounded by a wheel which was attached to a handle at one end. As the handle was turned, the wheel touched the strings, much like a circular bow. The pitches were changed by a stopping mechanism operated by a keyboard which was played by the other hand. The stopping device shortened the strings just as a violinist shortens the strings with the fingers of his left hand. The instrument also had two extra strings that sounded continuously, giving it a drone* effect.

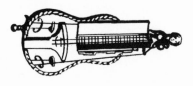

HYDRAULIS. An organ invented by the ancient Greeks. It was used widely by the Romans to provide music of a sort in their amphitheaters. Large and clumsy, the hydraulis used water pressure to force air into the organ pipes. The tone of the hydraulis was loud and unpleasant; so much so that it was used at times by Roman soldiers to frighten the enemy.

HYMN. In the Christian church a hymn is a song sung by the congregation in praise of God. Some of the earliest hymns were written by St. Ambrose in the fourth century. These and hymns composed up to the sixteenth century generally consisted of Latin poems set to plainsong* tunes. During the sixteenth century, Martin Luther, the German leader of the Protestant Reformation, decided that hymns should be sung in German rather than Latin. He himself wrote the words to many hymns, setting them to tunes taken from the old plainsong or to composed tunes. An example of one of these Lutheran hymns is the familiar *Ein feste Berg ist unser Gott* (A Mighty Fortress is Our God).

Calvin, the Protestant leader in England and Scotland, thought that the only proper songs to sing in church were songs based on Bible texts, so the hymns sung in the churches of those countries during the sixteenth and seventeenth centuries were translations of the Psalms, in which the words of the poems were made to rhyme, and were set to music. *Old Hundredth,* sung in many churches today, is an example of one of these Psalm tunes.

Early settlers in America brought many of the Lutheran and Calvinist hymns with them, and soon began to compose hymns of their own. In 1737 John Wesley, founder of the American Methodist Church, published his first volume of hymns in Charlestown, Georgia. Since that time, many more hymns have been written for use in various churches, and new hymns continue to be written.

I

IBERT (ee bair), **Jacques.** French composer, born in Paris on August 15, 1890.

Ibert's studies at the Paris Conservatory were interrupted by World War I, when he served in the French Navy. After the war he returned for another year's study at the Conservatory, then was awarded the *Prix de Rome.** While studying in Rome he wrote one of his best known works, a symphonic suite called *Escales* (Ports of Call). In 1937 he was appointed Director of the Académie de France in Rome, a position he held until 1955, when he became director of the Paris Opéra. Ibert's many works include operas, orchestral and chamber music, ballets, pieces for piano and organ, songs, and music for the theater, radio, and motion pictures.

IMITATION. A device that composers sometimes use in writing music in two or more parts or voices.* A pattern of notes in one voice is repeated or "imitated" by another voice (or voices)—sometimes exactly; sometimes in a slightly different form. For example, in the following excerpt from a two-part *Invention,* No. 8, by J. S. Bach, the pattern of notes in the first two measures of the treble part is repeated exactly, an octave lower, in the second and third measures of the bass part. In the writing of canons* and fuges,* imitation is used extensively.

IMPERFECT CADENCE. (See *Cadence.*)

IMPRESSIONISM. A term borrowed from painting, used to describe music that suggests rather than describes a subject. In the paintings of such impressionist artists as Degas, Monet, and Renoir, details are left to the imagination, and the subject is pictured vaguely. In music, the impressionists used new harmonies and new tonal progressions to achieve a similar "misty" effect. The whole tone scale* and parallel* chords* are two devices that impressionist composers used quite freely in their music. Impressionism in music was originated by Claude Debussy* with his *Afternoon of a Faun.* Some other composers of impressionistic music are Ravel,* Griffes,* Respighi,* and Falla.*

IMPROMPTU. The word *impromptu* describes something that is done on the spur of the moment, such as a speech that is given without any preparation. Certain composers of the Romantic period used the word as a title for some of their pieces. It probably means that the pieces were of a casual nature, composed somewhat as though they were being improvised.* Chopin, Schumann, and Schubert are examples of composers who wrote pieces they called *Impromptu.*

IMPROVISATION. (The same as *extemporization.*) To improvise or extemporize music is to make it up as one plays. In the seventeenth century, when the use of figured bass* (continuo) was common practice, the ability to improvise was an essential part of a keyboard player's musicianship. Organists competing for positions often were tested on their skill in improvising on a given bass. During his lifetime, J. S. Bach's* fame rested largely on his ability to improvise, and Handel,* Mozart,* and Beethoven* were renowned for their improvisations. Today the art of improvisation is practiced only by a few performing artists, mainly organists who may improvise on themes given them from the audience. Many jazz musicians are skillful at improvising solos against the background music played by the other musicians, and at "jam sessions" an entire group of jazz players will improvise arrangements of popular tunes.

INCIDENTAL MUSIC. Music written to accompany a play or a film. Many plays have music before and between the acts, songs that are sung during the play, and background music to set the mood. Most motion pictures and plays on television have "background" or incidental music, and many well-known composers have written such music for both the theater and motion pictures, radio, and television. For example, Mendelssohn* wrote the incidental music for Shakespeare's *Midsummer Night's Dream*; the *Peer Gynt* suites by Grieg* were written originally as incidental music for a play by Ibsen, *Peer Gynt*; Prokofievs' *Lieutenant Kije* suite was written first as music for a motion picture.

INDY (DAN dee), **Vincent d'.** French composer, teacher, and author, born in Paris on March 27, 1851; died there on December 1, 1931.

D'Indy was brought up by his grandmother who saw to it that he received an excellent education, including music. She herself taught him piano, and by the time he was fourteen he had shown so much talent that he began to study harmony under a famous teacher, one of Debussy's* masters, Albert Lavignac. He especially loved orchestral music and decided to devote his life to composing.

D'Indy was only nineteen when the Franco-Prussian War broke out. He enlisted at once and fought so bravely that he won several distinctions. At the end of the war he returned to music. He became a pupil and friend of César Franck* and made friends with many other musicians. In 1894 he helped to found the *Schola Cantorum* (originally a school for the study of church music), and he taught composition there until his death. In addition to composing music he wrote several books, including a two-volume study of composition and a biography of Beethoven.

D'Indy's works include a number of operas, incidental music, a large number of choral and orchestral works, chamber music, piano solos and duets, three organ works, and songs.

INSTRUMENTATION. (See *Orchestration.*)

INSTRUMENT. Any object other than the human voice that is used to produce musical sound is a musical instrument. The following chart lists the instruments most widely used today.

STRINGED INSTRUMENTS

violin
viola
cello
double bass (contrabass, bass viol)

} Played by bowing and plucking

autoharp
banjo
guitar
harp
mandolin   } Played by plucking or strumming
steel guitar
ukulele
zither

WOODWIND INSTRUMENTS

fife
flute
piccolo   } flue-voiced
pipe
recorder

bagpipe
bassett horn
bassoon
clarinet
English horn
harmonica   } reed-voiced
mouth harmonium
oboe
saxophone

BRASS INSTRUMENTS

alto horn   cornet   mellophone
baritone horn   euphonium   trombone
bass horn   flügelhorn   trumpet
bugle   French horn   tuba
                   helicon

KEYBOARD INSTRUMENTS

accordion   concertina   novachord
celesta   electronic organ   organ
clavichord   harpsichord   piano

PERCUSSION INSTRUMENTS

bell
chimes
glockenspiel
gong
marimba   } pitched
tam-tam
timpani (kettledrum)
vibraphone
xylophone

anvil
bass drum
blocks
bongo drums
castanets
claves
cymbals
maracas   } non-pitched
rattle
side drum (snare drum)
tabor
tambourine
triangle
whip

INTERMEZZO (in ter MET soh). An Italian word meaning "in the middle." Originally an intermezzo was a short play with music that was performed between the acts of a drama or opera. It is also an instrumental number played during an opera, as the *Intermezzo* performed while the singers are off the stage in Mascagni's *Cavalleria Rusticana.* Some composers, including Brahms* and Schumann,* have written short, rather light pieces for piano to which they gave the title *Intermezzo.*

INTERVAL. The distance between two pitches, counting both the top and bottom notes. The interval from C to D is a *second*; from E to G is a *third*; from D to G is a *fourth*; from A to E is a *fifth*; from E to C is a *sixth*; from C to B is a *seventh*; from D to D is an *octave* (*eighth*); from C to the second D above is a *ninth*; from G to the second B above is a *tenth*; and so on. Intervals are also named major,* minor,* augmented,* diminished* and perfect.*

Depending upon the number of half steps found between the upper and lower notes, fourths, fifths, and octaves may be *diminished, perfect,* or *augmented*; seconds, thirds, sixths, and sevenths may be *diminished, minor, major,* or *augmented.*

In the scale of C major C to D is a *major second* (one whole step), C to E is a *major third* (two whole steps), C to F is a *perfect fourth* (two and one-half steps); C to G is a *perfect fifth* (three and one-half steps); C to A is a *major sixth* (four and one-half steps); C to B is a *major seventh* (five and one-half steps); C to C is a *perfect octave* (six and one-half steps). The sequence of major and perfect intervals is the same in any major diatonic* scale, if the lower note is the tonic* or key note.*

An interval that is one-half step larger than the equivalent major or perfect interval is called *augmented.* For example, from C to G is a *perfect fifth*; from C to G-sharp or from C-flat to G would be an augmented fifth. (The letters remain the same.)

An interval that is one-half step smaller than the equivalent major interval is called *minor.* For example, C to A is a *major sixth,* so C-sharp to A or C to A-flat would be a *minor sixth.*

In interval that is one-half step smaller than the equivalent perfect or minor interval is called *diminished.* For example, C to F is a perfect fourth, so C to F-flat or C-sharp to F would be a *diminished fourth.*

Intervals that are written differently but sound the same on an equal-tempered instrument such as the piano are called *enharmonic* intervals.* For example, C to F-sharp and C to G-flat sound the same, yet C to F-sharp is an *augmented fourth* and C to G-flat is a *diminished fifth.*

INTONATION. The degree to which a performer sings or plays the correct pitch. For example, a singer is said to have good intonation if his pitches are accurate, and he is said to have poor intonation if he has a tendency to sing slightly above or below the correct pitch.

INVERSION. A chord is said to be inverted when its root is in a higher part instead of at the bottom. For example, the chord C-E-G becomes E-G-C in its first inversion, and G-C-E in its second inversion. A melody is inverted when each of the intervals through which it proceeds is changed to its opposite interval. For example, the melody in the second measure of the following is an inversion of the melody in the first measure.

INVERTIBLE COUNTERPOINT. Counterpoint* designed in such a way that any one of its upper parts or voices* can be moved to form a bass to the other parts. If it is in two parts it is called *double counterpoint*; if it is in three parts it is called *triple counterpoint*.

IONION MODE. (See *Modes.*)

ISAAC (EE zahk), **Heinrich.** Netherlands composer, born in Brabant about 1450; died in Florence, Italy, in 1517. (The exact dates are not known.)

Little has been discovered about Isaac's early life. He first came into prominence when he was appointed organist at the Medici Court in 1475 in Florence, Italy. He served later as teacher to Lorenzo de Medici's children. After ten years with the Medici family, and following visits to Rome, Ferrara, and Innsbruck, he entered the service of Maximilian I in Vienna. In 1514 he returned to Florence. His works include Masses,* motets,* and secular compositions.

ITALIAN SIXTH. An augmented sixth chord. (See also *Chords.*)

IVES, Charles. American composer, born in Danbury, Connecticut, on October 20, 1874; died in New York City on May 19, 1954.

Charles Ives is considered one of America's most original composers. His father was a teacher of theory, piano, and violin, and was conductor of an orchestra. When Charles was still a boy he played in his father's orchestra. Later he attended Yale University, where he studied under Horatio Parker.* Ives was not only an outstanding composer, but a successful business man as well. From 1916 to 1930 he was the senior member of the insurance firm of Ives and Myrick. Most of his compositions, however, were written before 1916.

Ives's works include eight choral compositions, four symphonies, many other works for orchestra, two string quartets, five violin sonatas, three sonatas for piano, and more than a hundred songs. In 1947 he was awarded the Pulitzer Prize for his Symphony No. 3, written in 1911.

J

JACKS. Long strips of wood to which the plectrums* or tongues of the harpsichord* are attached. The jacks rise when the keys are depressed, and the plectrums pluck the strings.

JANÁČEK (YAHN ah check), **Leoš.** Czech composer and conductor, born in Hukvaldy, Moravia, on July 3, 1854; died in Moravia, Ostrau, on August 12, 1928.

Janáček came from a musical family and he himself was talented enough to sing in the choir and study composition at the age of ten, when he became a pupil at the Augustine monastery at Brno. Nevertheless, he did not become well known as a composer until he was in his sixties, when his opera *Jenufa* was produced in Prague. Most of his life was devoted to teaching and conducting.

Janáček's music is strongly influenced by the native music of his area, a section of Moravia that lay near the Polish border where the people spoke a mixture of Czech and Polish. Some of his most interesting works are arrangements of folksongs of that section.

In addition to *Jenufa,* an opera that is especially popular in Europe, Janáček wrote nine other operas, a ballet based on Moravian folk dances, a large number of choral and orchestral works, church music, arrangements of folk songs, and many pieces for violin, for cello, and for piano.

JANISSARY MUSIC. The Janissaries were soldiers who guarded the Turkish Sultan in the days when Turkey was a monarchy. Their military bands included triangles, cymbals, bass drums, and an instrument called a *crescent.* Some of these instruments were adopted by military bands in Europe during the eighteenth century. Their sounds were considered very "Turkish," and several composers of that period used them in some of their works. Mozart, for example, used them in his opera *Die Entführung aus dem Serail* ("Abduction from the Harem"); Haydn used them in his Symphony in G Major, Opus 100, known as the *Military Symphony*.

JAQUES-DALCROZE (zhack dahl croze), **Émile.** Swiss composer and teacher, born in Vienna, Austria, on July 6, 1865; died in Geneva, Switzerland, on July 1, 1950.

Jacques-Dalcroze studied music in Paris, Vienna, and Geneva. He developed considerable skill as a composer, and during his lifetime wrote five operas, a number of orchestral and choral works, chamber music, songs, and piano pieces. However, he is best known for a system of rhythmic training that he developed and taught, called Eurhythmics.* In 1915 he founded the Jacques-Dalcroze Institute in Geneva where he and others taught the system. Eurhythmics became popular in both Europe and America, and schools to teach the system were established in Paris, Berlin, Vienna, Stockholm, New York, and other cities.

JAZZ. The name given to a particular type of popular music that originated in the United States about 1900 and spread over this country and Europe. Nobody knows exactly how it began, but it seems to have had roots in African music. It began to develop a definite system of its own as an outgrowth of ragtime* in New Orleans. It shifted to Chicago in the 1920's, and then to New York and other parts of the country.

The main characteristics of jazz are strong rhythm, syncopation, and "blue" notes (notes that are deliberately flattened, especially thirds and sevenths). Jazz players have extended the techniques of playing such instruments as the clarinet and trumpet. For example, they are able to get effects that in some ways seem to mimic certain "primitive" sounds of the human voice.

Jazz ensembles vary in size from small groups of musicians, who are especially adept at improvisation,* to the large dance bands whose specialty is "symphonic" jazz. Jazz orchestras employ a number of percussion instruments (including the piano) to supply the dominant rhythm. Stringed instruments are limited in most cases to bass viols that are plucked rather than played with a bow. The "solo" instruments are usually clarinets, trumpets, trombones, and saxophones.

JEW'S HARP. A small musical instrument popular in Europe. It consists of a metal frame shaped like a horseshoe with two parallel prongs down the center. Between the prongs is a vibrating strip of metal. The player holds the instrument in his mouth with the two prongs between his teeth, and strokes the vibrating strip with a finger. He plays different notes by changing the shape of his mouth in various ways.

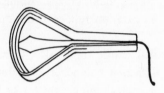

JIG. A lively dance popular for many centuries in the British Isles. Jig tunes may have three, six, nine, or twelve beats to the measure.

JOACHIM (yoh AHK him), **Joseph.** Hungarian violinist and composer, born in Kittsee on June 28, 1831; died in Berlin, Germany, on August 15, 1907.

Joachim was five years old when he began the study of violin. He made such rapid progress that two years later he was able to play a duet in public with his teacher, Serwaczynski, leader of an opera orchestra in Budapest. He then went to Vienna for further study, and two years later was sent to the famous Leipzig Conservatory in Germany. After a year in Leipzig he was advanced enough to begin a career as a virtuoso violinist. He was not quite thirteen years old when he played several concerts with great success in London. From that time on he made a great many public appearances both in England and in Europe, and became known as the greatest living violinist. The quartet he founded, and which was named after him, was considered the finest string quartet in the world.

Most of Joachim's compositions were for violin, but he also wrote several works for orchestra, some overtures, and songs.

JONGLEUR (zhong LEUR). A musician and entertainer of Medieval France, often in the employ of the trouvères* and troubadours.* The jongleurs traveled about the country, frequently in groups, playing, singing, dancing, juggling, and performing various acts for the entertainment of the people. Their instrument was the *vielle,** a kind of fiddle.

JOSQUIN DES PRÉS (zhos ken day PRA͜Y). Netherlands composer, born about 1450 (the date and place are not known); died in Condé on August 27, 1521.

Little is known of Josquin des Prés' early life, except that he sang in the choir of the Collegiate Church of St.-Quentin, and may have studied with the celebrated Ockeghem.* Most of his adult life was spent as a singer and choirmaster in various churches and in the service of royal families. One of the most celebrated musicians of all time, he is credited with some of the important innovations that distinguish Renaissance music from that of the Middle Ages. He wrote more than thirty Masses,* over fifty motets,* and many chansons.*

JOTA (HOE tah). A popular folk dance of northern Spain. It is written in 3/4 time and played in a moderately fast tempo. The *jota* is danced by couples facing each other, but without holding hands. Guitars,* castanets,* and sometimes triangles* are used to accompany the dancers.

K

K. (See *Köchel.*)

KABALEVSKY (cah bah LEFF skee), **Dmitri.** Russian composer, born in St. Petersburg (now Leningrad) on December 30, 1904.

Kabalevsky was a talented child who could play the piano by ear when he was only six years old. When his family moved to Moscow in 1918, he began to study music at the Scriabin Music School. He later attended the Moscow Conservatory, and since his graduation has devoted himself mainly to teaching and composing.

Kabalevsky has written three operas, two ballets, choral works, chamber music, four symphonies, songs, and piano pieces. His works for piano include a collection of easy pieces for children called *From Pioneer Life.*

KAPELLMEISTER (kah PELL mice ter). A German word meaning "master of the chapel." In the days of kings and noblemen in Europe, each court had a chapel and hired musicians to play religious music in the chapel and secular music for the entertainment of the court. The director of these musicians was the *Kapellmeister.*

KAZOO. A toy musical instrument consisting of a tube shaped like a cigar, with a strip of catgut on the inside. When the player hums or sings into the tube, the catgut vibrates, making a sound something like that made by humming through a comb covered with tissue paper.

KERN, Jerome. American composer, born in New York City on January 27, 1885; died there on November 11, 1945.

As a boy, Kern attended the New York public schools and studied music with his mother. Later, he studied piano and theory with several well-known teachers and eventually went to Germany for further study of composition. He returned to America in 1907 and took a job as pianist and salesman for a publishing firm. He had already published one popular song that became a hit, *How'd You Like to Spoon with Me?* In 1911, at the age of twenty-six, he wrote the music to a musical comedy, *The Red Petticoat,* that became an immediate success. From that time on he turned out one musical comedy after the other—some sixty stage shows altogether.

Kern's greatest success, *Show Boat,* has become an American classic among popular musical shows. Other highly successful Kern productions were *Sally, Sunny, Music in the Air, Roberta,* and *Very Warm for May.*

KETTLEDRUM. (See *Timpani.*)

KEY. (1) On keyboard instruments, such as the piano, a key is a black or white lever that is depressed by a finger to produce a tone. The organ has additional, larger keys that are depressed with the feet. (2) On woodwind instruments, such as the clarinet and oboe, a key is a lever that is depressed to open or close one of the air holes that produce the sounds. (3) In music itself, the term *key* is an important one. Most of the music written between about 1600 and 1900 is written in one of the twelve major or twelve minor keys. Each of these keys is "controlled" by a key-note* or tonic* center around which the other tones of the key are organized; each key is more or less governed by its particular scale.* For example, a tune written in the key of C-major would probably begin and end on the tonic note C, and most of the other notes in the tune would be found in the scale of C major. The same tune could be written in any one of the major keys and it would sound the same except for being lower or higher. If the tune were written in a minor key it would sound different, because minor scales have a different quality from major scales.

Many tunes have notes that are not included in the "basic" scale, but most of the notes and chords are in the scale and almost always a tune ends on the key note of the scale.

Longer works often involve more than one key; in fact two important musical structures, the fugue* and the sonata-form* movement, depend upon the relationships between different keys or tonal centers. However, tonal music usually begins and ends in the same key.

KEYBOARD. The complete set of keys on such instruments as the piano, organ, harpsichord, and accordion. The keys are arranged in groups of black and white keys, like this:

The keyboard of the organ is called a *manual*.* Some organs have as many as four different manuals, making it possible to get a great variety of tone colors and effects. The organ also has a keyboard called the *pedal keyboard* that consists of large keys played with the feet.

Keyboards are arranged with the black keys lying above and between the white keys in such a way that they do not take up any extra space. This makes it possible for the average sized hand to stretch at least as far as an octave (from C to the next higher or lower C, for example), and to play all the notes that lie between.

KEY-NOTE. (Also called the *tonic*.*) The tonic center and first note in the scale of any key. For example, C is the key-note of the scales of C-major and C-minor; B-flat is the key-note of the scales of B-flat major and B-flat minor, and so on.

KEY SIGNATURE. The sharps or flats printed at the beginning of each line of music to indicate the particular key of the piece. Following are the key signatures for all the major and minor keys:

D   G   C   F   B-flat   E-flat   A-flat

KHACHATURIAN (hah chah too ree AHN), **Aram.** Armenian (Russian) composer, born in Tiflis on June 6, 1903.

Unlike most gifted composers, Khachaturian did not have any particular interest in music until he was nineteen years old. Then he went to Moscow, where he studied cello, composition, and orchestration. He had several compositions published while he was still a student, and about the time he graduated his first major work, Symphony No. 1, was performed with great success. Since then he has composed steadily. He has written two symphonies, two ballets, choral works, several pieces for military band, chamber music, concertos, piano pieces, and a great deal of incidental music for plays and motions pictures. His works are strongly flavored with his native Armenian folk rhythms and melodies.

In Russia, Khachaturian is acclaimed for his *The Song of Stalin,* a work for symphony orchestra and chorus, and for a ballet, *Happiness.* Outside Russia he is better known for his popular piano concerto and his violin concerto.

KIT. A tiny violin, small enough to be carried in a pocket. It was played by dancing masters in the sixteenth century, and perhaps even earlier. The body of the kit was sometimes shaped like a violin, but with a proportionately longer and wider neck to make it easier to finger. More often it was shaped like a *rebec.**

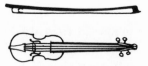

KITHARA. A musical instrument popular in ancient Greece. It was shaped something like a lyre, and was played by plucking the strings with the fingers. The Greeks used the kithara to accompany singers and also as a solo instrument. (Illustration on page 154.)

KLAVIER (klah VEER). The German word for piano (or, formerly, other keyboard instruments).

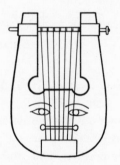

KÖCHEL (KUR shell). The name of a man who catalogued the works of Mozart. When the letter K is used with a number, as K.546, the K is an abbreviation of Köchel. When Mozart died, his manuscripts were in such a mixed-up state that it was easy for one work to be confused with another. Köchel sorted them out, as well as he was able to, according to when each was written, and gave each work a number. Altogether, Mozart wrote more than 600 works, including forty symphonies. Sixteen of the symphonies are in the key of D major. Now each one of the sixteen can be identified as Symphony in D, K.45; Symphony in D, K.81; Symphony in D, K.133; and so on.

KODÁLY (KOH dah ee), **Zoltán.** Hungarian composer, folklorist, and teacher, born in Kecskemet on December 16, 1882.

Kodály began to take regular piano lessons when he was nine years old and soon afterwards he took up the violin. During most of his school years he sang in the cathedral choir. He liked to read about music, and spent many hours in the music library reading books about such famous composers as Beethoven and Mozart, and studying their music. He began his career as a composer by writing a Mass and an *Ave Maria* when he was sixteen years old. He graduated from the Budapest Conservatory of Music, and beginning about 1907 taught composition there.

In addition to teaching and composing, Kodály has spent a great deal of time collecting Hungarian folk music, much of it in collaboration with his close friend, Béla Bartók.* Many of his own compositions have a marked folk-music flavor. He has written an enormous number of works including three operas, church music, more than fifty choral works (including several for children's voices), orchestral works, chamber music, and solos for voice and for stringed instruments. He has also written a great many books and articles about music, most of them on the subject of folk music.

KORNGOLD, Eric. Austrian composer, born in Brno on May 29, 1897; died in Hollywood, California, on November 29, 1957.

Korngold, the son of a Vienna music critic, showed a remarkable talent for composition while he was still very young. He was only twelve when a piano trio he wrote was published. About the same time he wrote a pantomine called *Der Schneeman* (The Snowman) that was performed at the Vienna Court Opera. During the next six years he had compositions performed in Leipzig, Munich, and Vienna by the most prominent symphony orchestras. His opera *Die tote Stadt* (The Dead City) was produced with great success in Hamburg, Germany, when he was twenty-three years old, and soon afterwards it received performances in opera houses all over the world. His later works include another opera, orchestral works, chamber music, violin pieces, piano pieces, and songs.

When Austria was taken over by the Nazis during World War II, Korngold was forced to leave the country. He came to the United States and settled in Hollywood, California. He was naturalized in 1943. The remainder of his life was devoted to composing music for motion pictures.

KOVEN, Reginald de. American composer, born in Middletown, Connecticut on April 3, 1859; died in Chicago, Illinois, on January 16, 1920.

De Koven was educated in Europe, first at Oxford University in England. After obtaining his degree there in 1879 he studied piano, harmony, and composition in various European cities. In 1902 he organized the Philharmonic Orchestra in Washington, D.C., and remained as its conductor for several years.

De Koven was most successful as a writer of operettas. He also wrote two grand operas, *The Canterbury Pilgrims* and *Rip Van Winkle*. One of the most popular of all wedding songs, *Oh Promise Me,* was written for the London performances of his operetta *Robin Hood*. In addition to some twenty operettas and other works for the stage, de Koven wrote more than 400 songs.

KREISLER, Fritz. Austrian violinist and composer, born in Vienna on February 2, 1875; died in New York City on January 29, 1962.

Kreisler's father was a physician, but also an enthusiastic amateur musician. When he realized that his son Fritz was gifted musically, he encouraged him to study, and entered him in the Vienna Conservatory when the boy was only seven years old. Three years later he won the Gold Prize for violin playing. He then went to Paris to study at the

Paris Conservatory, and again astonished everyone by winning the *Grand Prix* (the highest honor) when he was twelve. Two years later he toured America as a professional violinist.

Then a curious thing happened. He dropped violin playing and returned to Vienna to study medicine. He also studied art in Rome and Paris. He next joined the Austrian Army, where he served as an officer. Once more he took up the violin, and when he appeared in Berlin in 1899 he created a sensation with his amazing performance. From then until 1914 he toured Europe and America, appearing in many cities with great success. When World War I broke out he rejoined the Austrian Army. He was wounded shortly afterwards, but fortunately his wounds were not serious enough to interfere with his playing of the violin, and at the end of 1914 he returned to the United States and resumed his career as a concert violinist and composer.

Kreisler wrote a large number of pieces for violin (many of them under other composers' names, signing himself simply as "editor"). He also wrote two operettas and a string quartet. Two of his best known works are *Caprice Viennois,* a rather short piece for violin, and the highly successful operetta *Apple Blossoms.*

KŘENEK (kjreh nek), **Ernst.** Austrian composer, born in Vienna on August 23, 1900. He became a naturalized citizen of the United States in 1945.

Křenek entered the Vienna Conservatory of Music when he was sixteen years old, where he studied composition with a famous teacher, Schreker. When Schreker became Director of the Berlin Academy of Music, Křenek followed him. During his teens Křenek composed a number of works that were more or less traditional in style, although they showed a good deal of originality. Later he composed in a free atonal* style, and finally he adopted the twelve-tone technique* of Schoenberg.*

From about 1920 to 1938 Křenek worked as a conductor and director of opera theatres in Europe and became well known as a concert pianist. When the Nazis became powerful in Austria, he migrated to the United States, where he has taught in a number of colleges and universities, and has continued to compose.

Křenek's most famous work is the opera *Jonny spielt auf* (Jonny Strikes Up), in which he combined elements of jazz* with atonal style very successfully. He has also written several other operas, choral works, ballets, five symphonies, concertos, chamber music, several works for piano, and a number of songs and song cycles.

KYRIE (KEE ree ay). Short for *Kyrie eleison,* Greek words which mean "Lord have mercy." These words, which are often set to music, occur in the first part of the Ordinary of the Roman Catholic Mass. (See also *Mass.*)

L. or **L.H.** The abbreviation for *left hand*. In music for keyboard instruments, the notes marked *l.h.* are played by the fingers of the left hand. Often the fingers to be used are indicated by numbers, and when the left and right hand are used alternately, the abbreviation *r.h.* (for right hand) is used also.

LA. (Sometimes spelled *lah*.) In the system of *movable do*,* the syllable name given to the sixth note of the major scale. In the fixed do* system, the note A. (See also *Do*.)

LA FORGE, Frank. American pianist, composer, and teacher, born in Rockford, Illinois, on October 22, 1879; died in New York City on May 5, 1953.

La Forge began his study of piano as a boy in his home town. He later studied in Vienna, Austria, with the great pianist and teacher, Leschetizky. During the early part of his career he made a reputation as an outstanding accompanist, touring with such well-known singers as Marcella Sembrich and Schumann-Heink. When he was thirty-two years old he settled in New York and devoted himself to teaching voice and coaching singers. Among his pupils were such noted concert artists as Lawrence Tibbett, Richard Crooks, and Marian Anderson.

La Forge's compositions include many songs and a number of pieces for piano.

LA HALE, Adam de. (Sometimes spelled Halle.) French trouvère,* born in Arras about 1240; died in Naples about 1286. (The exact dates of his birth and death are not known.)

Adam de la Hale (nicknamed "The Hunchback of Arras") was one of the most famous of the many trouvères of the twelfth and thirteenth centuries. He wrote many chansons* as well as polyphonic* works, usually composing the poems as well as the music himself. Of his many works that have been preserved, the most interesting is a pastoral drama, *Le Jeu de Robin et de Marion* (The Play of Robin and Marion), first performed about 1275 for the French court in Naples. The play has recently been translated and published in English.

LALO (LAH low), **Victor Antoine Édouard.** French composer (of Spanish descent), born in Lille on January 27, 1823; died in Paris on April 22, 1892.

As a boy, Lalo studied violin and cello at the conservatory in his home town. When he was sixteen he was sent to Paris to study violin at the Paris Conservatory with Professor Haveneck. At the same time he studied composition privately. He was in his twenties when his first songs were published, and from that time on he wrote a great many works. They include three operas; two ballets; orchestral works; chamber music; pieces for cello, for violin, and for piano; and many songs. He is best known today for his symphony for violin and orchestra called *Symphonie espagnole,* a brilliant composition that is often performed by concert violinists.

LAMENT. A piece that expresses sorrow or mourning, usually for a death. In Scotland and Ireland laments are pieces written for the bagpipe. Each clan has its own lament that is played at the funeral of a clan member.

LÄNDLER (LENT lerr). A German word meaning "slow waltz." The dance originated in rural Austria. *Ländler* have been written by a number of composers, including Mozart, Beethoven, and Schubert.

LARGAMENTE (lahr gah MEN tay). An Italian word meaning "broadly." It indicates that the music should be performed rather slowly and deliberately. (See also *Tempo.*)

LARGHETTO (lahr GET toh). An Italian word meaning "slow." It indicates that the music should be performed slowly, but not as slowly as music marked *largo.* (See also *Tempo.*)

LARGO (LAHR goh). An Italian word meaning "large" or "wide." (1) It indicates that the music should be played very slowly. (2) A movement whose basic tempo is *largo.* (See also *Tempo.*)

LASSUS (LAH soos), **Roland de.** (Also known as Orlando di Lasso.) Netherlands composer, born in Mons in 1532; died in Munich, Bavaria, on June 14, 1594.

As a boy chorister in Mons, Lassus was kidnapped three times because of his exceptionally beautiful voice. Then his parents agreed to let him go to Italy in the service of the Viceroy of Sicily. When his voice broke at the age of eighteen, he became choirmaster at St. John Latern in Rome. Six years later he accepted the important post of *Kapellmeister** to the Bavarian Court in Munich, and there he remained for the rest of his life. One of the most celebrated composers of all time, he wrote numerous Masses,* Magnificats,* and Passions.* His secular works include French chansons,* Italian madrigals,* and German *Lieder.**

LEADING NOTE. The seventh note in all major and some minor scales. In the scale of C major, for example, the leading note is B (a half tone below C). It is called *leading* because it gives the feeling in the scale of leading naturally upward to the note a half tone above it, the tonic.*

LEADING TONE. (See *Leading Note.*)

LEDGER LINES. (Sometimes spelled *leger.*) Short lines used above and below the staffs* to show the position of notes that are too high or too low to be placed on the staffs themselves. Middle C lies halfway between the highest note on the bass staff and the lowest note on the treble staff, so it is always placed on a leger line. Other examples are the second E above Middle C, and the second C below Middle C:

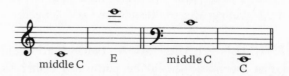

LEGATO (leh GAH toh). An Italian word meaning "bound together." Legato indicates that the music should be performed smoothly, one note following another with no break between the sounds. Legato is the opposite of staccato.*

LEGEND. A name sometimes given to pieces that suggest some legendary character or happening. Liszt,* for example, wrote two pieces for piano which he called *Légendes*. No. 1 is based on the legend of St. Francis of Assisi and the birds; No. 2 on the legend of St. Francis of Paula walking on the waters.

LEGNO (LAYN yoh). An Italian word meaning "wood." It is used frequently as *col legno* (with the wood) as a direction to players of stringed instruments to tap the strings with the stick of the bow instead of the usual method of bowing with the hairs.

LÉHAR (LAY harr), **Franz.** Hungarian composer, born in Komárom on April 30, 1870; died in Bad Ischl, Austria, on October 24, 1948.

Léhar first studied music with his father, the leader of a military band, and later at the Prague Conservatory. His first professional jobs were as leader of military bands in several Central European countries. In 1902 he settled in Vienna, and from that time on he proceeded to win fame as a composer of operettas. Altogether, Léhar wrote more than thirty such works for the stage. Most of them were first produced in Vienna, but they soon became popular in other cities. His best known work is *The Merry Widow,* an operetta which has been produced hundreds of times all over the world.

LEITMOTIV (LITE moh teef). A German word meaning "leading motif or theme." A short musical theme that symbolizes a certain character, place, idea, or object that is used recurrently throughout a musical work. Although recurring themes had been used in operas by earlier composers, Mozart's *Don Giovanni,* for example, the term *Leitmotiv* was first used in reference to Wagner's* extensive use of leading themes in his *Ring* cycle.

LENTO (LEN toh). An Italian word meaning "slow" or "sluggish." Lento indicates that the music is to be performed slowly. (See also *Tempo.*)

LEONCAVALLO (lay on cah VAHL loh), **Ruggiero.** Italian composer, born in Naples on March 8, 1858; died in Montecatini on August 9, 1919.

Leoncavallo attended the Conservatory in Naples, where he studied piano, harmony, and composition, until he was eighteen. From that time on he devoted himself to writing operas. He wrote a great many operas, but only one of them gained any measure of success. That was *I Pagliacci* (The Clowns), one of the most popular operas that has ever been written.

LIADOV (lee AH doff), **Anatol Constantinovich.** Russian composer, born in St. Petersburg (now Leningrad) on May 11, 1855; died in Novgorod on August 28, 1914.

Liadov first studied music with his father, a professional theater musician. Later he studied at the St. Petersburg Conservatory. He made such a brilliant record there that he was invited back to teach harmony and composition after he graduated.

Liadov wrote a number of orchestral works, choral works, and a ballet. But he is best known for the many charming pieces he wrote for the piano, and for the arrangements he made of more than a hundred Russian folk songs he had collected from various parts of the country.

LIBRETTO (lee BRET toh). An Italian word meaning "booklet." A libretto is the text (the words) of an opera or oratorio. With a few exceptions, composers of operas write only the music. A librettist writes the story, and the composer fits music to the words. For example, the music for the opera *Hansel and Gretel* was written by Humperdinck,* but the libretto was written by his sister Adelheid. Richard Wagner was one of a few opera composers who wrote their own librettos (Italian plural, *libretti*).

LIED (LEED). A German word meaning "song." (The plural is *Lieder.*) In English-speaking countries *lieder* are usually thought of as art songs written by such composers as Franz Schubert, Robert Schumann, Johannes Brahms, and Hugo Wolf. Such songs are settings, for solo voices, of poems with highly artistic piano accompaniments. Some examples of great lieder are Schubert's *The Erl King,* Schumann's *The Nut Tree,* Brahms' *The Disappointed Serenader,* and Wolf's *Secrecy* (*Verborgenheit*).

LIGATURE (LIG a tyoor). (1) The name sometimes given to the curved line, or "slur" used in songs to show all the notes that are to be sung on one syllable. (2) The metal band that fastens the reed to the mouthpiece on such instruments as the clarinet and the saxophone. (3) See *Notation.*

LISZT (list), **Franz.** Hungarian pianist and composer, born in Raiding on October 22, 1811; died in Bayreuth, Germany, on July 31, 1886.

Liszt began his study of piano with his father, an excellent amateur musician. By the time the boy was nine he played well enough to give concerts in public. In fact, he played so well that several noblemen who heard him offered to pay his expenses for six years in order that he might study in Vienna. There he took piano lessons from the eminent teacher Czerny,* and at the same time studied composition. He was only eleven when he gave his first public concert in Vienna and was hailed at once as a great prodigy. A year later he went to Paris, hoping to enter the Conservatory. Although he was not admitted because of his foreign birth, he continued to study and to give highly successful concerts in France, England, and Switzerland. He became the greatest virtuoso pianist of his day and at the same time wrote an enormous number of works.

Liszt was just thirty-seven years old when he became musical director of the Court in Weimar, Germany. Thirteen years later he went to live in Rome. There he stayed for eight years, composing a number of works including his two oratorios. During that time he took minor orders in the Roman Catholic church, and although he did not follow up with a religious career, he became known as the "Abbé Liszt."

In his later years he returned to Weimar. By then he had become so famous that young musicians from all over Europe flocked to his home, hoping to play for him. He gave encouragement and even lessons to a great many pianists who later became famous themselves.

Altogether, Liszt wrote more than 1300 works, including about four hundred piano arrangements of other composers' compositions. Most of his works were for piano, but he also wrote a number of choral and orchestral numbers (including twelve symphonic poems,* of which he was the innovator), some seventy songs, and even an opera.

LITANY. In the Roman Catholic and Anglican churches, a litany is a prayer for help. It usually consists of sentences said by the priest and answered by the congregation with some such response as "Lord, have mercy." Litanies have been set to music by many composers, including Palestrina,* Tallis,* and Mozart.*

LOCATELLI (loh cah TELL ee), **Pietro.** Italian violinist and composer, born in Bergamo on September 3, 1695; died in Amsterdam, Holland, on March 30, 1764.

Locatelli was an exceptionally talented child. When he was still very young he was sent to Rome to study under the great violinist and teacher, Corelli.* He traveled widely for many years as a concert violinist, then finally settled in Amsterdam, Holland.

He wrote many works for stringed instruments, including concertos, sonatas, trios, and technical studies for the violin. He also wrote sonatas for flute.

LOCO (LOH coh). An Italian word meaning "place." Loco is a direction to the player to perform the music at the pitch notated on the staff. It cancels some previous direction, such as *all' ottava* or *8va* (to be played an octave higher) or *8va bassa* (to be played an octave lower).

LOEFFLER, Charles Martin. American (by adoption) violinist and composer, born in Mulhouse, Alsace, on January 30, 1861; died in Medfield, Massachusetts, on May 19, 1935.

Loeffler spent his boyhood partly in Russia, partly in Hungary, and partly in Switzerland. When he was fourteen he decided to become a professional violinist. The great violinist and composer Joachim* was so impressed with his talent that he accepted him as a student in Berlin. Later he studied in Paris. He played in a number of European orchestras, then in 1881, when he was still only twenty years old, he came to America where a year later he became a member of the Boston Symphony Orchestra. In 1903, at the age of forty-two, he resigned from the orchestra to devote his time to composing.

Although most of Loeffler's compositions are for violin, he wrote several works for orchestra, several for chorus, some chamber music, and a number of songs.

LOESSER, Frank. American composer, born in New York on June 29, 1910.

Loesser began writing songs while he was a student at the College of the City of New York. During his U.S. Army service in World War II he wrote a number of Army songs that became extremely popular. They include "What Do You Do in the Infantry," "Praise the Lord and Pass the Ammunition," and "They're Either Too Young or Too Old." After the war he continued to write popular songs. Among the highly successful broadway plays for which he wrote the music are *Where's Charley, Guys and Dolls,* and *The Most Happy Fella.*

LOEWE (LEUR veh), **Karl.** German composer, born in Löbejün on November 30, 1796; died in Kiel on April 20, 1869.

Loewe studied first with his father, a cantor* and schoolmaster. Karl had a fine singing voice and was offered a place in the court chapel choir of

Cöthen when he was ten years old. Two years later he entered the Franke Institution of Halle, where he studied with Türk, the Institution's head. His talent brought him to the attention of Jerome Bonaparte, who granted him an annual stipend of 300 Thaler, a sum that enabled him to devote himself to composition. He had begun to compose as a boy, and before long had built a substantial reputation as a composer of German ballads.* In addition to some 150 ballads, Loewe composed several operas, oratorios, a cantata, chamber music, songs, piano pieces, and works for orchestra.

LOEWE (LEUR veh), **Johann Jakob.** German composer, born in Vienna in 1628; died in Lüneburg in September, 1703. (The exact dates are not known.)

Loewe studied with the famous composer Heinrich Schütz* in Dresden, and in 1655 accepted the post of *Kapellmeister** at Wolfenbüttel. After service there and in Zeitz, he was appointed organist of St. Nicholas' Church at Lüneburg in 1682, a post he retained until the end of his life. He is noted for having composed some of the first German songs for solo voice. Besides his many songs, his works include ballets, instrumental suites, and two operas.

LORTZING (LORT sing), **Gustav Albert.** German singer, conductor, and composer, born in Berlin on October 23, 1801; died there on January 21, 1851.

Lortzing's parents were actors, and as a boy he traveled all over Germany with them. His mother taught him some music, and he studied with others for a short time. But for the most part his knowledge of music came from hearing it in the theater and watching conductors at rehearsals. He had a good tenor voice and frequently sang roles in the same musical productions that his parents appeared in. Often when the theater managers needed songs or incidental music, young Lortzing wrote it for them. He had a gift for operas of the light and comic kind, and by the time he was in his middle thirties he had written several works that were successfully produced. He held various positions in Germany as an opera conductor, and for two years he conducted the orchestra at the famous *Theater an der Wien* (Vienna).

Lortzing wrote fourteen light operas—both the music and the librettos—and most of them were popular with German audiences. His *Czar and Carpenter* (*Zar und Zimmermann*) is widely performed in Germany and Austria today.

LUENING, Otto. American composer, flutist, and conductor, born in Milwaukee, Wisconsin, on June 15, 1900.

Luening's first music teacher was his father. He began at an early age, and by the time he was six he was already composing. He was just twelve when his parents took him to Germany, where he entered the State Music Academy in Munich. Five years later he enrolled in the Municipal Conservatory of Zurich, Switzerland, where he studied composition and played flute in the local symphony and opera orchestras. He was seventeen when his works were performed in public for the first time.

After his return to the United States, Luening continued to compose and began a teaching career. He has taught at a number of schools, including the Eastman School of Music, University of Arizona, Bennington College, Barnard College, and Columbia University.

His compositions include one opera, *Evangeline,* for which he wrote his own libretto, several choral and orchestral works, chamber music, solo works for instruments, and several works for tape recorder. His electronic* compositions include *Poem in Cycles and Bells* for tape recorder and orchestra, and two works for tape recorder alone, *Low Speed* and *Suite from King Lear.*

LULLY (lü lee), **Jean-Baptiste.** Italian composer, born in Florence on November 28, 1632; died in Paris, France, on March 22, 1687.

Not much is known about Lully's early childhood in Italy. A monk gave him some music lessons, and he proved so talented that he was taken to Paris when he was about eleven. There he worked as a kitchen helper in the home of a noblewoman who allowed him to spend a good deal of time composing music and playing the violin. She fired him, however, when he wrote some satirical songs making fun of her. He was then employed by the young King Louis, and soon became a favorite and eventually the head musician of the court. There he remained, composing and conducting the court orchestra until his death, which resulted from an odd accident. In those days it was the custom for the conductor to beat time by pounding the floor with a long staff. One day Lully accidentally hit his foot with the end of the staff. The wound became infected and eventually caused his death. Lully wrote a great many ballets for the court, some fourteen operas, incidental music for plays, comedies, other stage works, and some religious music.

LUTE. A stringed instrument, popular in the sixteenth and seventeenth centuries. It was made in various sizes, ranging from small lutes held like a guitar, to large lutes that rested on the floor. The long fingerboard had frets,* and the peg box (where the tuning pegs were located) was turned back. It has eleven strings, ten of them tuned in pairs (called *courses*), and was played by plucking the strings with the fingers.

The lute was used widely for accompanying songs, and many song arrangements as well as solo and ensemble compositions were written for it. J. S. Bach wrote several pieces for the lute, and Haydn wrote two works which included the lute as one of the instruments.

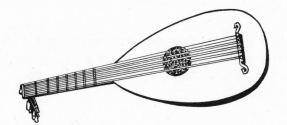

LUTHER, Martin. German religious reformer and musician, born in Eisleben on November 10, 1483; died there on February 18, 1546.

A man of strong moral character, Luther devoted most of his life to reform of the Christian church, including the music of the church. He changed the order of the Mass and substituted German for the Latin texts. He was a skillful musician who loved to sing and could perform on the lute and the flute. It is said that he composed chorale melodies on the flute, and that his *Kapellmeister** and cantor* wrote them down. No one knows for sure which of the hymn tunes that bear his name were actually composed by Luther, but he did write the words to a great many and probably composed the music for some of them. Among the hymns ascribed to Luther is the familiar *Ein' feste Burg ist unser Gott* (A Mighty Fortress is Our God).

LYDIAN MODE. (See *Modes.*)

LYRE. A stringed instrument that was widely used in ancient Greece to accompany singers and sometimes dancers. The body, made of tortoise shell or wood, had two curved arms that extended from the body and were joined by a cross bar. The strings, which numbered anywhere from three to twelve, were made of gut and were stretched between the cross bar and the bottom of the sounding board. The instrument was played by being plucked with the fingers or with a plectrum* made of ivory, horn, or wood.

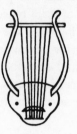

LYRIC. A word stemming from the Greek word *lyre.** It usually means something that pertains to singing, as the lyric theater (opera, operetta, etc.); a lyric tenor (light, flexible tenor voice). The plural form, *lyrics,* means the words to songs.

M

M. The letter M (or *m*) is often used with other letters as an abbreviation in music. Some of the more important abbreviations are these:

m.d. Right hand in keyboard music (abbreviation of the French *main droite,* and of the Italian *mano destra*).

mf Moderately loud (abbreviation of the Italian *mezzo-forte*).

m.g. Left hand in keyboard music (abbreviation of the French *main gauche*).

M.M. Indicates the metronome* setting for the proper tempo, as M.M. (abbreviation for Maelzel's Metronome) ♩ =60.

M.Mus. Master of Music. A college or conservatory degree that is the next higher after Bachelor of Music (B.Mus.).

mp Moderately soft (abbreviation of the Italian *mezzo-piano*).

m.s. Left hand in keyboard music (abbreviation of the Italian *mano sinistra*).

m.v. About half way between loud and soft (abbreviation of the Italian *mezzo voce*).

MACDOWELL, Edward Alexander. American composer, born in New York City on December 18, 1861; died there on January 23, 1908.

As a boy, MacDowell was a gifted pianist, and when he was fifteen his mother took him to Paris, where he was accepted as a student at the Paris Conservatory. Later he studied in Germany. He was only twenty years old when he became the chief piano teacher at the Darmstadt Conservatory. He stayed in Germany, teaching and composing, until he was twenty-nine, when he returned to the United States and settled in Boston. Six years later he accepted a position as Professor of Music at Columbia University. He remained there until 1904, a disagreement with University policy causing him to resign. A year later his musical career came to an end when his health failed and he became hopelessly insane. He died three years later.

MacDowell was one of America's greatest composers. His music was highly romantic in style, much of it reflecting his interest in nature, and some of it his concern with native Indian musical ideas. In addition to a great many piano pieces and songs, he wrote two piano concertos, a "Romance" for cello and orchestra, and several orchestral works.

MACHAUT (mah SHOH), **Guillaume.** French poet and composer, born in Champagne about 1300; died in Rheims in 1377. (The exact dates are not known.)

Machaut became an ordained priest while he was young, and was made secretary to the King of Bohemia when he was twenty-three. His later patrons included the King of Navarre, the King of France, and the Duc de Berry. From 1337 until his death he was canon of Rheims. Machaut, considered the leading French composer of the fourteenth century, was the first single composer to write a setting of the Mass.* He also wrote many motets* and polyphonic* chansons.

MADRIGAL. A kind of two-, three-, four-, or five-part song. A madrigal is contrapuntal in style; that is, the different voices* (melodies) weave in and out among one another and often imitate each other. Originally, just one singer sang each part, but later it became common to have several singers for each part.

The madrigal originated during the fourteenth century in Italy, but it reached its greatest height of popularity in England during the Elizabethan period.

The madrigal was secular* rather than religious, and the lyrics were usually based on themes of love. It was written without any instrumental accompaniment, but sometimes instruments were used to "double" some of the vocal parts.

In many colleges today madrigal groups are formed to sing these lovely old songs. The singers usually sit informally around a table as they sing, sometimes wearing Elizabethan costumes.

MAESTOSO (mah ess TOH soh). An Italian word meaning "majestic." It is a direction to perform the music in a dignified way.

MAESTRO (mah ESS troh). An Italian word meaning "teacher." In Italy, and sometimes in other countries, it is a title used in addressing distinguished conductors, composers, and teachers, as Maestro Toscanini.

MAGNIFICAT. Hymn of the Virgin Mary taken from the Book of Luke. It is sung in the Roman Catholic service at Vespers, and in the Anglican church at Evening Prayer. The text has been set to music by many composers. One of the most famous is Bach's *Magnificat* written in the form of a cantata.* A more recent setting is Vaughan Williams' *Magnificat* for soprano, women's chorus, and orchestra.

MAHLER (MAHL er), **Gustav.** Austrian (Bohemian) composer and conductor, born in Kališt on July 7, 1860; died in Vienna on May 18, 1911.

As a child, Mahler showed a great interest in music, and by the time he was fifteen he was advanced enough to attend the Vienna Conservatory. Four years later he left Vienna to take up his first professional post, that of *Kapellmeister** at Hall, a small town in Austria. From that time on his life was devoted to composing and conducting. Some of the famous organizations that he conducted were the Budapest Opera, the Hamburg Opera, the Vienna Opera, the Metropolitan Opera, and the New York Philharmonic Orchestra.

Although Mahler was a great opera conductor and served in some of the world's most famous opera houses, he wrote only one opera that was produced. His greatest works were written for orchestra and for voice. He wrote nine symphonies (a tenth symphony was unfinished at his death), and more than forty songs. One of his most beautiful works is *Das Lied von der Erde* (The Song of the Earth) for orchestra, with tenor and contralto solo voices.

MAJOR-MINOR. The names applied to certain contrasting scales, keys, chords, and intervals.

(1) *Scales.* Major and minor scales are the two basic scales used in music composition since about 1700. The arrangement of whole and half steps within a major or minor scale is always the same, no matter which note is the key note.* The scale of C major, ascending and descending, is:

C D E F G A B C B A G F E D C

There are three minor scales, natural minor, melodic minor, and harmonic minor. Only the melodic minor has different notes in its descending form.

The natural minor and the harmonic minor have the same notes ascending and descending. The three minor scales in C are:

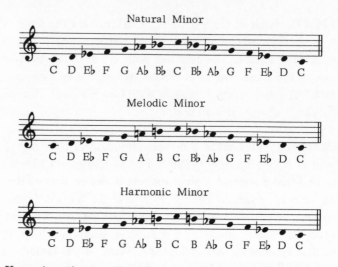

Natural Minor

C D Eb F G Ab Bb C Bb Ab G F Eb D C

Melodic Minor

C D Eb F G A B C Bb Ab G F Eb D C

Harmonic Minor

C D Eb F G Ab B C B Ab G F Eb D C

(2) *Keys.* A major or minor key corresponds with the major or minor scale that begins on a particular note. For example, the key of C major is the key in which the notes of the scale of C major are "normal." Similarly, the key of C minor is the key in which notes of the scale of C minor are normal. (There is only one type of minor key, although there are three types of minor scale.)

(3) *Chords.* Major and minor chords are built from corresponding major and minor scales. The common chord of C major, for example, is C-E-G, while the common chord of C minor is C-Eb -G.

(4) *Intervals.* The intervals of the second, third, sixth, and seventh are classified as either major or minor, the minor intervals being a half tone smaller than the major. For example, with the lower tone as C, C-D is a major second and C-Db is a minor second; C-E is a major third and C-Eb is a minor third; C-A is a major sixth and C-Ab is a minor sixth; C-B is a major seventh and C-Bb is a minor seventh. (See *Chords, Intervals,* and *Keys.* See also *Melodic Minor* and *Natural Minor.*)

MALAGUEÑA. A Spanish folk dance, with words, named after the town where it originated, Málaga. The music is lively, in 3/4 time, and usually begins and ends on the dominant (fifth) note of the scale. The name has been used also by composers for pieces they have written in the style of the original folk music. An example is the popular *Malagueña* by the Cuban composer, Lecuona.

MANDOLIN. (Also spelled *mandoline.*) A stringed instrument of the lute* family. It is played by brushing a small plectrum* rapidly back and forth across the strings. It has four pairs of strings, each tuned like the corresponding string on the violin.* The mandolin has been popular since the early part of the eighteenth century, especially in Italy, as an instrument for accompanying singers. Mozart wrote a mandolin accompaniment for the famous serenade, "Deh vieni alla finestra" (Come here to your window), in his opera *Don Giovanni.*

MANUAL. A keyboard on the organ that is played by the hands. (The keyboard played by the feet is called a *pedal keyboard.*) Some organs have only one manual. Large organs usually have two or three manuals, and the largest organs may have even more. (See also *Organ.*)

MARACAS (mah RAH kas). A percussion instrument that originated in Cuba. It is usually made of a dry gourd filled with dry seeds that rattle when the instrument is shaken, though some maracas are made of other materials that give the same effect. Maracas are used mainly in dance bands that play Latin-American music.

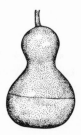

MARCATO (mar CAH toh). An Italian word meaning "marked." It is a direction to accent the notes strongly.

MARCH. A piece written in a regular, accented style, designed for marching groups or processions. Fast marches are usually written in 4/4 or 2/2 time. Slow marches, such as wedding or funeral marches, in either 2/4 or

6/8 time. Many marches have been written for non-military use. Verdi wrote a stirring "Triumphal March" for the big scene in his opera *Aida*; Beethoven wrote a funeral march for his Symphony No. 3; Mendelssohn wrote a famous *Wedding March*. The most eminent composer of military marches was John Philip Sousa,* an American.

MARCHING BAND. (See *Band.*)

MARCIA (MAHR chah). An Italian word meaning "march." It usually appears in the phrase *alla marcia,* a direction to play the music in strict time, with a well-accented rhythm, in the style of a march.

MARIMBA. A percussion instrument that resembles the xylophone. The "keys" are bars of wood mounted over hollow boxes that make the sound resonate. The instrument is played by striking the bars with hammers held in the hands. The marimba originated in Africa, and later became popular in Latin-American countries. It is used mainly in dance bands, but occasionally in orchestras.

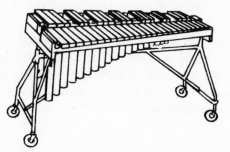

MARTELÉ (mar tuh LAY). A French word meaning "hammered." In piano music martelé indicates that the keys should be struck quickly and energetically. In music for stringed instruments it indicates that the notes should be played with short, sharp strokes of the bow. (See also *Bowing.*)

MARTIN, Frank. Swiss composer, born in Geneva on September 15, 1890.
Martin studied music in his home town, then spent a number of years in Rome, Paris, and Zurich. He held several important positions, and for many years taught at the Jaques-Dalcroze* Institute. In 1946 he went to live in Amsterdam, and in 1950 he was appointed Professor of Composition at the Cologne, Germany, Conservatory of Music. He is consid-

ered one of Switzerland's most important composers, and his works have been performed in many parts of the world. They include ballets, orchestral and choral works, compositions for solo instruments and orchestra, chamber music, piano pieces, and songs.

MARTINŮ (MAR tin oo), **Bohuslav.** Czech composer, born in Polička (Bohemia) on December 8, 1890; died in Liestal, Switzerland, on August 28, 1959.

Martinů began his study of music when he was six years old. His instrument was the violin, and by the time he was eight he could play rather difficult works. He was only ten when he wrote a string quartet. He entered the Prague Conservatory when he was sixteen, and seven years later joined the Prague Philharmonic Orchestra as a violinist. In 1923 he settled in Paris, and there he remained for seventeen years devoting himself to composition. His works began to attract more and more attention, and were performed under such conductors as Münch in Paris and Koussevitzky in the United States. From 1941 to 1945 Martinů lived in the United States, and during that time composed four symphonies in addition to other works. In 1945 he accepted a position as a professor of composition at the Prague Conservatory, but he remained in his native country for only a brief period. In 1957 he became resident composer at the American Academy in Rome, and there he stayed until shortly before his death. Martinů wrote a great many works, including, besides the four symphonies, a number of orchestral works, ballets, operas, chamber music, pieces for solo instruments and orchestra, piano solos, and songs.

MARZIALE (mahrt zee AHL lay). An Italian word meaning "martial." It indicates that the music should be played in a march-like, military style.

MASCAGNI (mahs CAHN yee), **Pietro.** Italian composer, born December 7, 1863, in Leghorn; died in Rome on August 2, 1945.

Mascagni studied music in his home town of Leghorn until he was eighteen. He then entered the Milan Conservatorio where he studied with the well-known composer Ponchielli.* He soon tired of the difficult course of study, however, and found himself a job as conductor of a traveling opera company. For many years he lived a hard life of travel with various opera companies and had little time for composing. He is famous today for his one-act opera *Cavalleria Rusticana*. It won first prize in a competition in 1889, and was first performed with enormous success in Rome in 1890. He later attempted other operas, but none of them enjoyed the success of *Cavalleria*.

MASON, Daniel Gregory. American composer and teacher, born in Brookline, Massachusetts, on November 20, 1873; died in Greenwich, Connecticut, on December 4, 1953.

Daniel was the grandson of another prominent American musician, Lowell Mason,* and the son of one of the founders of the Mason and Hamlin Piano Company. Daniel graduated from Harvard University when he was twenty-two, then continued his study of music. For many years he taught music at Columbia University, finally becoming head of the music department. His works include piano pieces, songs, chamber music, choral music, and a number of orchestral works. He wrote three symphonies, the most famous of which is the third, called *A Lincoln Symphony*. In addition to his musical compositions, he wrote a number of books about music.

MASON, Lowell. American organist and educator, born in Medfield, Massachusetts, on January 24, 1792; died in Orange, New Jersey, on August 11, 1872.

Young Lowell taught himself music and learned by himself to play a number of instruments, including the organ. He spent a good many years playing organ and conducting the choirs in various churches, and he helped to compile a collection of hymns that was published in Boston in 1822. He was one of the founders of the Boston Academy of Music, where he devoted much time to the training of teachers for teaching music in the public schools. Because of his lasting influence on public school music, he is often called "The father of music education in America." Lowell Mason was the grandfather of another eminent American musician, Daniel Gregory Mason.*

MASQUE. An elaborate type of entertainment popular in the sixteenth and seventeenth centuries in England. The masque, which was designed primarily for entertaining the nobility, combined dancing, poetry, and music, and frequently was staged with elaborate scenery and costumes. One of the most famous masques, *Comus,* was written by the great poet Milton with music composed by Henry Lawes, a musician in the service of the English court.

MASS. The Mass is the communion service of the Roman Catholic church.

Low Mass is spoken; High Mass is sung. There are two musical parts of the Mass, the Proper and the Ordinary. The Ordinary has been set to music by a great many composers. It consists of five parts: *Kyrie eleison* ("Lord have mercy"), *Gloria in excelsis Deo* ("Glory be to God on high"), *Credo* ("I believe"), *Sanctus* and *Benedictus* ("Holy, Holy; Blessed is he that cometh"), and *Agnus Dei* ("Lamb of God"). Some of the most beautiful choral works of all time have been Masses. Two examples are Beethoven's *Missa Solemnis* ("Solemn Mass") and Bach's *Mass in B Minor*. Among the modern composers who have set the Mass to music are Stravinsky and Vaughan Williams.

MASSENET (mah sen NAY), **Jules Émile Frédéric.** French composer, born in Montaud on May 12, 1842; died in Paris on August 13, 1912.

The Massenet family moved to Paris when Jules was five years old. His father was in poor health, and his mother helped support the family by giving piano lessons. Jules studied with her until he was eleven, when he was accepted as a student at the Paris Conservatory. There he studied with a number of famous teachers. During his student days he helped to support himself by playing the triangle and the drums in theater orchestras. Later he taught composition at the Conservatory.

Although Massenet wrote a great many songs, a piano concerto, and some suites for orchestra, his greatest talent was for stage works. These include three ballets, incidental music for a number of plays, and twenty operas. His most popular operas were *Hérodiade, Manon, Le Cid, Werther,* and *Thaïs.*

MASTERSINGERS. (German spelling *Meistersinger.*) Members of a school or "guild" of singers prominent in Germany during the fifteenth and sixteenth centuries. They followed, more or less, the tradition of the earlier *Minnesinger,** except that they were craftsmen and tradesmen rather than aristocrats. The guild was organized along strict lines, with rigid rules about the kinds of songs sung and the way they were to be sung. It was the custom of the Mastersingers to meet each Sunday after church. Once a year they held a festival at which prizes were awarded for the best singing. Hans Sachs,* a shoemaker in Nuremburg, was the most famous of all Mastersingers. Richard Wagner's* famous opera, *Die Meistersinger von Nürnberg* (The Mastersingers of Nuremberg), tells the story of Hans Sachs and the great festival of the Mastersingers.

MAZURKA. A country dance that was popular in Poland in the eighteenth and nineteenth centuries. It is moderately fast and in either 3/4 or 3/8 time. It is often strongly accented on the second or third beat. Its characteristic rhythm is: ♫. ♪ ♩. ♪ . Chopin was the first composer to adapt the Mazurka to concert music. He wrote more than fifty Mazurkas that more or less follow the style of the original Polish dance music.

MEASURE. A measure of music is the same as a *bar** of music. It includes the notes and rests that lie between one bar line and the next.

MECHANICAL INSTRUMENTS. Instruments in which the sounds are produced by mechanical means. The phonograph is the most widely used mechanical instrument. Some others are the player piano, the barrel organ, musical clocks, and music boxes.

MEDIANT. (1) The name given to the third note of the diatonic scale. For example, in the scale of C major, E is the mediant. In the scale of A minor, C is the mediant. (2) The chord built on the third degree of the scale.

MELLOPHONE. A brass instrument that resembles the French horn, but is simpler in design and easier to play. It is sometimes used in dance bands, and often in school bands.

MELODIC MINOR. (See *Major-Minor.*)

MELODY. A melody is a succession of musical tones organized horizontally into a musically meaningful entity. There are two aspects of this horizontal organization—rhythmic patterning and pitch-line patterning—but the two fuse to such an extent that they create a unified whole. Rhythmic patterning (patterning in time) results from likenesses and differences in the duration (length) of the individual tones and usually also from the metrical scheme upon which they are superimposed. Pitch patterning in different periods has resulted in different modes of organization. Most of the music we know—music composed from the seventeenth century through the second decade of the present century—is organized around tonal centers in major* or minor* keys. Prior to the seventeenth century, modes* were used by composers as the bases of their melodic organization, and in the twentieth century some composers have resumed this practice. While some contemporary composers still employ major and minor keys and church modes, the trend is toward the use of other bases of organization, the most prevalent of which is the use of tone rows as series made up of particular arrangements of the twelve tones of the chromatic* scale. (See *Atonal Music*.)

Melody may occur in music with or without any additional element. In monophonic* music it stands alone. In polyphonic* music it is combined with one or more additional melodies. In homophonic* music it is supported by harmonies.

MENDELSSOHN (MEN dell sohn), **Felix.** (Full name: Jakob Ludwig Felix Mendelssohn-Bartholdy). German composer, born in Hamburg on February 3, 1809; died in Leipzig on November 4, 1847.

Mendelssohn's parents recognized their young son's unusual musical talent and saw to it that he studied with the very best teachers of piano, violin, and composition. He was only eight years old when he gave his first public piano recital, and only ten when one of his choral works was performed.

Mendelssohn's father was strict with his children and insisted that they practice and study for long hours every day. This did not seem to bother Felix as it did the others. He actually spent so much time composing that his mother worried about him. In one year, his twelfth, he composed several symphonies and fugues for stringed instruments, as well as a number of songs and piano pieces. He was seventeen when he composed the beautiful "Overture" to Shakespeare's *A Midsummer Night's Dream,* one of the greatest of all works for orchestra.

Mendelssohn made his first visit to England when he was twenty years old. He became a great favorite there and returned many times. He also travelled widely in Germany, Austria, Italy, France, and Switzerland, playing and conducting with great success. In 1829 he conducted Bach's *St. Matthew Passion* in Leipzig, an event that led very likely to a revival of Bach's works. In 1835, at the age of twenty-six, he was appointed conductor of the famous *Gewandhaus Orchestra* in Leipzig, and seven years later became Director of the newly-formed Leipzig Conservatory, a school which he helped to build into one of the finest music schools in the world.

Although Mendelssohn died young, he left to the world a great many beautiful works. These include five symphonies, six overtures for orchestra, two oratorios (*Elijah* and *St. Paul*), other religious works, a violin concerto, two piano concertos, nineteen chamber works, several sonatas for organ, a great many solos for piano, and more than eighty songs, as well as the music for *A Midsummer Night's Dream*.

MENNIN, Peter. American composer, born in Erie, Pennsylvania, on May 17, 1923.

Mennin began his study of music when he was seven years old, and about the same time started writing music. During his student days at the Oberlin Conservatory he wrote his first symphony, his first chamber music work, and several songs. He later studied composition at the Eastman School of Music, where he earned the Bachelor's, Master's, and Ph.D. degrees. He was just twenty-two years old when he won the Gershwin Memorial Award for part of his second symphony. Two years later he was awarded a Guggenheim Fellowship. In 1958 he became Director of the Peabody Conservatory in Baltimore, and in 1962 he accepted the Presidency of the Juilliard School of Music in New York.

Mennin's works have been performed by many of this country's leading orchestras. He has written six symphonies and other works for orchestra, a violin concerto, a piano concerto, chamber music, a number of choruses, piano pieces, and songs.

MENO (MAY noh). An Italian word meaning "less." It usually is written as *meno mosso,* which means "less movement," or "slower."

MENOTTI, Gian-Carlo. Italian-American composer, born near Milan, Italy, on July 7, 1911.

Menotti is well known to the American television audience as the composer of the one-act opera *Amahl and the Night Visitors,* given every year during the Christmas season.

As a boy in Italy, Menotti studied music with his mother, a talented musician. By the time he was eleven he had written his first opera, *The*

Death of Pierrot. Soon after that he wrote another, *The Little Mermaid.* Neither of these operas was ever produced, but his mother recognized his unusual talent and took him to Milan to study at the Conservatory. There he spent three years studying counterpoint, harmony, and other musical subjects. His father died when he was seventeen, and soon afterward he was sent to the United States for further study at the Curtis Institute of Music in Philadelphia.

The first of Menotti's many operas to be produced was *Amelia Goes to the Ball.* It was an immediate success, and the following season, when Menotti was just twenty-six years old, it was given at the Metropolitan Opera in New York. Other highly successful operas of his are *The Medium, The Telephone, The Consul, The Saint of Bleeker Street, Maria Golovin, The Last Savage,* and two operas written expressly for television, *Amahl and the Night Visitors* and *Labyrinth.* One of his most recent works is a kind of cantata-opera based on the story of the Children's Crusade of the Middle Ages, *The Death of the Bishop of Brindisi.*

MENUET. (Same as *Minuet.**)

METER. (Sometimes spelled *Metre.*) The basic pattern of accented notes or beats in a piece of music. The meter is usually indicated by a time signature* such as 3/4, 4/4, 6/8, and so on. The meter of a waltz, for example, is an underlying beat of *1*-2-*3*, *1*-2-*3*. The meter of a march will be a steady *1*-2-*3*-4, *1*-2-*3*-4, with the third beat accented less strongly than the first beat.

METRONOME. An instrument invented by a man named Maelzel, a friend of Beethoven, to indicate the exact speed (or tempo*) at which a piece should be played. Maelzel's metronome consists of a triangular shaped box in which a small rod is set in such a way that it swings from side to side, like a pendulum, making a clicking noise at the end of each swing. A weight on the rod can be adjusted down or up to increase or decrease the width of the swing for faster or slower tempos. The speeds can be varied from thirty clicks per minute (very slow) to 180 clicks per minute (very fast). The various tempos are marked on the rod of the metronome.

Metronome speed settings are given at the beginning of many pieces. For example, $\quarternote=100$ indicates that quarter notes should be played at the rate of 100 per minute.

More recently an electric metronome has been invented. This is equipped with a dial with a small "hand" that can be set at the speed desired.

MEYERBEER (MY er bair), **Giacomo.** German composer, born in Berlin on September 5, 1791; died in Paris, France, on May 2, 1864.

Meyerbeer started his musical career as a pianist when he was very young. He studied for some time with the famous piano teacher Clementi, and gave his first public recital when he was nine years old. Before he was in his teens he was considered one of the most promising pianists in Berlin. At the same time he became deeply interested in composition, and one of his operas had already been performed when he reached his twentieth birthday. On a visit to Italy, he heard for the first time the operas of Rossini. He became interested in the Italian style of opera and decided to remain in Italy. He stayed for a number of years and succeeded in having several of his own operas performed with great success. Later he settled in Paris, and there, too, he wrote operas that were "hits" of the day. Before long his operas were being performed widely in Europe.

In addition to sixteen operas, Meyerbeer wrote a number of other musical works for the stage, choral works, songs, and several instrumental pieces. His best known operas are *Robert le Diable* (Robert the Devil), *Les Huguenots, Le Prophète,* and *L'Africaine.*

MEZZO (MED zoh). An Italian word meaning "half" or "middle." Thus, *mezzo forte* means "medium loud"; *mezzo voce* means that roughly half the power of the voice is to be used; *mezzo soprano* means a voice with a range halfway between soprano and contralto.

MI (mee). In the system of *movable do,** the syllable name given to the third note of the major scale. In the *fixed do* system, the note E.

MICROTONE. An interval that is smaller than a half-step. Microtones cannot be played on the piano because the distance between one note and the next is a full half-step or semitone. They can be played only on stringed instruments and certain kinds of wind instruments, or on specially constructed instruments, including some electronic instruments. Several modern composers have written music that calls for microtones.

MIDDLE C. The note C that is closest to the middle of the piano keyboard. It is notated on the first ledger line* above the bass staff* or the first ledger line below the treble staff.

MILHAUD (MEE yoh), **Darius.** French composer, born in Aix-en-Provence on September 4, 1892. Milhaud was only three years old when his mother found him picking out tunes on the piano. But since he was a delicate child, his parents did not allow him to have formal lessons until he was seven. Then he began the study of violin. By the time he was twelve he played so well that his teacher invited him to play in his own string quartet. In 1909 he entered the Paris Conservatory. At first he concentrated on violin, but he was drawn gradually to composing. He was an outstanding student and soon began to win recognition. He became a member of an influential group of young composers known as *Les Six* (The Six*), and he made friends with a number of prominent literary figures. Among these was Paul Claudel. When Claudel was appointed French Minister to Brazil he took Milhaud with him as Secretary. Milhaud returned to France in 1918 and remained in Paris, composing a great many works, until 1940. He taught at Mills College in California until 1947, when he again returned to France to become a professor of composition at the Paris Conservatory.

Milhaud has been able to write music successfully in many different styles. His works include several symphonies, concertos, and other orchestral works; operas; ballets; chamber music; and pieces for piano.

MILITARY BAND. A military band differs from a brass band* in that it includes woodwind as well as brass instruments. Usually, but not always, a military band is associated with one of the armed forces, and is used mainly to accompany parade marches, but may also give regular concerts. A military band, such as the United States Air Force Band, is capable of performing some very difficult and beautiful works. The best known writer of music for the military band in recent times was John Philip Sousa.*

MINNESINGER (MIN eh zing er). The Minnesinger (the plural spelling is the same as singular) were the forerunners of the Mastersingers.* They were poet-musicians, usually of noble birth, prominent from the middle of the twelfth century to the middle of the fifteenth century. They composed songs and held singing contests, much as the Mastersingers did later. Walther von der Vogelweide and Tannhäuser were two of the most celebrated of the *Minnesinger.* Wagner's opera *Tannhäuser* is based on a singing contest that actually took place in 1207 and in which Tannhäuser, a *Minnesinger,* took part.

MINOR. (See *Major-Minor.*)

MINSTRELS. Musician-entertainers prominent in northern France during the Middle Ages. They originally "ministered" to the Troubadours,* accompanying their singing on stringed instruments. In America the term *minstrel* has been applied to a kind of humorous entertainment in which white entertainers disguised themselves as Negroes and imitated their singing, dancing, and so on. Minstrel shows were popular for some forty years before the motion picture began to take the place of "live" shows.

MINUET. A dance in 3/4 time that became popular in France in the seventeenth century. Composers of the Baroque* period used it in their suites and sonatas, and it eventually became a standard part of compositions written in classic sonata-form.* It occurred often in a three-part form of minuet-trio-minuet. Mozart used it in a five-part form, minuet-trio I-minuet-trio II-minuet. Beethoven elaborated the minuet and called it *scherzo.* Many composers have written minuets, some as parts of larger works; others as pieces for piano or other instruments.

MISSA (MEE sah). The Latin word meaning *Mass.**

MIXED VOICES. In choral music, a term which indicates that both men's and women's voices are used.

MIXOLYDIAN MODE. (See *Mode.*)

MODE. Used in the broad sense, the term means a series of tones organized into a scale which is used as the tonal material for musical compositions. In a more restricted sense, the term refers to the church modes which served as the tonal bases of the Gregorian chant* and of most early music until the seventeenth century.

The church modes consist of octave segments of the diatonic scale, the difference between one mode and another depending upon (1) the tone upon which the mode begins and (2) the patterning of whole and half steps within the octave.

The octave range of a mode is called *ambitus,* and the key or center tone is called *finalis.* There are six finalis in what is considered the complete system of the modes: D (Dorian); E (Phrygian); F (Lydian); G (Mixolydian); A (Aeolian); C (Ionian). Each *finalis* has two modes: (1) an *authentic* mode, whose *ambitus* begins on the *finalis* and ends an octave higher, and (2) a *plagal* mode, whose *ambitus* begins a fourth* below the *finalis* and ends a fifth* above. To distinguish the plagal from the authentic modes, the prefix *hypo* is used.

The twelve modes subdivided into the two groups, with first the *finalis* and then the *ambitus* indicated in parentheses, are as follows:

Authentic: Dorian (D; D-D); Phrygian (E; E-E); Lydian (F; F-F); Mixolydian (G; G-G); Aeolian (A; A-A); Ionian (C; C-C).

Plagal: Hypodorian (D; A-A); Hypophrygian (E; B-B); Hypolydian (F; C-C); Hypomixolydian (G; D-D); Hypoaeolian (A; E-E); Hypo-ionian (C; G-G).

A useful means of grasping the modes is to play them on the piano, stressing the *finalis*.

The Aeolian and Ionian modes (and their corresponding plagal modes) correspond to the present day natural minor* and major* scales in C. These modes did not appear in the literature about the modes until the middle of the sixteenth century. It is possible that this addition to the modes was the beginning of the major-minor* system which dominated the organization of music for about three hundred years.

MODERATO (moh dehr RAH toh). An Italian word meaning "moderate." Used with other terms that indicate speed, it serves to "moderate" the other terms. For example, *allegro moderato* means moderately fast—not so fast as *allegro*; *adagio moderato* means moderately slow—not so slow as *adagio*. (See also *Tempo*.)

MODULATION. Changing from one key to another within a composition or a section of a composition. Music which stays in one key throughout an entire piece—especially in a fairly long piece—tends to sound monotonous. Even in a short piece there is often a change to one other key, and then a return to the original key. In longer works changes may be made into a number of different keys before returning to the main key. Learning to modulate smoothly from one key to another involves a knowledge of key relationships and other aspects of harmony* and tonality.*

MOLTO (MOHL toh). An Italian word meaning "very." It is used with other words, as *allegro molto* (very fast); *molto adagio* (very slow); and so on.

MONOCHORD. A word taken from the Greek, meaning "one string." An ancient instrument consisting of a single string stretched over a wooden box between two bridges, and equipped with a movable fret.* The monochord was used by the ancient Greeks to study the laws of acoustics* and to determine the intervals in the ancient modes.* During the Middle Ages it was used to study the relation between musical intervals and the divisions of the string.

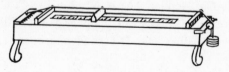

MONODY. A word taken from the Greek, meaning "one song." It refers to music written for solo voice, with or without accompaniment.

MONOPHONY. A word taken from the Greek, meaning "a single voice." Monophonic music consists of a single-voiced melody, without accompaniment. Examples of monophony can be found among folk songs* and in plainsong.*

MONOTONE. A Greek word meaning "one tone." In music it means singing on a single tone without any change in pitch. The term is sometimes applied to a person who has no sense of pitch and sings along on the same tone.

MONTEMEZZI (mon tah MEHD zee), **Italo.** Italian composer, born in Vigasio on August 4, 1875; died there on May 15, 1952.

Montemezzi studied piano as a child, but he did not show any particular talent. He was sent to a technical school in Milan to study engineering, but suddenly became interested in music. He attended the Milan Conservatory and graduated when he was twenty-five. During his student days in Milan he heard a great deal of opera at the famous La Scala, and he became interested in writing an opera himself. His first opera, *Giovanni Gallurese,* was produced both in Turin, Italy, and at the Metropolitan Opera in New York. The opera for which he is best known was his third, *L'Amore dei Tre Re* (The Love of Three Kings).

MONTEVERDI (mon tah VEHR dee), **Claudio.** Italian composer, born in Cremona (baptized May 15), 1567; died in Venice on November 29, 1643.

As a child Monteverdi sang in the choir of the cathedral in Cremona and studied organ and the viol* with his choirmaster. By the time he was fifteen he had already published a collection of three-part motets.* In 1590 he was employed by the Duke of Mantua as a madrigal* singer and viol player. For some twenty years he remained in the Duke's service, following him during a number of military campaigns in several European countries. During that time he wrote a great deal of music, including the opera *Orfeo*. A year after the Duke's death in 1612 Monteverdi was appointed *maestro di cappella* (chapel master) at San Marco in Venice, a position he held until his own death. During his lifetime he wrote a great many works in every style of vocal music, and he exerted a great deal of influence on the development of opera through his own experimentation with new devices. In addition to some 250 madrigals, two settings of the Magnificat, many Masses, and other vocal works, he wrote seventeen operas. The best known of his operas today are *Orfeo* (Orpheus), *The Combat of Tancred and Clorinda,* and *The Coronation of Poppaea.*

MOORE, Douglas Stuart. American Composer, born in Cutchogue, New York, on August 10, 1893.

Moore studied music at Yale University with Horatio Parker, a distinguished American composer and teacher, and graduated with a Bachelor of Music degree in 1917. During the first World War he served in the Navy as a lieutenant, and then went to Europe for further musical study. In Paris he worked with Vincent d'Indy,* Nadia Boulanger,* and Ernest Bloch.* He then returned to the United States and began his brilliant career as a teacher, organist, and composer. After appointments in several other institutions, he joined the faculty of Columbia University in 1926, and in 1940 succeeded Daniel Gregory Mason* as head of the Music Department. Some of the honors he has received are the Guggenheim Fellowship, the Pulitzer Scholarship, and the Eastman School Publication Award.

Moore has written a great many works, including a folk opera, *The Ballad of Baby Doe*; a full-scale opera, *The Devil and Daniel Webster*; an operetta, *The Headless Horseman*; and other works for the stage. His works for orchestra include *The Pageant of P. T. Barnum, Moby Dick, Overture on an American Tune,* and *Symphony in A major.* He has also written music for chamber groups and a piano trio.

MORDENT. A kind of inverted trill that is played rapidly and sharply.

The length of the trill depends on the length of the note below the mordent. This is how it is designated, and how it is played:

MORESCA. A dance that originated in Spain during the time when the Moors occupied the country. It became popular throughout Europe in the fifteenth and sixteenth centuries, and found its way to England where it became known as the Morris Dance.* In its original form it represented a battle between the Moors (who were Mohammedans) and the Spanish Christians. Later it evolved into a dance where the performers darkened their faces, attached bells to their legs, and danced to the accompaniment of the pipe* and the tabor.*

MORLEY, Thomas. English composer and theorist, born in 1557; died in 1602. (The exact places and dates are not known.)

Morley studied music with the famous English organist and composer, William Byrd.* In 1591 he was appointed organist at St. Paul's Cathedral in London; a year later he became a Gentleman of the Royal Chapel. His compositions include a great deal of church music, many madrigals, pieces for viols* and for virginals,* and solo songs with lute* accompaniments. He was the author of the first textbook on music theory to be published in England (1597), *A Plain and Easy Introduction to Practical Music.*

MORRIS DANCE. An old English dance derived from the Spanish moresca.* The performers wore bells and dressed in costumes that represented the Queen of the May, knights, ladies, fools, and so on. It was traditionally danced on the Village Green on May Day.

MOSSO (MOH soh). An Italian word meaning "movement." It generally indicates speed, and is most often used with other words, as *più mosso* (more movement, or faster) and *meno mosso* (less movement, or slower). By itself, *mosso* means "faster."

MOSZKOWSKI (mohs KOV ski), **Moritz.** German pianist and composer, born in Breslau on August 23, 1854; died in Paris, France, on March 4, 1925.

Moszkowski studied music first in Dresden, then in Berlin. He became a teacher at the Kullak Academy there, and gave his first public performance in Berlin when he was nineteen years old. He toured widely throughout Europe as a pianist, and sometimes as a conductor, and finally settled in Paris. His reputation as a pianist and teacher gradually dwindled, and he died in poverty.

Moszkowski wrote a number of large works, including an opera, a piano concerto, and a violin concerto. But he is remembered today mainly for his compositions for piano, and especially for his *Spanische Tänze* (Spanish Dances). These were originally written as piano duets, but they became so popular that solo arrangements for piano were made from them.

MOTET (moh TET). A word derived from the French word *mot,* meaning "word." The motet originated in Medieval times and became an important music form during the Renaissance. The Medieval motet was usually in three voice parts: *tenor, motetus,* and *triplum.* The tenor (the lowest voice part), ordinarily consisted of a *Cantus Firmus,* a melody taken from Gregorian chant,* and was usually sung in Latin. The other two parts were sung to other words, usually in the language of the particular country. The Renaissance motet was a sacred composition in which all voice parts (usually five) contained the same Latin text. But, since the composition was usually polyphonic,* the words frequently appeared at different times in the various parts. J. S. Bach wrote motets for unaccompanied double chorus, for five-part chorus, and for four-part chorus with organ continuo.* Among later composers who wrote motets, both with and without accompaniment, were Mendelssohn and Schubert.

MOTION. The changes of pitch in a melody. The motion may be *ascending* (going up), *descending* (going down), *conjunct* (moving step by step), or *disjunct* (moving up or down by larger intervals). In music for two voices or parts, the term *parallel motion* is used when the parts remain at the same distance from each other; *contrary motion* when they move in opposite directions; and *oblique motion* when one voice moves and the other remains on the same note.

MOTIVE. The shortest possible melodic or rhythmic figure that is recognizable as a unit in a composition. One theme* or subject* may be made up of several motives, as in the following theme that opens the fourth movement of Beethoven's Symphony No. 7. (The motives are indicated by the brackets above the notes.)

MOTO (MOH toh). Italian word meaning "motion." It is usually used with the word *con,* as *con moto* (with motion), meaning that the music should be performed rather quickly.

MOUSSORGSKY. (See *Mussorgsky.*)

MOUTH ORGAN. (See *Harmonica.*)

MOVABLE DO. A system of solmization* in which the syllables, do-re-mi-fa-so-la-ti, are given to degrees* of the scale, regardless of the key note* of the scale, as opposed to the fixed do* system, in which C is always *do* and F is always *fa,* and so on.

MOVEMENT. One of the major units in a large composition such as a symphony, sonata, string quartet, concerto, or suite. Each movement in such a composition is a self-contained piece in itself, although it is not necessarily independent of the other movements. The number of movements varies from two to six. Mozart wrote several symphonies in three movements; eight of Beethoven's nine symphonies have four movements, the sixth has five.

MOZART (MOH tsart), **Wolfgang Amadeus.** Austrian composer, born in Salzburg on January 27, 1756; died in Vienna on December 5, 1791.

Mozart, one of the greatest composers the world has ever known, began to show his immense talent when he was only three years old. He paid close attention to his sister's harpsichord lessons and soon began to pick out tunes. When he started lessons himself, his progress was so rapid that by the time he was six his father Leopold, who was an important musical figure of the time, took him and his sister on a concert tour. The children were so sensationally successful that the tours became more and more frequent, and they travelled to Germany, Belgium, Paris, London, and Holland. They became favorites in the courts of Europe, especially in

Vienna, where young Wolfgang played with the little princess who later became Queen of France, Marie Antoinette.

By the time the Mozarts returned to Salzburg, the ten-year-old Wolfgang had already written three symphonies and a good many other works. In 1769, his father took him to Italy. During the two years they stayed there Mozart studied with the great teacher Martini and continued to compose. The Prince Archbishop of Salzburg gave him a position in his court, but as time went on Mozart became dissatisfied with procedures there, and when he was twenty-five, he resigned. He went to Vienna, settled down, and married. The Emperor gave him a small position, and the operas he wrote were produced with great success, but he still did not make much money and was constantly worried about making ends meet. He was not yet thirty-six years old when he became ill and died, so poor that he was buried in a pauper's grave.

With the possible exception of Johann Sebastian Bach, who lived to be almost twice the age of Mozart, no other composer in such a short time wrote such a vast amount of music of the highest order—music that constitutes an important part of the world's repertoire of great music.

In all, Mozart wrote forty symphonies, twenty-two operas, over fifty concertos for various instruments, twenty-three string quartets and other chamber music, seventeen piano sonatas, church music, and many other works. Among his greatest operas are *The Marriage of Figaro, Don Giovanni,* and *The Magic Flute.* His last three symphonies, the E-flat major, the G minor, and the "Jupiter" (C major) stand high among all the great symphonies ever written; his inspired *Requiem** (unfinished at the time of his death and completed by a pupil) and his great *Mass in C minor* have never been excelled. In fact, all of Mozart's music is a reflection of the highest artistic genius, and remains to this day as delightful as when it was written, almost two hundred years ago.

MUSETTE (mew SET). (1) An instrument resembling a bagpipe* that was popular in the seventeenth and eighteenth centuries in France. (2) A dance of the same period, usually in 2/4, 3/4, or 6/8 time. Rather pastoral (rural) in style, the music consisted of a drone* bass that accompanied a graceful melody.

MUSIC DRAMA. A term that Wagner* used to describe those of his operas that followed *Lohengrin.* He felt that the term "opera" did not express adequately the nature of the works he had now begun to write.

These works were different from the traditional operas with their separate arias, duets, choruses, and so on. They were more unified dramatically and musically, and there was a feeling of continuity in them that most operas of his day lacked.

MUSICAL COMEDY. A light play with spoken dialogue as well as solo songs, duets, and choruses. It usually includes dancing. The music is likely to be closer in style to jazz or popular music than to "serious" music, and the story is frequently based on some typically American theme. A few of the better-known American composers of musical comedy are Irving Berlin,* George Gershwin,* Jerome Kern,* Cole Porter,* Richard Rodgers,* and Leonard Bernstein.*

MUSICOLOGY. The scholarly and scientific study of all aspects of music. A musicologist is a researcher. He studies the history and literature of music, styles of music, the acoustics and the mathematical basis of music. He may trace the development of music from earliest times to the present. He searches for old music manuscripts, then transcribes the obsolete notation to modern notation and edits the works. He searches for new facts about the lives and the work of composers, performers, and publishers of music. He often writes books and articles based on his research. These are only a few of the kinds of research and writing a musicologist does. To become a musicologist requires years of study and preparation and the kind of inquiring mind that is necessary for any scientific career.

MUSSORGSKY (moo SORG skee), **Modest Petrovich.** Russian composer, born in Karevo on March 21, 1839; died in St. Petersburg (now Leningrad) on March 28, 1881.
   Mussorgsky began to study piano with his mother at a very early age, and by the time he was nine was advanced enough to play a concerto before a sizable audience. His family was wealthy, however, and insisted that he follow the custom of such families and enter an officer training school. He finished cadet school when he was seventeen, and at once became a member of a regiment of guards. About this time he met several musicians who took an interest in him. They included Borodin,* Cui,* and Balakirev,* members of a group that later became known as "The Five," or "The Mighty Handful" because of their influence on Russian music. Mussorgsky decided to devote himself to music and resigned his military mission. He became interested in the peasants (serfs) who were fighting for their

freedom, and this interest is reflected in a number of his compositions, particularly in his masterpiece, the opera *Boris Godunov*.

Although Mussorgsky never studied enough to gain an adequate knowledge of form, counterpoint, and orchestration, he was able to write powerful and expressive music. In addition to his great opera *Boris Godunov*, he left several operas unfinished at the time of his death. His orchestral works include the tone poem, *Night on the Bare Mountain*. His best known work for piano is *Pictures at an Exhibition*, later transcribed by Ravel* and others for orchestra. He is noted also for his many songs.

MUTE. A device used for muffling or softening the sound of an instrument. The mute used for stringed instruments is a small comb-like attachment with prongs that clamp onto the bridge. The mute for brass instruments is a pear-shaped piece of wood that is inserted into the bell. Kettledrums are muted by placing a cloth over the skin or by using drumsticks with sponge heads. The piano is muted by pressing the "soft" pedal, which causes the hammers to shift so they strike only one string.

N

NABOKOV (nah BOH kawf), **Nikolay.** Russian composer, born in Lubcha on April 17, 1903.

When Nabokov was eight years old his family moved to St. Petersburg (now Leningrad). He studied music there until after the Revolution in 1918, then moved to Yalta, where he studied for two years with Rebikov. He later attended the Stuttgart Conservatory in Germany, and finally went to the *Hochschule für Musik* in Berlin for study with the eminent teacher Busoni.* When he was twenty-three years old he went to Paris, where he met the famous dance impressario, Diaghilev. Diaghilev commissioned him to write a ballet-oratorio, *Ode*. This work, which was performed in Paris, London, and Berlin, launched him on his distinguished career as a composer. In 1933 he emigrated to the United States, and three years later accepted a position as teacher of composition at Wells College. During World War II he was employed by the United States State Department as chief editor of the Russian Section of the International Broadcast Division. Since 1952, when he organized the Paris Festival of Twentieth-Century Music, he has spent most of his time in Paris.

His compositions include several ballets, the most important of which is *Union Pacific*; choral and orchestral works; some chamber music; and a number of songs.

NARDINI (nar DEE nee), **Pietro.** Italian violinist and composer, born in Leghorn on April 12, 1722; died in Florence on May 7, 1793.

Nardini first studied music in his home town of Leghorn, then later was accepted as a pupil by the master, Tartini,* at Padua. In 1753 he was named soloist at the court of the Duke of Stuttgart, Germany. He stayed there for fourteen years, playing and composing. When Tartini became ill in 1767, Nardini returned to Italy and remained with him until his death. He then went to Florence to accept a position as director of music at the ducal court of Tuscany.

Nardini's works include six violin concertos, six violin solos, sonatas for violin and bass, duets, string quartets, and flute trios.

NATIONAL ANTHEM. A patriotic song or hymn that has been adopted by a particular country as its official anthem. *The Star-Spangled Banner,* for example, was made the official anthem of the United States in 1931 by an Act of Congress.

NATIONALISM. The term refers to a movement on the part of certain composers to write works that reflected the characteristics of their own countries rather than the classical German-Austrian style of composition. They accomplished this by drawing upon native folksong and dance forms, folk legends, and historical events. Some examples of nationalism in music are the opera *Boris Godunov* by the Russian composer Mussorgsky;* *The Three-Cornered Hat* by the Spanish composer de Falla;* *My Country* by the Czech composer Smetana;* *Rumanian Rhapsodies* by the Rumanian composer Enesco;* *Peer Gynt* by the Norwegian composer Grieg;* *Finlandia* by the Finnish composer Sibelius.*

NATURAL. The sign (♮) placed before a note to cancel a flat or sharp previously used for the same pitch (in the same measure or in the key signature). By extension, a note that is neither sharp nor flat.

NATURAL MINOR. (See *Major-Minor.*)

NEUMES. (See *Notation.*)

NEVIN, Ethelbert. American composer, born in Edgeworth, Pennsylvania, on November 25, 1862; died in New Haven, Connecticut, on February 17, 1901.

Nevin began his study of music while he was very young, first in his home town and a few years later in Pittsburgh. He was fifteen years old when he went to Dresden, Germany, to study voice. He studied later with Hans von Bülow in Berlin. Although he died young, Nevin enjoyed great popularity during his lifetime. His works, mostly for piano and for voice, include the popular *Narcissus,* a piano solo, and the two songs, *Mighty Lak' a Rose* and *The Rosary*.

NICOLAI (NEE koh lye), **Carl Otto.** German composer, born in Königsberg on June 9, 1810; died in Berlin on May 11, 1849.

Nicolai's early childhood was unhappy, and he was only too glad to get away from his tyrannical father, a teacher of singing, when a protector sent him to Berlin at the age of sixteen to study with a famous teacher, Zelter. He did extremely well, and a few years later the Prussian Ambassador to Rome invited him to go to Rome as organist at the Prussian Embassy there. This gave him the chance to make a thorough study of Italian music. He was twenty-seven years old when he was appointed music director of the Kaertnertor Theater in Vienna, and while he was in that city he founded the Philharmonic Concerts, chiefly to give proper performances of Beethoven's works. In 1847 he became Director of the Court Opera in Berlin, and two years later he died there of a stroke. Although he wrote several operas, two symphonies, chamber music, and some church music, he is famous today for just one work, the opera *The Merry Wives of Windsor*.

NIELSON, Carl August. Danish composer, born in Nörre Lyndelse on June 9, 1865; died in Copenhagen on October 2, 1931.

The Nielson family was poor, and the children had to earn their own living while they were still very young. Carl became a shepherd, but the father was an amateur musician who played for village dances, and through him Carl learned to play the violin. By the time he was fourteen, he was able to earn enough money by playing in various local bands and orchestras to enter the Copenhagen Conservatory for further study of violin and composition. When he won the Ancker Award, he used the money for more study in Germany, France, and Italy. He eventually became well-known as a conductor in Europe, and also as a gifted composer. His many works include operas, symphonies, choral and orchestral works, a great deal of chamber music, and piano and vocal solos. Although Nielson was one of Denmark's most noted composers, his music is not well known in the United States.

NIENTE (nee EN tay). An Italian word meaning "nothing." It usually appears as *a niente,* often after this sign: (———————), to indicate that the music is to die away completely.

NINTH. An interval of an octave plus a second. A ninth with C as its lower note looks like this: (See also *Chords* and *Intervals.*)

NOBLE, Thomas Tertius. English organist and composer, born in Bath on May 5, 1867; died in Rockport, Massachusetts, on May 4, 1953.

When Noble was fourteen years old, an old friend of the family, the Rector of All Saints Church in Colchester, recognized the boy's unusual talent. He took him into his own home, supervised his musical education, and later gave him his first appointment as a church organist. Most of Noble's life was spent in the service of the Protestant church, and most of his compositions were of a sacred nature. In 1914 he became organist and choir director at St. Thomas's Church in New York City, where he founded its famous boys' choir. His compositions, which include organ works, anthems, and other church music, are performed regularly as a part of the Episcopal Church's service across the nation.

NOCTURNE. A rather slow, quiet, and lyrical piece. Chopin borrowed the title from John Field, who wrote a number of *Nocturnes* for the piano. Many composers have used the title, among them Debussy for his suite of three orchestral pieces, Fauré for thirteen piano solos, and Chopin for nine piano pieces.

NOËL. A French word meaning "Christmas." Noëls, therefore, are Christmas carols, usually of French origin. Many collections of Noëls have been made since the sixteenth century, and some have been preserved from even earlier times. One of the oldest and most famous is *Pros de l'ane,* which dates from the twelfth century.

NONET. A composition for nine instruments. It is usually written for a string quaret or quintet plus various wind instruments, but is sometimes for wind instruments alone.

NOTATION. The writing down of music. Our present well-developed system of notation on the staff has evolved over the centuries from early forms that were too vague to express clearly the musical ideas of the composers.

One of the most important of the early forms of notation was the *neume.* Neumes, used in chanting of medieval music notated in the early church modes,* were signs or symbols written over the words to indicate one or more notes and the general direction of the melody, sometimes up, sometimes down, and sometimes in both directions. The signs helped the singers remember the general direction of the melody, but they had to memorize the music by ear in order to sing it accurately.

The next step in the evolution of notation was the square note. At first only a one-line staff was provided with the square notes, then gradually more lines were added. Under the name of *ligatures,* square notes were adopted for the notation of polyphonic* music.

Finally, after centuries of experimentation, our present-day system of notating music came into being. It is now used universally. In addition to the notes themselves, modern notation makes use of staffs,* clefs,* time signatures,* bar lines,* accidentals,* (sharps, flats, natural signs), ties,* dots,* and rests.*

The following chart shows (1) the neumes, with their Latin names, their equivalents in square notes, and finally the direction of the notes in modern notation: (2) the later development of square notes into diamond shaped symbols; (3) present forms of notes and their corresponding rests.

Neumes	Later Development of Square Notes into Diamond-Shaped Symbols:	Present Forms (American Names)	Corresponding Rests
Punctum	maxima		
Virga	longa		
Podatus or Pes	brevis		
	semibrevis	Whole Note	
Clivis	minima	Half Note	
Scandicus	semiminima	Quarter Note	
	fusa	Eighth Note	
Climacus		Sixteenth Note	
Torculus		Thirty-second Note	
Porrectus		Sixty-fourth Note	

NOTE. The symbol that stands for a particular pitch.* (See also *Notation.*)

NOVACHORD. An electronic instrument similar to the electric organ, but with only one manual and a much simpler mechanism for producing tone. It has a six-octave keyboard, pedals for controlling the loudness and softness of the tone, and controls for varying the tone quality.

NUT. (1) A small strip of ebony or ivory attached to the upper end of the neck of a stringed instrument. Its purpose is to keep the strings raised slightly above the fingerboard. (2) A kind of screw-like device at the lower end of the bow used to play stringed instruments. The player can adjust the tension (tightness) of the hairs by turning the nut.

O

OBBLIGATO (ah bli GAH toh). Italian word meaning "obliged" or "compelled." A melody separate from the main melody written to be played by a different instrument, as a song with flute obbligato. In some present-day music, the obbligato may be omitted without seriously hurting the composition, but in earlier times, especially during the Baroque* period, an obbligato was an essential part of the composition.

OBLIQUE MOTION. (See *Motion.*)

OBOE. One of the most important instruments of the modern orchestra. It has a two-foot pipe with a conical bore, and is blown through a double reed.* The tone of the oboe is mellow and can be quite melancholy. Its range is from the B-flat below Middle C upward for more than two and one-half octaves. Other modern instruments related to the oboe are the bassoon,* and the English horn,* both with lower pitches than the oboe. (See also *Woodwinds.*)

OCARINA (ah cah REE nah). A small wind instrument with holes for the fingers, usually made of clay, metal, or plastic material, and played by blowing into a mouth hole. Different pitches are made by placing the fingers over the various holes in the front and back. The ocarina's tone is straight, with little or no vibrato. For this reason it is not considered an "artistic" instrument, and its use is generally restricted to that of a toy.

OCTAVE. From the Latin word *octavus,* which means "eight." An octave consists of the first and eighth notes of the diatonic scale, as Middle C and the next C above or the next C below. (See also *Intervals.*)

OCTET. A piece of chamber music for eight instruments or a piece for eight voices. A group of eight performers is also called an octet.

ODE. A word derived from the Greek "to be sung." An ode usually consists of a musical setting of a rather long poem, often for chorus, orchestra, and soloists. A famous example is the "Ode to Joy," which forms the last movement of Beethoven's *Symphony No. 9.* It is a setting of a poem, *Ode to Joy,* by the German poet, Schiller.

OFFENBACH (OFF en bach), **Jacques.** German composer, born in Cologne on June 20, 1819; died in Paris, France, on October 4, 1880.

Offenbach's father, a cantor* of the Jewish synagogue in Cologne, recognized his son's musical talent and sent him to Paris to study cello at the Conservatory. He remained in school there for only a year, but he had already become a good enough musician to find employment in an orchestra. He later became director of an orchestra, and then manager of a theater. This theatrical experience was an important factor in his success as a composer of operettas. He wrote more than a hundred operettas, of which several have remained highly popular to this day, especially in Europe. One opera, *The Tales of Hoffmann,* was performed more than a hundred times during its first year in Paris, and is still one of the most popular of all operas.

OFFERTORY. In the Roman Catholic church the Offertory is a part of the Mass.* It is the fourth of the five items of the Proper of the Mass.

In the Anglican church it is the anthem* sung during the offertory (collection of offerings); in other Protestant churches it is a religious song sung at that time in the service.

OKEGHEM (OCK egg em), **Johannes.** Flemish composer, born in Flanders about 1430; died in Tours about 1495. (The exact dates are not known.)

Okeghem was a boy chorister in the Antwerp Cathedral, and later in the chapel of Duke Charles of Bourbon. He studied with Dufay* in Cambrai, and subsequently served as a chorister in the chapel of the King of France in Paris. He remained in the royal service as composer and chaplain under three different monarchs until his death. Okeghem was famous as a teacher as well as a composer. One of his most illustrious pupils was Josquin des Prés,* and he taught many others. In addition to some nineteen Masses,* and more than one hundred motets,* he wrote a large number of secular chansons.*

OP. Abbreviation for *opus.**

OPEN NOTES. On stringed instruments an open note is a note that is played without stopping* the string on which it is played. An open string is indicated on the music by a small o placed above the note. On wind instruments, open notes are those notes which are played without using keys or valves or without placing the hand in the bell.

OPEN STRINGS. (See *Open Notes.*)

OPERA. An Italian word meaning "work." In English-speaking countries, it means "a musical work." Actually, an opera is a play set to music. It has all the features of a play—acting, costumes, lighting, scenery, often ballet, and always music. There are different types of opera. Some, like Wagner's *Parsifal,* are very long; some, like Milhaud's *Trois Operas-Minutes* (Three Minute-Operas), are very short. Some operas have several acts and as many as fifteen or twenty changes of scene; others have only one scene. Some operas, as Strauss's *Salome,* require an enormous orchestra; others, like Menotti's *The Telephone,* can be performed quite satisfactorily with just a piano accompaniment. Operas such as Wagner's *Mastersingers of Nuremberg* require a large cast of soloists and several choruses, while others may be written for a very small cast. There is almost no end to the variety found in opera.

The first operas were produced in Italy about 1600 by two composers in Florence, Peri* and Caccini.* In fact, the first publicly performed opera whose score has survived to the present time was *Euridici,* written by Jacopo Peri for the wedding festivities of Henry IV and Marie de Medici in the year 1600. From Florence, opera spread to Venice, where Monteverdi* produced several operas and where the first opera house was built in 1637. From Venice, then Rome, the opera movement was taken up in France, with Lully* and Rameau* its chief composers. Purcell,* toward the end of the seventeenth century, and then Handel,* in the eighteenth century, brought opera to a high peak in England.

An important scene of operatic action was in Italy, in the city of Naples, where such outstanding composers as Scarlatti,* Pergolesi,* and Cimarosa* turned out operas that were enormously popular in their day. Then, around 1750, came a "revolt" against the Neapolitan type of opera because of its lack of dramatic force. The great "reformer" was an Austrian-born composer, Gluck,* in whose opera *Orfeo* dramatic action became of greatest importance. It set a new style of Italian opera. Closely following Gluck was Mozart,* with his masterpieces, such as *The Marriage of Figaro* and *Don Giovanni.* Mozart was in his own day and remains to the present time a "giant" in the history of opera. The period of "romantic" opera began with his *Magic Flute,* a German opera. During this period the important composers of opera were Cherubini,* Weber,* Donizetti,* and Rossini.*

The nineteenth century brought a number of changes in opera. For one thing, there was an emphasis on "nationalism" in opera. This brought forth operas whose plots and music were centered specifically on the cultures of individual countries. The plots of these operas involved historical happenings and native customs, and their music was frequently based on the folk music of the people. Examples of national opera are Mussorgsky's* *Boris Godunov,* and Smetana's* *The Bartered Bride.*

Another important development of the nineteenth century was the emergence of Giuseppi Verdi* as the greatest Italian composer of opera. During his long life, Verdi wrote operas that range all the way from his early, rather simple musical settings of plays to what is considered by some as a perfect blend of music and drama. In the 1850's alone Verdi produced four operas that have become a standard part of the repertory throughout the world: *Rigoletto, Il Trovatore, La Traviata,* and *A Masked Ball.* Later to come were *Don Carlo, Aïda, Othello,* and *Falstaff.*

While Verdi was creating his masterpieces in Italy, a German composer, Richard Wagner,* was initiating a new style of opera with his "music-dramas." Beginning with *Lohengrin,* he wrote operas that did away with the old "number" system in which the arias,* recitatives,* and choruses* were numbered and could be omitted without doing too much damage to the plot. Instead, he wrote a continuous kind of work in which the music and drama were unified as they had never been before.

In Italy, the successors to Verdi became interested in a style called *verismo* (realism). Puccini, with *La Bohème, Tosca,* and *Madame Butterfly*; Leoncavallo with *I Pagliacci*; Mascagni with *Cavalleria Rusticana,* for example, wrote operas with realistic plots and highly dramatic music that have made them popular the world over.

The influence of Wagner carried over to the present century, especially in the early works of Richard Strauss, whose most popular works are *Electra, Salome,* and *Der Rosenkavalier.* The operas of other composers of the twentieth century reflect the new developments in music. Debussy's *Pelleas et Melisande* is highly impressionistic.

Examples of some of the more recent operas, written in modern or ultra-modern musical idioms, are *Bluebeard's Castle* by Bartók, *Wozzeck* by Alban Berg,* *The Consul* by Menotti,* *Peter Grimes* by Britten,* *The Rake's Progress* by Stravinsky,* and *Moses and Aaron* by Schoenberg.*

Opera has become one of the most important art mediums of entertainment in the world. In Europe practically every major city has its own opera house where opera is presented nightly almost the year around. In South America every capital city has its opera house, and in the United States the interest in opera is growing fast. Thanks to television, motion pictures, radio, and recordings, American audiences are becoming more familiar with and learning to enjoy opera more and more. The Metropolitan Opera in New York, which gave its first performance in 1883, is one of the great opera companies of the world. The City Center Opera, also in New York, is noted for its excellent productions, particularly of newer works with American singers in leading roles. The Chicago and San Francisco companies are well established, and there are many other growing opera companies throughout the country, including such well-known summer opera groups as the Summer Opera of Cincinnati, Ohio; the Sante Fe, New Mexico, and the Central City, Colorado, companies.

OPERA BUFFA (BOO fah). An Italian term meaning "comic opera." Examples of opera buffa are Mozart's *The Marriage of Figaro* and Rossini's *The Barber of Seville.*

OPÉRA COMIQUE (aw pay ra caw MEEK). A French term meaning comic opera.*

OPERETTA. A light, usually humorous play set to music. It differs from opera in several ways: It has much spoken dialogue, the music is usually gay, appealing, and "singable," and the plot is highly romantic. The operetta originated in Vienna with Franz von Suppé* and in Paris with Offenbach.* Some examples of famous operettas are *Die Fledermaus* (The Bat), by the Viennese composer Johann Strauss, Jr.;* *The Mikado,* by the English composer, Arthur Sullivan,* and his librettist, W. S. Gilbert; *The Merry*

Widow by Franz Léhar;* *The Firefly* by Rudolf Friml;* and *Babes in Toyland* by Victor Herbert.*

OPUS. A Latin word meaning "work." The term is used with numbers, usually to indicate the order in which a composer's works were published. Thus, *Opus 1* means that a composition was the first published work of a particular composer—or at least the first of his works that he wanted to number. The abbreviation for *Opus* is *Op.*

ORATORIO. A large work written for soloists, chorus, and orchestra or organ (or sometimes both). Oratorio differs from opera* primarily in its method of presentation; whereas opera involves staging, scenery, costumes, dramatic action, and often ballet,* an oratorio is usually presented without theatrical effects. Most oratorios are based on religious subjects, whereas operas more frequently deal with secular subjects. Oratorio originated in Italy in 1600 and soon spread to Germany and England. Some of the most famous of all oratorios are Haydn's *The Creation* and *The Seasons,* Handel's *The Messiah,* Mendelssohn's *St. Paul* and *Elijah,* Berlioz' *L'Enfance du Christ,* and César Franck's *Beatitudes.* Some important oratorios composed during the twentieth century are Elgar's *The Dream of Gerontius,* Walton's *Belshazzar's Feast,* Honegger's *King David,* and Stravinsky's opera-oratorio *Oedipus Rex.*

ORCHESTRA. A large group of players of various musical instruments. The *symphony orchestra,* which may have as many as a hundred or more players, is the largest, and is made up of stringed instruments, woodwinds, brass, and percussion instruments. A *chamber orchestra* may have the same kinds of instruments, but is smaller in number. A *string orchestra* is made up of stringed instruments alone. A *theater orchestra* resembles a chamber orchestra, but is small enough to fit comfortably into an orchestra pit and may also include such instruments as the saxophone, which is not frequently included in a chamber or symphony orchestra.

From early times instrumentalists have played together to accompany dancers and stage presentations, but the first organized group of musicians to perform regularly was the famous group that performed under the direction of Lully* at the French court during the seventeenth century. This organization was called "Les Vingt-quatre Violons du Roi" (The twenty-four violins of the King). It was not until about a century later that the instruments of the orchestra began to resemble what we think of today as an orchestra.

The typical modern symphony orchestra employs approximately one hundred instruments, distributed as follows:

Strings	Woodwinds	Brass	Percussion
18 first violins	3 flutes	6 French horns	4 timpani
16 second violins	1 piccolo	4 trumpets	1 glockenspiel
12 violas	3 oboes	4 trombones	tenor drums
10 cellos	1 English horn	1 tuba	bass drum
8 double basses	3 clarinets		xylophone
2 harps	1 bass clarinet		
	3 bassoons		
	1 double bassoon		

The celesta,* chimes,* triangle,* cymbals,* and various other percussion* instruments may be required by certain composers, and the piano is frequently used as well.

Today many of the large cities in Europe and in North and South America support at least one symphony orchestra, and many of the largest, such as Paris, London, and Vienna, have several. Some of these world-famous orchestras go on tours where they play in cities and towns that cannot afford orchestras of their own. Most of them make recordings and many of them appear on television and radio. This has made it possible for people almost everywhere to enjoy the world's greatest music performed by the finest orchestras.

ORCHESTRATION. The art of writing or arranging music to be performed by an orchestra. This involves (1) a thorough knowledge of each of the orchestral instruments—its range, its tone color, its possibilities, and its limitations; (2) a knowledge of how the various instruments sound when played in combination and how they can be best used to express musical ideas.

Through the ages instruments have been improved and changed, and new instruments have been invented. As these changes have taken place, composers have become more concerned with composing orchestral works so as to achieve the finest possible performance from the orchestra. One of the first composers to experiment with new orchestral effects was Monteverdi,* who introduced tremolo* and pizzicato* effects in the string section for the first time. Haydn* and Mozart* used great imagination in exploiting the possibilities of the instruments of their day. Beethoven* gave the orchestra a majesty it had not known before by the broadness and magnitude of his ideas. Mendelssohn* introduced a marvelous clarity and lightness with his skillful use of instruments. Berlioz,* who wrote a famous book on orchestration, had some daring ideas that were far ahead of his time. Wagner* wrote demanding and rich orchestrations and achieved powerful effects that have seldom been rivaled. Ravel* and Debussy* introduced new orchestral color in their impressionistic works. Richard Strauss,* Bartók,* and Stravinsky* experimented with great energy and achieved some radically new and daring instrumentations. The possibilities for new tonal effects are almost unlimited, and will continue to be one of the most challenging aspects of a serious composer's work.

ORDINARY. (See *Mass.*)

ORFF, Carl. German composer, born in Munich on July 10, 1895.

Practically all of Orff's musical education was in Munich. From an early age he was interested in music education, and between 1930 and 1933 he published a series of music textbooks for children called *Schulwerk* (School Work). He had previously helped to found the Günter School in Munich, and he taught there until 1936. Orff has written a number of works that have been widely performed. In them he has striven for simplicity of melody and texture. He makes strong use of percussion instruments, and his compositions are highly rhythmic. His best-known works are *Carmina Burana,* a stage work with songs from old manuscripts found in a monastery in southern Bavaria; an opera, *Die Kluge* (The Clever Girl), based on one of Grimm's fairy tales; and *Antigonae,* an opera that was first produced at the Salzburg Festival of 1949.

ORGAN. There are two types of organs, electronic organs (See *Electronic Organ*) and pipe organs, in use today. The pipe organ is a keyboard instrument in which the sound is produced by wind blown through pipes by means of bellows. The modern organ has keys for both the hands and the feet. The performer plays by depressing the keys and by operating stops—that is, by pulling buttons or levers that control the pipes. In former times the pipes were made to vibrate by pumping air through them by means of hand- or foot-operated bellows. If the organ was large, one or more persons operated the bellows while the organist manipulated the keys and stops. Most modern organs are equipped with an electrical machine for supplying air to the pipes, and in some organs even the depression of the keys is operated electrically.

Modern organs have a great many pipes, which are divided into series. Each series, called a *rank* or *register,* is controlled by stops. An organ may have from two to seven keyboards (called *manuals*), and each manual plays a certain number of these pipes. There is only one *pedal-board* (the keyboard played by the feet) on any organ, regardless of its size. Through the use of the stops, which control the volume and a great variety of tone colors, an accomplished organist can achieve a wide range of expression.

The use of the organ for religious services began early in the Christian era. It reached a high peak during the days of Buxtehude* and J. S. Bach,* who wrote an enormous number of organ works. Since Bach's time many composers have written for the organ. Two of the most outstanding were Césare Franck* in France and Max Reger* in Germany. Probably the world's greatest organist and composer of music for the organ today is Marcel Dupré.*

ORGANUM. An early form of part-writing for voice. It consisted of two, three, or four parts, and was based on a plainsong.* It flourished from the ninth century to about the middle of the thirteenth century, when the motet* took its place.

ORGATRON. An electronic instrument invented in the United States in 1934. It is a keyboard instrument with a sound similar to the pipe organ, electrically produced from vibrating reeds.

ORNAMENTS. In general, these are extra notes, sometimes written, sometimes not, that embellish or "decorate" a melody. Before the French harpsichordists attempted to standardize ornaments by a system of signs (about 1650), there was no standard procedure. Sometimes the extra notes were written out, but more often the performer was expected to use his own discretion, which led to a good deal of confusion. Today, however, composers usually write exactly the notes they wish used for ornaments, and in the case of older music the editors have supplied the ornaments either by notation or by using signs that are now well standardized. The following table lists some of the more common signs for ornaments along with a notation to show how they should be performed:

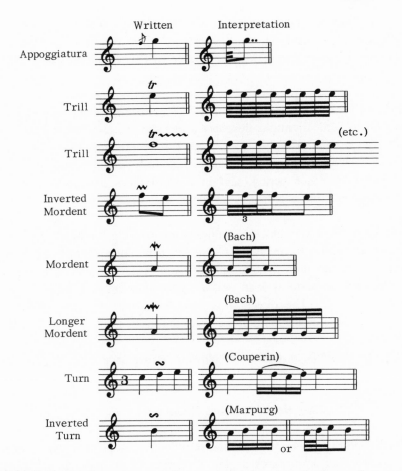

ORPHEUS (OR fay us). According to a Greek myth, Orpheus, the son of Apollo, was the "inventor" of music. He was said to have descended into the underworld to try and regain his wife Eurydice, who had died. He charmed Pluto, ruler of the underworld, so well with his singing and playing of the lyre* that he was allowed to lead Eurydice back to earth if he would promise not to look back. He failed to keep his promise, and when he looked back Eurydice was lost to him forever. The myth has been the source of a number of operas and operettas, and the name *Orpheus* itself has been used as a title of numerous publications, musical organizations, and so on.

OSSIA. A word formed from the Italian *o sia,* which means "or it may be." A composer may sometimes write a simpler version of a difficult passage in small notes above the treble or below the bass along with the word *ossia*. This means that the performer may substitute the easier version if he wishes.

OSTINATO (oss tee NAH toh). An Italian word meaning "obstinate" or "stubborn." This, in music, describes a melodic figure that is repeated over and over, usually at the same pitch level. It occurs most frequently in the bass, in which case it is called *basso ostinato* or *ground bass*. It was popular during the Baroque period, and in modern times has been revived in American jazz in such figures as the *boogie-woogie* bass.

OTTAVA (ot TAH vah). An Italian word meaning "octave." The direction *all' ottava* (at the octave) indicates that the notes are to be performed an octave higher than written. *Ottava bassa* (octave lower) indicates that they should be performed an octave lower. The musical abbreviation is *8va.* . . . . The direction is cancelled when the word *loco** (in place) appears, indicating that the notes are again to be played as written.

OVERBLOWING. A method of blowing harder on a wind instrument in order to play the overtones* or harmonics* of the fundamental* tones.

OVERTONE. (See *Harmonics* and *Acoustics.*)

OVERTURE. (1) An instrumental introduction or prelude* to an opera, an operetta, an oratorio, or a play. Overtures to the early Italian operas often had nothing to do with the operas themselves. In the nineteenth century, however, composers began to use them to set the mood, and often to expose the major themes of at least the first act of the opera that followed. Mozart wrote some of the greatest operatic overtures of the Classic period, and many overtures are in themselves complete enough compositions and beautiful enough so they have become standard works in orchestral repertories. Some examples of overtures that are performed frequently by themselves are Beethoven's *Leonora* Overtures, Wagner's Overture to *Die Meistersinger,* and Mendelssohn's Overture to *A Midsummer Night's Dream.* (2) The name has also been used for compositions written for orchestra, which have no connection with a stage work. These are sometimes called "concert overtures." Examples of this type are Brahms's *Academic Festival Overture* and Dvořák's *Carnival Overture.*

P

P. Abbreviation for the Italian word *piano,* which means "soft." The abbreviation *p* indicates a soft tone; *pp* indicates very soft; *ppp* indicates extremely soft.

PADEREWSKI (pah der REF skee), **Ignacy Jan.** Polish composer, pianist, and statesman, born in Kurylówka (Russian Poland) on November 18, 1860; died in New York on June 29, 1941.

Paderewski showed unusual musical talent when he was only three years old. He played duets with his sister when he was four, and by the time he was twelve he and his sister were playing in public. Meanwhile, his father had lost his fortune in a revolution and the family lived in poverty. Some wealthy people heard the boy play, however, and sent him to Kiev for study. Later he entered the Warsaw Conservatory, but after a year he was expelled because he rebelled against having to study some instruments in which he was not interested. He cared only for the piano. He went on tour for a time, then was allowed to enroll again in the Conservatory. Upon graduation he was engaged there as a teacher. When he was twenty-three he met the famous actress Modjeska, who encouraged him to become a concert pianist. In fact, she sponsored his studies with the great teacher Leschetizky in Vienna from 1884 to 1887. In 1889 he made his debut as a soloist in Vienna. He was a great success, and from that time on his life was filled with one triumph after another. He became one of the most successful concert pianists that the world has ever known. He had a remarkable career also, as a statesman. He served as Premier of the first Polish Republic, and during World War II he was President of the Polish Government in Exile when it moved to Paris following the Nazi occupation.

In his autobiography, *The Paderewski Memoirs,* Paderewski explains how he happened to write the original version of his *Minuet in G.* It seems that a group of friends for whom he often played were ardent admirers of Mozart, claiming that no one could write music to equal his. To play a joke on them, Paderewski wrote a minuet more or less in the style of Mozart and proceeded to play it for them the next time they begged him to play some Mozart. They were enchanted until, having finally been convinced that the composition had indeed been composed by their young friend, they were greatly put out by the trick that had been played on them.

Besides his celebrated *Minuet in G,* Paderewski wrote many piano pieces, an opera, a symphony, a piano concerto, a piano sonata, some chamber music, and songs.

PAGANINI (pah gah NEE nee), **Niccolo.** Italian violinist and composer, born in Genoa on October 27, 1782; died in Nice, France, on May 27, 1840.

Paganini, who was to become the most famous violin virtuoso the world has ever known, was the son of a poor shopkeeper. He received his first music lessons from his father, who was an excellent mandolin player. Soon, however, the boy had learned all that his father could teach him and he was sent to study with better teachers. At the age of eight he composed a violin sonata, and when he was nine he gave his first public concert. This concert was soon followed by another, at which he played one of his own compositions. He continued to study, next with a celebrated teacher in Parma, and in 1797, when he was just fifteen years old, he left with his father for a concert tour. His father was very strict and demanded so much of the boy that when he was sixteen he ran away and launched out on a tour by himself. By this time he had already acquired so much technical skill on the violin that everywhere he played in Italy people flocked to hear him. In spite of his successful concerts, he was often hard up for money. For one thing, he liked to gamble and he was careless in other ways about finances. On one occasion he was without a violin with which to play a concert because he had been forced to pawn it to pay a debt. Fortunately, a wealthy nobleman came to his rescue and loaned him a fine Guarneri (a violin made by the famous Giuseppe Guarneri*) for the concert, and later gave him the instrument. In later years he owned several valuable violins, but that Guarneri remained his favorite.

Until 1828, Pagnini remained in Italy, playing, studying, and composing. Then he gave his first concert in Vienna, and from that time on he enjoyed endless triumphs—especially in the great capitals of Europe: Berlin, Paris, London. In 1832 his health, which had always been frail, began to fail and he was able to play only occasionally. Fortunately, he had learned to take better care of his money and had invested enough of the great fortune he made from his playing to enable him to spend the last years of his life in relative comfort.

Pagnini's fame rests largely upon his tremendous contribution to the art of violin playing. He played higher than anyone had before by mastering the difficult use of *harmonics.** He proved that it was possible to play double notes in extremely high passages. One of his favorite tricks was to use one or two worn and frayed strings on his violin, and when they broke to continue to play as brilliantly as before. The music he wrote for the violin demanded the same high degree of technical virtuosity that he himself displayed, and much of it has become an important part of the violin repertory. His *Caprices* especially are popular. Some of his themes appealed so strongly to other composers of his day that they used them in compositions of their own. Schumann and Busoni transcribed some of his works for piano; Brahms wrote *Variations on a Theme of Paganini*; Liszt wrote a work for piano based on the *Campanella* theme from Paganini's B minor violin concerto, to name only a few.

PAINE, John Knowles. American organist, composer, and educator, born in Portland, Maine, on January 9, 1839; died in Cambridge, Massachusetts, on April 25, 1906.

Paine studied music in his home town until he was nineteen, when he went to Europe for three years of study in Berlin. The organ was his favorite instrument, and he played so well that he was able to give a number of successful concerts in Germany before he returned to the United States. Shortly after his return home he was appointed to a teaching position at Harvard University, and in 1875 he was made a full professor of music—the first such appointment to be made in an American university. He held the position for twenty years, during which time he made a unique contribution. In addition to being the University organist, he gave frequent piano lecture recitals and worked hard to familiarize the students with the great works of music. His compositions include a Mass, two symphonies, symphonic poems, cantatas, and many other works.

PALESTRINA (pah less TREE nah), **Giovanni Pierluiga da.** Italian composer, born in Palestrina about 1525; died in Rome on February 2, 1594.

(His family name was Pierluigi, but he preferred to call himself by the name of the town where he was born.)

Palestrina's initial musical study was as a choir boy, first in the cathedral of Palestrina, next in the Church of Santa Maria Maggiore in Rome. He studied as a chorister until his voice broke, then he studied composition. He was just nineteen when he was appointed organist and choirmaster in the Cathedral of St. Agapit in Palestrina, and four years later was made a member of the great Papal Choir in Rome.

During the famine and plague that raged through Italy between 1572 and 1580 Palestrina suffered great personal losses. Two of his three sons, two brothers, and his wife died. He was so overcome with grief that he seriously considered entering the priesthood, and went so far as to apply for permission of Pope Gregory. The Pope, anxious to secure the services of the great Palestrina for the Basilica of St. Peter, granted him permission to prepare himself for holy orders. But before he took the final step he remarried.

Palestrina, considered to be the greatest writer of liturgical music for the Roman Catholic church, was a master of polyphonic style. Although most of his music was written for the church, he composed some 150 madrigals as well. His complete works, which include more than ninety Masses and almost two hundred motets, fill thirty-four volumes.

PALMGREN, Selim. Finnish composer, conductor, and pianist, born in Pori, Finland, on February 16, 1878; died on December 13, 1951, in Helsinki.

Palmgren first studied music in Finland, graduating from the Helsinki Conservatory in 1899. He then went to Germany and Italy for more advanced study with Ansorage, Berger, and the eminent teacher, Busoni.* When he returned to Finland he was appointed conductor of the Finnish Students' Choral Society, the first of several distinguished positions he held during his lifetime. In addition, he toured extensively as a pianist and conductor. His works include five piano concertos, choral music, operas, and a great many songs and piano pieces.

PANDORA. (Sometimes spelled *pandur*.) (1) An ancient Greek instrument of Oriental origin that resembled the lute.* It had a long neck, a pear-shaped body, and from one to three strings. It was played by being plucked. Its prototypes appear often in illustrations in ancient manuscripts and in old carvings and statuary of Egypt, North Africa, and various empires of ancient Near Eastern civilizations. (2) A plucked stringed instrument, now obsolete, invented in England in the mid-sixteenth century.

PANPIPES. (Sometimes called "Pandean Pipe.") An ancient instrument of the wind family dating back at least as far as the ancient Greeks, who called it "syrinx." Panpipes are still used today in such widely scattered places as Rumania and the mountainous areas of South America. The instrument consists of anywhere from three to twenty-five pipes of different lengths, made of cane reeds, pottery, or even soapstone, that are bound together. Each pipe produces just one tone, and melodies can be played by moving from pipe to pipe as the pitches change.

PARALLEL MOTION. (See *Motion.*)

PARKER, Horatio William. American composer, organist, and music educator, born in Auburndale, Massachusetts, on September 15, 1863; died in Cedarhurst, New York, on December 18, 1919.

Parker did not begin to study music until he was fifteen years old. He was highly gifted, however, and made such rapid progress that he was sent to Germany to study with Rheinberger* when he was nineteen years old. When he returned to the United States he was appointed organist and professor of music at the Cathedral School in Garden City, New York. He taught later at the National Conservatory, where Dvořák* was director, and in 1894 he was asked to fill the chair of music at Yale University. He remained at Yale for the rest of his life.

Parker's most famous work is the oratorio, *Hora Novissima,* the libretto of which was translated from the French by his mother. He wrote a number of other oratorios, cantatas, and choral works, two operas, some orchestral works, songs, and pieces for piano.

PARLANDO (par LAHN doh). An Italian word that means "speaking." In vocal music, *parlando* indicates a rather free style of singing with more or less the same inflections used in speaking the words. In instrumental music it indicates expressiveness.

PART. (1) An individual line in music written for more than one voice or instrument, as the soprano part, the clarinet part, and so on. (2) The individual "voice" or part in contrapuntal* music, as in a three-part invention or a four-part fugue. (3) A section of a large work, such as a symphony written in three-part form.

PARTIAL. (See *Harmonic Series*).

PARTITA (par TEE tah). An Italian word that was originally used in the plural (*partite*) in the titles of sets of variations composed in the sixteenth century. It has since been used by a number of composers in that sense, including J. S. Bach* in his Chorale Partitas for the organ. Bach also used it in the sense of *suite** for a set of six suites for harpsichord and for his suites for violin.

PART MUSIC. Music written for vocal or instrumental ensembles in such a way that each part consists of a good melodic line. A madrigal* is an example of part music. (See also *Counterpoint*.)

PART SONG. A song written for several vocal parts, rather than for solo or unison singing, in which the highest voice part carries the chief melody while the other parts provide a chordal type of accompaniment. Schumann's five *Jaglieder* (Hunting Songs) for men's voices are examples of part songs.

PASSACAGLIA (pah sah KAH lyah). Music in which one theme, usually in the bass, is repeated over and over again. It was originally a dance, possibly originating in Spain. Bach,* Buxtehude,* and Couperin* were all skillful writers of passacaglia. A famous example is Bach's Passacaglia in C minor for organ.

PASSEPIED (pahs PYAY). A French word meaning "stick out the foot." The passepied is a dance that originated in northern France and later was made a part of the ballet at the court of Louis XIV. During the Baroque* period it was used in suites for keyboard instruments. It was written in fast 3/4 time and slightly resembled the minuet, but was much livelier and gayer.

PASSING NOTE. A note taken scalewise that occurs between two notes that are consonant* with the harmony. For instance, in the following example the passing note D is discordant, while the E and the C are in harmony with the basic chord.

PASSION MUSIC. A musical setting of the story of the Crucifixion of Christ, usually as the events were related by one of the four Evangelists. Passion music settings are usually concerned with the series of events that led up to the Crucifixion, but some deal with short episodes. An example of the latter is *The Seven Last Words,* set first by Schütz and later by Haydn.* Other great Passions are J. S. Bach's* *Passion according to St. John* and *Passion according to St. Matthew.* The role of Christ in Bach's works, as in most other Passions, is sung by a low voice; that of the Evangelist by a tenor. Other roles are sung by individual singers, and the chorus is used in a variety of interesting and beautiful ways.

PASTICCIO (pah STEE choh). An Italian word meaning "patch work" or "pasted together." In music it means a kind of operatic entertainment that reached its peak of popularity in the eighteenth century. It was a conglomeration of tunes by different composers. An example is the opera *Love in a Village,* arranged by Arne,* with music by sixteen other composers as well as himself.

PASTORAL. A term applied to music that gives the impression of a rural or rustic setting. Examples are Beethoven's* Symphony No. 6 (the Pastoral Symphony) and Vaughan Williams'* Symphony No. 3, *A Pastoral Symphony.*

PATTER SONG. A song of a humorous nature characterized by extremely fast singing of syllables. Donizetti,* Rossini,* and Mozart* all used patter songs effectively in their operas. Two famous examples are "Largo al factotum" from Rossini's *Barber of Seville* and "Madamina" from Mozart's *Don Giovanni.*

PAUSE. (See *Fermata.*)

PAVANE (pah VAN). French name for a rather slow and stately dance that originated in Spain and was introduced into instrumental music in the sixteenth century. Later, it was often followed by a galliard.* It became popular in England among writers of music for the virginal,* and was used in suites* by German composers during the first half of the seventeenth century. Two more recent pavanes are Faure's *Pavane,* written in 1887, and Ravel's *Pavane pour une infante défunte* (Pavane for a Dead Spanish Prince), which was first composed in 1899 for piano, and arranged by the composer for orchestra in 1912.

PED. Abbreviation for pedal. In piano music it indicates that the sustaining (loud) pedal should be used. In organ music it indicates that the pedal keyboard (for the feet) should be used.

PEDAL. A lever operated by foot and used in various musical instruments. (1) The modern piano has three pedals. The soft pedal, on the left, softens the tone by shifting the action so the hammers strike fewer strings. The sustaining pedal, in the middle, "sustains," or holds the sound of a single note or chord because it raises the dampers for only the key or keys that are depressed when the pedal is used. The loud or *forte* pedal, on the right, removes the dampers from the strings and allows them to vibrate fully with all their overtones. The abbreviation for *pedal* is *Ped.* The sign (*) shows when the pedal is to be released. (2) On the organ, the pedals are keys operated by the feet, and for organ music the pedal notes are written on a separate staff. On some organs, a *combination* pedal (sometimes called a *composition* pedal) is used to draw in or throw out groups of stops.* The *swell* pedal is used for increasing or decreasing the volume of sound. (3) Harpsichord pedals are registers (or stops*) operated by the feet, and sometimes by the knee. (4) The pedal on the harp changes the pitch of the strings. (See also *Harp.*)

PEDAL BOARD. The row of large "keys" on the organ, operated by the feet.

PEDAL POINT. A note, usually in the bass, that is sustained (held) for a long period while the harmonies above it change. If the sustained note occurs in the treble, while the harmonies in the bass change, it is called an *inverted pedal.*

PEGS. The wooden pins set in the neck of a stringed instrument. They are used to tighten or loosen the strings.

PENTATONIC SCALE. The word *pentatonic* is taken from two Greek words, *penta* (five) and *tonos* (tone). The scale consists of five notes only, and dates from ancient times. (See also *Scales.*) The most common form of the pentatonic scale is represented by C-D-F-G-A on the piano or by the five black keys, C-sharp, D-sharp, F-sharp, G-sharp, A-sharp.

PERCUSSION INSTRUMENTS. The instruments of an orchestra or band that are, in most cases, struck or shaken. They fall roughly into two varieties: (1) instruments with surfaces made of stretched skins, and (2) instruments with plates, bars, or other kinds of resonating surfaces made of wood or metal. Percussion instruments can be further classified in two ways: (1) those which have definite pitch (timpani, celesta, xylophone, chimes, bells, glockenspiel, etc.), and (2) those which have no definite pitch (bass drums, side drum, tambourine, wood blocks, castanets, cymbals, gong, etc.). (See also *Instruments.*)

Three examples of works that make striking use of percussion instruments are Bartók's *Music for String Instruments, Percussion, and Celesta*; Stravinsky's *Les Noces,* scored for chorus, soloists, four pianos, and seventeen percussion instruments; and Milhaud's *Concerto for Percussion and Small Orchestra.*

PERFECT. (See *Cadence* and *Intervals.*)

PERGOLESI (payr goh LAY see), **Giovanni Battista.** Italian composer born in Jesi on January 4, 1710; died in Pozzuoli on March 16, 1736.

Although Pergolesi came of a poor family and was always a frail person, he showed great talent for music and studied under several teachers in his home town while still a boy. When he was in his middle teens a wealthy nobleman became interested in him and sent him to Naples to study at the Conservatory. Little is known about his work there, but he undoubtedly was a gifted student, for he soon became known for his violin and organ playing as well as for his compositions. His most famous work, *La serva padrona* (*The Maid as Mistress*), was written originally as an intermezzo* to accompany his serious opera, *Il prigioner superbo* (The Proud Prisoner). Other works that have survived to this day are his *Stabat Mater,* a religious work for female voices, and his two well-known songs, *Se tu m'ami* and

Tre giorni son che Nina. Stravinsky's* ballet *Pulcinella* is based on themes of Pergolesi.

PERI (PAY ree), **Jacopo.** Italian composer, born in Florence on August 20, 1561; died there on August 12, 1633.

Peri came of a noble family and spent much of his musical life in the employ of noble families. Not much is known about the details of his life except that he was interested in new ideas and was responsible for some important musical innovations. His first opera, *Dafne,* was performed during the Carnival of 1597 in Florence, and he himself sang an important role. Unfortunately, the opera has been lost. His next opera, *Euridice,* is famous as the first opera that has come down to us in complete form. It was composed in 1600 for the wedding celebration of Henry IV of France and Maria de' Medici.

PEROTIN or **PEROTINUS MAGNUS.** French composer of the twelfth and thirteenth centuries. (The dates and places of his birth and death are not known.)

Almost nothing has been learned about Perotin's life except that he became chief composer at Notre Dame in Paris about 1180 and retained that important post for some fifty years. He is famous as a composer of *clausulae* (sections of compositions in which the rhythm was measured) a form that evolved into the Medieval motet.* Perotin wrote much beautiful music for the church and contributed greatly to the development of mensural notation.*

PERSICHETTI, Vincent. American composer, born in Philadelphia on June 6, 1915.

Persichetti was so gifted as a child that by the time he had reached the age of eleven he was already performing with orchestras. At fifteen he received an appointment as organist in a Philadelphia church. Among the schools which Persichetti attended were Combs College, the Curtis Institute, the Philadelphia Conservatory, and Colorado College. In 1939 he was appointed head of the composition department at Combs College, and in 1942 he accepted a similar position at the Philadelphia Conservatory. He later joined the staff of the Juilliard School of Music.

Persichetti's music has been widely performed, and he has been awarded several distinguished prizes in composition. His works include four symphonies, a great deal of chamber music for various combinations of instruments, choral music, piano solos, and songs.

PESANTE (pay ZAHN tay). An Italian word meaning "weighty" or "heavy." *Pesante* indicates that a passage or section should be played with a rather heavy tone, usually quite sustained and slow.

PHILHARMONIC. A word taken from the Greek, meaning "friend of music." It is used widely as a name for orchestras, choral societies, music halls, and so on. Although it is often used as the name of certain symphony orchestras, as the New York Philharmonic Symphony Orchestra, it does not necessarily denote a particular kind of orchestra, as the word *symphony* does.

PHRASE. A group of notes that forms a distinct unit of melody. It may be long or short, involving several measures or just a few notes. In any case, the performer "feels" the phrases and makes the slightest of breaks or pauses between one phrase and another. Phrases are sometimes indicated by curved lines called *phrase-marks* or *slurs.**

PHRASING. The proper division by the performer of musical lines or subjects. This includes the proper starting and ending of phrases and other musical divisions. It includes also highlighting various musical ideas with crescendoes* and diminuendoes.* Helpful signs are slurs* (curved lines), crescendo* and diminuendo signs,* accent* marks, staccato* marks, and so on. In music for strings, bowing* signs are helpful, as are breathing marks for vocal music and music for wind instruments.

PHRYGIAN (See *Modes.*)

PIANISSIMO (pyah NEE se moh). An Italian word meaning "very soft." The abbreviations used most often in music are *pp* or *ppp.* (See also *Dynamics.*)

PIANO. (1) An Italian word meaning "soft." The abbreviation is *p.* (2) The common term, used almost exclusively in America, for the pianoforte.*

PIANOFORTE. An Italian word derived from *piano* (soft) and *forte* (loud). It was first used as the name of an instrument invented in Florence, Italy, in 1709 by Bartolomeo Cristofori. Actually, the entire name he gave to his invention was *gravecembalo col piano e forte,* meaning a cembalo (Italian harpsichord*) that was capable of playing both soft and loud.

Cristofori's instrument led to the modern piano. It was the first string-keyboard instrument on which it was possible to sustain or hold tones by means of pedals. It took almost a hundred years for it to be improved to the point where it displaced the harpsichord.

The modern piano has a complicated mechanism. The standard instrument has eighty-eight keys. Each key, when depressed, causes a string to be struck in such a way that vibrations are set up. Actually, each "string" consists of one, two, or three strings: one heavy string for each of the lowest tones; three strings for each tone in the center register; two strings for each of the higher tones. When a key is depressed, a small felt-covered piece of wood called a *damper* is lifted from the string, allowing the string to vibrate. When the damper pedal (loud pedal) is depressed, all of the dampers are raised. A flat sheet of wood called a *sounding board* lying under the strings on the grand piano, and behind the strings on an upright piano, has a great deal to do with the *tone* of a piano. The larger the piano, the larger the sounding board, and the longer the strings. Consequently, a nine-foot concert grand piano is capable of a much larger and richer tone than a small upright.

The "soft" pedal, on the left, softens the tone by shifting the action so the hammers strike fewer strings. Some pianos have a third pedal between the "loud" pedal and the "soft" pedal. This third pedal raises the dampers for only the keys that are depressed, making it possible for individual notes to be held as long as the pedal is depressed.

The piano has become possibly the most important musical instrument of all times. Certainly more music has been written for it than for any other, and by most of the world's greatest composers of the last two hundred years.

PIANOLA. A mechanical piano played by pumping large treadles with the feet. Attached to the front of the instrument is a cylinder with a slit corresponding to each piano key. A roll of paper with perforations that duplicate a musical composition passes over the cylinder. Air pumped by a kind of bellows passes through the perforations and sets the proper keys in motion. Actual performances by well-known pianists, both classical and popular, have been re-recorded on such paper roles for playing on the player piano. However, the instrument is not capable of much expressiveness, and as modern disc and tape recordings have taken its place, the pianola has become practically extinct.

PIANO QUARTET. A composition for piano and string trio.* Its form is usually the same as that of a string quartet or symphony.

PIANO QUINTET. A composition for piano and string quartet. Its form is usually the same as that of a string quartet or symphony. Sometimes the instrumental quartet that accompanies the piano may be slightly different from the standard quartet of two violins, viola, and cello. An example is Schubert's* "Trout" quintet, written for piano, violin, viola, cello, and double bass.

PICCOLO (PICK koh loh). The highest pitched wind instrument of the modern orchestra. It is of the flute family, but has a range one octave higher than the regular flute. (See also *Flute*.)

PIPE. (1) A hollow tube or cylinder in which air vibrates, as in a pipe organ. (2) A simple wind instrument, usually with three finger holes, used in combination with a small drum called a tabor* as a dance accompaniment in some sections of Spain at the present time, and as early as the fourteenth century in England.

PISTON, Walter. American composer and teacher, born in Rockland, Maine, on January 20, 1894.

Piston did not study music seriously until after he had graduated from an art school at the age of sixteen. When he did take up the piano and violin he made rapid progress and was soon performing in public. During World War I he played saxophone in a navy band; after the war he attended Harvard University where he majored in music. After his graduation from Harvard he studied in Paris with the famous teacher, Nadia Boulanger,* and in 1926 he was appointed to the music faculty at Harvard.

Piston is famous not only for his compositions, which have been widely performed, but also for his textbooks on harmony, counterpoint, and orchestration. His works to date include seven symphonies, other compositions for orchestra, a great deal of chamber music, a violin concerto, and a ballet.

PITCH. The highness or lowness of a tone. Pitch can be measured scientifically by means of the number of vibrations per second, but a performer— especially a singer or a player of stringed instruments—must develop through practice a high degree of sensitivity to accurate pitch if he is to sing or play "in tune." The accuracy of a pitch depends upon its relationship to the pitch of notes that follow or precede it. The problem of tuning the instruments of the orchestra so they will all play "in tune" with each other has been largely solved by agreement on a universal pitch. That is, they generally tune to an A (just above Middle C) that vibrates at 440 vibrations per second. (See also *Absolute Pitch* and *Acoustics.*)

PITCH PIPE. A small reed pipe used for giving the pitch to unaccompanied choral groups. Before the invention of the tuning fork,* which is a more reliable instrument, the pitch pipe was used to give the pitch to stringed instruments.

PIÙ (pee YOU). An Italian word meaning "more." It is used in music with other terms, as *più allegro* (more fast, or faster), *più forte* (louder), and so on. The opposite of *più* is *meno* (less).

PIZZETTI (peet SAY tee), **Ildebrando.** Italian composer, born in Parma on September 20, 1880.

Pizzetti's father was a piano teacher, but the boy was more interested in the theater than in music, and did not begin seriously to study harmony, counterpoint, and composition until he was fifteen years old. Even so, his interest in the theater influenced his music to the degree that he wished to concentrate on opera. His first opera, *Fedra,* was set to a libretto by the famous Italian poet, Gabriele d'Annunzio. He has since written seven more operas (all to librettos that he wrote himself), a considerable amount of orchestral music, chamber music, concertos, choral works, and songs. Pizzetti is also widely known as a teacher. He has taught composition and harmony at several leading conservatories, has been director of the Milan Conservatory, and has held master classes at the famous Accademia di Santa Cecilia in Rome.

PIZZICATO (pit see CAH toh). An Italian word meaning "pinched." It is a direction for players of stringed instruments to pluck the strings instead of bowing them. *Pizzicato* is usually indicated for the right hand, but occasionally the left is used to get special effects. The abbreviation for pizzicato is *pizz.* To cancel the direction and show that the strings are again to be bowed, the word *arco** (bow) is used.

PLAGAL CADENCE. (See *Cadence.*)

PLAIN CHANT. (See *Plainsong.*)

PLAINSONG. (Sometimes called *Plain Chant.*) The general term given to unaccompanied chanting of liturgy, especially the chanting by priests in the Roman Catholic service. It originated in the the Medieval church, and in its final form as used today is called Gregorian Chant.* It consists of a single line of melody that is not divided into measures, and has a special notation of its own.

PLECTRUM. A small piece of flexible material used in strumming or plucking stringed instruments of the lute* and lyre* families. Plectrums may be made of horn, metal, plastic, shell, and so on. The mandolin, the zither, and sometimes the banjo, are played with plectrums. A different kind of plectrum is used for plucking the strings of the spinet* and the harpsichord.*

POCO (POH coh). An Italian word meaning "little" or "somewhat." The term is used in music with other terms, as *poco a poco dim* (little by little getting softer), *rit. poco* (a little slower), and so on.

POLKA. A lively dance in 2/4 time that originated in eastern Bohemia in the early part of the nineteenth century. It soon spread to other European countries and into serious music, especially the music of the Czech composer Smetana, who wrote polkas into his operas and some of his other works. The polka is to this day the favorite folk dance of Czechoslovakia.

POLONAISE (paw law NEZ). A French word meaning "Polish." It is a stately court dance in 3/4 time that originated as a folk dance in ancient times in a part of Europe that is considered the "cradle" of the Polish nation. During the seventeenth and eighteenth centuries it was used in Baroque suites by Couperin,* Telemann,* Bach,* and others. Its basic rhythm is generally a ♩ ♫♩ ♩ ♩ ♩ . As time passed, the polonaise took on more elaborate rhythmic patterns, especially in Chopin's* thirteen polonaises.

POLYMETER. Two or more different meters that are used at the same time in a composition; for example, 3/4 in the treble part and 4/4 in the bass part. This is sometimes called *polyrhythm,* and occurs most often in twentieth century music by such composers as Hindemith* and Schoenberg.*

POLYPHONY. A word derived from the Greek word *polyphonia,* mean-

ing "many voices." It is used in a general way to describe part music.*
The origin of polyphonic writing goes back to the eleventh century, when
one or more parts, or voices,* were added to the single part of a plainsong.*
In the course of centuries more and more voices were added and the individual parts became more and more elaborate. Some important forms of
polyphonic writing are the motet,* the round,* the canon,* the chanson,*
and the fugue.* Two great masters of polyphonic writing were Palestrina*
and J. S. Bach.* (See also *Counterpoint.*)

POLYTONALITY. The use of two or more different keys simultaneously
in the same composition. Although a few composers experimented with
polytonality before the 20th century (Mozart used some polytonal effects
in a composition called *Ein musikalischer Spass* (A Musical Joke)), it
was not until recent times that it was used seriously by such modern composers as Stravinsky and Bartók.

POMPOSO (pohm POH soh). An Italian word meaning "pompous" or
"overly dignified." It indicates that the music is to be performed in a rather
heavy, dignified, and slow fashion.

PONCHIELLI (ponk KYELL lee), **Amilcare.** Italian composer, born in
Paderno Fasolaro, near Cremona, on August 31, 1834; died in Milan on
January 16, 1886.

Ponchielli entered the Milan Conservatory when he was nine years old
and remained there for eleven years. His first stage work, written with three
other students, was an operetta called *Il sindaco babbeo.* It was produced
in Milan in 1851. After leaving the Conservatory, Ponchielli held a number
of positions, including that of organist in Cremona, *Maestro di cappella*
(director of music) at the Bergamo Cathedral, and teacher of composition
at the Milan Conservatory. He wrote nine operas, including *La Gioconda,*
the only one to achieve any lasting popularity. The well-known "Dance
of the Hours" is from a ballet in the third act of that opera. He also wrote
ballets, cantatas, and church music.

PONTICELLO (pon tee CHELL oh). An Italian word meaning "little
bridge." It is the Italian name for the bridge on instruments of the violin
family. The term is often used as *sul ponticello,* a direction to players of
stringed instruments to bow as close to the bridge as possible. This produces a rather brittle tone with very little vibration.

POPPER, David. Czech (Bohemian) composer and cellist, born in Prague on June 16, 1843; died in Baden, near Vienna, on August 7, 1913.

Popper was educated at the Prague Conservatory, where he showed remarkable talent for the cello. By the time he was twenty he had begun to tour Germany as a virtuoso artist, and he soon rose to a high position as a performer. At the age of twenty-two he won acclaim as soloist at the Karlsruhe Music Festival, and later was appointed *Kammervirtuoso* (top performer) at the court of Prince Hohenzollern. In 1868 he became first cellist of the Vienna Court Opera, and in 1896, after extensive concert tours throughout Europe, he joined the staff of the Budapest Conservatory, where he taught until his death.

Popper's works include four cello concertos, many cello solos, a *Requiem* for three cellos, a number of shorter works, and two books of studies for the cello.

PORTAMENTO (poor tah MEN toh). An Italian word meaning "carrying." The term is used mainly for bowed instruments and vocal music, and indicates that the sound is to be carried over smoothly from one note to the next. It is more "slurred" than legato,* but not so much as glissando.*

PORTER, Cole. American composer of musical comedies; born in Peru, Indiana, on June 9, 1893; died in Santa Monica, California, on October 15, 1964.

Porter attended Yale University and took a Bachelor of Arts degree there in 1913. Later he studied music at Harvard University. During World War I he served in the French Army, and after the armistice continued his study of music at the Schola Cantorum in Paris. After his return to the United States he devoted himself with great success to writing musical comedies. Among some of his better known shows were *Panama Hattie, Something for the Boys, Kiss Me Kate,* and *Silk Stockings.* Many of his songs became great hits. Among his most popular were *Begin the Beguine, Night and Day, Don't Fence Me In,* and *Wunderbar.*

PORTER, Quincy. American violinist, teacher, and composer, born in New Haven, Connecticut, on February 7, 1897.

Quincy Porter grew up in an intellectual atmosphere; both his father and grandfather were professors at Yale University. He showed considerable talent for music and his family encouraged him to continue his studies at Yale, where he studied composition with Horatio Parker.* At the same time he kept up his study of the violin, which he had started when he was seven. After graduating from Yale he went to Paris for further study, and when he returned to the United States he did advanced work in composition with Ernest Bloch.* For some time he earned a living by playing violin in theater orchestras. Later he taught at the Cleveland Institute of Music, and still later at Vassar College. In 1946 he became a professor of music at Yale University. His works include a symphony, several other works for orchestra, a good deal of chamber music, pieces for violin and for viola, piano pieces, organ pieces, and songs. His *Concerto Concertante* for two pianos and orchestras won the Pulitzer Prize in 1954.

POSITION. (1) In referring to the way the notes of a chord are arranged, we say that the chord is in *root position* or *first position* if the key note, or root of the chord is at the bottom. For example, the chord C-E-G-C is in first (or root) position. If the E is at the bottom, the chord is in first inversion; if the G is at the bottom the chord is in second inversion. Also, when the notes of a chord are as close as possible (C-E-G-C), the chord is said to be in close position. When the notes of a chord are otherwise, the chord is in open position. (2) In playing bowed stringed instruments, the fingers of the left hand are placed in different positions. For example, in the first position on the G string, A is played by the first finger, in the second position B is played by the first finger, and so on. (3) In playing the trombone, the slide changes position as the pitch changes. When the slide is closed it is in first position. As it is extended, it is in second, third, etc., positions.

POSTLUDE. A piece played at the end of a service, as an organ postlude in a church service. It is the opposite of a prelude.*

POT-POURRI (poh poor REE). A French word meaning "a jar or pot filled with some kind of mixture." In music it refers to a medley of tunes, as a piece for orchestra made up of popular melodies from light opera played one after the other.

POULENC (poo LAHNK), **Francis.** French composer, born in Paris on January 7, 1899; died there on January 30, 1963.

As a boy, Poulenc was much more interested in music than he was in getting a classical education, as his parents wished. They did allow him to study piano and he proved to be exceptionally talented. At the same time he studied composition and was equally gifted at that. By the time he was eighteen he had written a composition for voice and chamber orchestra called *Rapsodie nègre*. A year later he played in a concert sponsored by Erik Satie,* a prominent French composer who took an interest in Poulenc and influenced him greatly. Soon Poulenc was associated with the group of influential French composers known as *Les Six*.* His works include ballets, chamber music, many piano pieces, choral works, a cantata, and a great many songs. He also wrote two operas, *Les Mamelles de Tiresias* and *Les Dialogues des Carmelites*. The latter is performed frequently in Europe and has become increasingly well known in America.

POWELL, John. American composer and pianist, born in Richmond, Virginia on September 6, 1882.

Powell's first musical study was at home. His mother was an amateur musician, and his sister a pianist with whom he took his first lessons. He later studied with a pupil of Liszt. While he was a student at the University of Virginia he continued his musical studies, and after graduation in 1901 he went to Vienna. There he studied piano for five years with the eminent teacher Leschetizky and composition for three years with Navratil. His first appearance as a concert pianist was in Berlin in the year 1907. From that time on he toured widely, both in Europe and in the United States. His works include choral compositions, a symphony, orchestral pieces, a piano concerto, a violin concerto, two sonatas for violin and piano. His *Rapsodie Nègre,* a work for piano and orchestra which was commissioned by the conductor of the Russian Symphony Orchestra in 1917, is his best known work. He himself played the piano part at its New York premiere, and later played it with several orchestras in Europe and the United States.

PRELUDE. A title that is sometimes used for a composition that precedes a larger work (as the *prelude* to an opera) or the opening hymns in a church service (as an *organ prelude*), and sometimes simply as the title of an independent composition. J. S. Bach* wrote forty-eight preludes, one to precede each of the fugues in his *Well-tempered Clavier*.* Chopin wrote twenty-four preludes that were not designed to precede anything. Other composers who have written sets of preludes are Scriabin* with twelve, Debussy* with two sets of twelve, and Shostakovich* with twenty-four.

PRESTISSIMO (pray STEE see moh). An Italian word meaning "very

lively." As a direction in music, it indicates a speed faster than *presto**
(fast), or as fast as a performer can play or sing the passage. (See also
Tempo.)

PRESTO (PRAY stoh). An Italian word meaning "lively." It indicates that
the passage should be fast. It is often used with other terms, as *più presto*
(go faster) and *meno presto* (not so fast—slow down). (See also *Tempo.*)

PRIMA (PREE mah), **PRIMO** (PREE moh). Feminine and masculine
forms of an Italian word meaning "first." It is always used with another
word, as *prima volta* (first time), *prima donna* (first, or leading lady),
primo movimento (first, or original, speed), *prima parte* (first part or
section), and so on.

PRIMA DONNA. (See *Prima.*)

PRIX DE ROME (pree d' Rome). In English, the Rome Prize. A prize
awarded each year by the French government to students of music (and
other fine arts). The competition is conducted by the *École des Beaux-Arts*
(School of Fine Arts) in Paris, and is open to students between the ages of
fifteen and thirty. The prize consists of a four-year scholarship in Rome,
plus living expenses. The *Prix de Rome* was established in 1666 by King
Louis XIV, but it was not open to music students until 1803. Both Belgium
and the United States now have similar prizes.

PROGRAM MUSIC. Music that interprets or describes an event, that suggests a mood, that relates a tale, that imitates nature, and so on. It is the
opposite of absolute music.* Sometimes the subject is actually given in
the title by the composer, as Debussy's *La Mer* (The Sea) or Stravinsky's
Rite of Spring. Often a title that suggests a subject is given by music editors
or writers of program notes to music the composer intended to be absolute
music. Program music was written as far back as the sixteenth century,
when a composer named Jannequin wrote chansons* with such titles as
Song of the Birds, The War, The Hunt. In the seventeenth century Rameau*
and Couperin* gave such titles as *La Villageoise* (The Villager) and *Les
Papillons* (The Butterflies) to their pieces for harpsichord. An example of
eighteenth century music is J. S. Bach's *Capriccio,* on the departure of a
brother, written for the clavier. Program music reached its height in the
nineteenth century, when most of the great composers wrote descriptive

music. Some examples are Tchaikovsky's *1812 Overture*, Berlioz's *Symphonie fantastique* (Fantastic Symphony), Mendelssohn's *Overture to A Midsummer Night's Dream*, Schumann's *Kinderscenen* (Scenes from Childhood). Some examples of program music written by composers of the twentieth century are Sibelius' *Finlandia* and Prokofiev's work for narrator and orchestra, *Peter and the Wolf*.

PROKOFIEV (pro KOH fyeff), **Sergei.** Russian composer and pianist, born in Sontsovka on April 23, 1891; died in Moscow on March 5, 1953.

Prokofiev was an unusually gifted child. He first studied piano with his mother, who was an amateur musician. By the age of six he could play quite well, and soon was trying his hand at composition. He was just nine when he finished the piano score for an opera he called *The Giant*. At thirteen he entered the St. Petersburg Conservatory, and there he studied with such famous teachers as Rimsky-Korsakov,* Liadov,* and Tcherepnin.* He graduated from the Conservatory in 1914 with the highest honors for a pianist. From that time on he devoted himself mainly to composition, and soon made a name for himself. His famous *Classical Symphony* was completed when he was just twenty-six. That and other works, some of which he played himself, were soon being played widely in Europe. Soon after the first performance of the *Classical Symphony* he left Russia and traveled by way of Siberia and the Pacific to the United States. For two years he performed his own works in such cities as Chicago and New York, then went to Paris, where he became associated with the ballet impressario, Diaghilev, who produced his ballet, *The Buffoon*. In 1921 he returned to the United States for the production of his opera, *The Love for Three Oranges*, a work that is performed frequently in the major capitals of the world. Six years later he returned to Russia where he remained for the rest of his life, except for occasional trips to other countries. One of his most interesting works, *Peter and the Wolf*, was written in 1936 especially for a children's concert. This work is familiar to young people in America through recordings and frequent stage productions. It was written originally to acquaint young people with the different instruments of the orchestra, but it proved to be clever enough to be highly entertaining as a musical story alone.

Prokofiev wrote a great many works, including seven operas, seven symphonies, several shorter orchestral works, five piano concertos, six ballets, two violin concertos, a cello concerto, two string quartets, solo piano pieces, and a number of songs.

PROPER. (See *Mass.*)

PSALM. One of the sacred hymns in the Book of Psalms of the Old Testament. The Psalms have provided musicians with a source of text material for centuries. A large percentage of chants in the Roman Catholic liturgy, for example, are settings of texts drawn from among the 150 Psalms. Originally there were three ways in which Psalms were sung or chanted: (1) A Psalm was sung straight through from beginning to end by one or several voices in unison;* (2) in *antiphone,* that is, one group singing a single line in response to another group singing an entire verse; (3) a choir or congregation singing in response to a cantor* or soloist. In more recent times, the Psalms have been used by many composers as texts for compositions, both for solo voice and for chorus. Among the great composers of the nineteenth and twentieth centuries who have set Psalms to music are Schubert,* Mendelssohn,* Liszt,* Dvořák,* and Stravinsky.*

PSALTERY. An instrument of medieval times that resembled the dulcimer.* The strings were arranged in groups of three, all the strings in a group being tuned alike. The player plucked the strings with his fingers. The psaltery was a forerunner of the spinet* and harpsichord.*

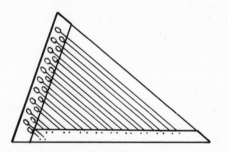

PUCCINI (poo CHEE nee), **Giacomo.** Italian composer, born in Lucca on December 22, 1858; died in Brussels, Belgium, on November 29, 1924.

Puccini's father, his grandfather, his great-grandfather, and even his great-great-grandfather all were composers, so it is not surprising that the young Giacomo inherited a great love for music and talent for writing it. While he was still a boy, the Queen of Italy granted him a pension that made it possible for him to attend the Conservatory of Milan. There he studied with Ponchielli,* who encouraged him to write his first opera, *Le Ville.* Although it was not a success, it indicated clearly that Puccini had a gift for melody. It was not until his third opera, *Manon Lescaut,* was produced that Puccini really began to make a name for himself. From that time on he continued to write operas that are among the world's best loved and most frequently produced. The three that are heard most often are *La Bohème, Tosca,* and *Madame Butterfly.* Less well known, but still quite frequently performed are his *La Fanciulla del West* (The Girl of the Golden West) and his *Il Trittico* (The Triptych, or group of three one-act operas): *Il Tabarro, Suor Angelica,* and *Gianni Schicci.* His last opera, *Turandot,* was finished except for the final duet when Puccini died. It was completed by Alfano and produced at the famous La Scala in Milan in 1926. Puccini's operas, ranging from the light comedy of *Gianni Schicci* to the heavy drama of *Tosca* and of *Turandot,* show the great talent he had for beautiful melody, impressive orchestration, and powerful dramatic effects.

PUGNANI (poo NYAH nee), **Gaetano.** Italian violinist and composer, born in Turin on November 27, 1731; died there on July 15, 1798.

Not much is known about Pugnani's boyhood, except that he showed great talent for the violin and was a pupil of a master teacher of that day, Somis. When he was twenty-one years old he was appointed violinist of the Sardinian Court. Two years later he began touring as a concert violinist and did a great deal of composing. Later, when he settled in Turin, he was much sought after as a teacher. The most famous of his many fine pupils was Viotti,* whose name is known to any serious violinist. In addition to violin concertos and sonatas, quintets, and other chamber music, Pugnani composed several operas, ballets, and cantatas. However, his fame rests today not on his compositions, but rather on the continuity he supplied to the great style of violin playing of the early Italian masters.

PURCELL, Henry. English composer, born in London about 1659; died in London on November 21, 1695.

As a child, Purcell sang in the choir of the Royal Chapel, and by the time he was ten years old he was already composing music for the choir. He stayed with the choir until his voice broke, and then began serious study with John Blow, the organist of the famous Westminster Abbey. He himself was appointed to that position in 1679, when he was only about twenty years old. Three years later he became organist of the Chapel Royal. In the meantime he had become interested in writing incidental music for the theater. During his lifetime he wrote a great many works and became famous as the greatest British composer of his day. His fame continued after his death, and even the great Handel did not overshadow his memory. In fact, he is one of the famous men of history who are buried in Westminster Abbey.

Purcell's most famous work is his opera, *Dido and Aeneas*. First produced in 1689, it is still a favorite in today's opera repertory. In addition to *Dido and Aeneas,* he wrote several other operas, a great deal of incidental music and songs for plays; anthems, Psalms, canons, and other sacred music; catches, vocal duets, violin pieces, and a great many solo songs with continuo* accompaniment.

QUADRILLE. A French dance that became popular in the eighteenth century, was introduced later into England, and then into Germany. It was danced by two or four couples in the form of a square, and consisted of five parts, alternating between 6/8 and 2/4 time. The music was ordinarily taken from popular tunes or operatic airs of the period.

QUADRUPLET. A group of four notes (or notes and rests) of equal time value that are played in the space of three, as indicated by the time signature.

QUANTZ (kvants), **Johann.** German flutist and composer, born in Oberscheden on January 30, 1697; died in Potsdam on July 12, 1773.

Quantz was so gifted musically that he started performing when he was only eight years old. He started out by playing the double bass,* but soon became skillful on various instruments, including the clavier,* the oboe,* and the violin.* After serving a five and a half year apprenticeship, he held a number of high positions, including that of musician in the chapel of the King of Poland. It was not until he was twenty-one that he took up study of the flute.* In 1728, after years of successful touring in Europe, he performed before the Crown Prince of Germany, who later became

Frederick the Great. The Prince was so charmed with Quantz's playing that he decided to study the flute, and Quantz traveled from Dresden to Berlin twice a year to give him lessons. When the Prince became King he hired Quantz as head court musician. There his chief duties were to conduct the court orchestra, in which the King played the flute, and to compose flute pieces for the King and others to play. Quantz remained at the German court until his death. During that time he wrote most of his works. They include some three hundred concertos for flute, many flute solos, a large number of trios and quartets, hymns, and songs. He wrote some important works on flute playing, and he made important improvements on the instrument by adding a second key and a device for tuning it.

QUARTER NOTE. The note (♩) that represents one fourth the value of a whole note. In music written in 4/4 time, there are four quarter notes (or the equivalent in notes and rests) to the measure; in 3/4 time there are three quarter notes, and so on. In England the quarter note is called a *crotchet.*

QUARTER TONE. A tone equal to one quarter of a whole tone (or one half of a half tone). (See also *Microtone.*)

QUARTET. (1) A group of four instrumentalists or four singers who specialize in playing or singing music especially written for that combination. A string quartet consists of two violins, cello, and viola. A piano quartet consists of piano, violin, viola, and cello. A mixed vocal quartet usually consists of soprano, alto, tenor, and bass; a male quartet of two tenors, baritone, and bass; and a female quartet of two sopranos and two altos. (2) Music written for four instruments or four singers. (See also *Chamber Music.*)

QUASI (KWAH zee). An Italian word meaning "as if" or "almost." It is used with other terms, as *andante quasi allegretto* (moderate speed, but almost moderately fast) or *quasi niente* (almost nothing, or extremely soft).

QUAVER (KWAY ver). The name used in England for the eighth note: (♪ ♫). The quaver rest is the same as the eighth rest: (𝄾).

QUILTER, Roger. English composer, born in Brighton on November 1, 1877; died in London on September 21, 1953.

After graduating from Eton College, Quilter went to Frankfurt-am-Main in Germany to study composition with Knorr. He had a special gift for melody and wrote many beautiful songs, using as lyrics some of the world's greatest poetry. In addition to nearly a hundred songs, he wrote three light operas, two ballets, incidental music to two plays, twelve choral works with orchestra, seven smaller orchestral pieces, and piano solos.

QUINTET. (1) A group of five instrumentalists or five singers who specialize in playing or singing music especially written for that combination. A string quintet usually consists of two violins, two violas and a cello, or of two violins, one viola, and two cellos. A piano quintet usually consists of piano, two violins, viola, and cello. A woodwind quintet usually consists of flute, oboe, clarinet, bassoon, and horn. (2) Music written for five instruments or five singers. (See also *Chamber Music.*)

QUINTUPLET. A group of five notes (or notes and rests) of equal time value that are played in the space of one (or more) notes, as indicated by the time signature.

R

RACHMANINOFF (rahk MAHN yee nawf), **Sergei.** Russian composer, born in Oneg (a district in Novgorod) on April 1, 1873; died in Beverly Hills, California, on March 28, 1943.

Rachmaninoff was nine years old when he entered the St. Petersburg Conservatory of Music. Three years later he transferred to the Moscow Conservatory, where he studied piano with Zverev and Siloti, and composition with Tanyeyev and Arensky. He was nineteen years old when he won a gold medal for composition; and in the same year he began to tour as a concert pianist. From that time on he concertized widely and attained great success as a composer. His second piano concerto is especially popular. In 1917 the Russian Revolution forced him to leave Russia, and from then on he divided his time between the United States, Paris, and Switzerland.

As a concert pianist Rachmaninoff had few equals. He possessed a technical skill and mastery of the instrument that was of the highest order. As a composer, he achieved great beauty in many of his works, especially in his piano pieces and songs. In addition to these works, he composed three operas, three symphonies, several tone poems and other works for orchestra, four concertos, a rhapsody for piano and orchestra, choral works, and chamber music.

RAGTIME. An early type of jazz that was extremely popular in the United States from about 1895 to 1915. It was usually written in 4/4 or 2/4 time and had a peculiar syncopated rhythm of its own. An example is Irving Berlin's *Alexander's Ragtime Band.* Stravinsky* wrote two works in which he used ragtime rhythms, *Ragtime for Eleven Instruments* and *Piano Rag-Music.*

RALLENTANDO (rah lehn TAHN doh). An Italian word meaning "slowing down." Rallentando is a direction to slacken or slow down the speed of the music gradually. It is abbreviated *rall.*

RAMEAU (rah MOH) **Jean-Philippe.** French composer and theorist, born in Dijon and baptized there on September 25, 1683; died in Paris on September 12, 1764.

Rameau's father, a church organist, gave his son lessons on the harpsichord and the organ and some instruction in music theory while the boy was quite young. The father had wanted his son to become a lawyer and sent him to the university; but when he realized that the boy possessed unusual talent for music he allowed him to leave the university and go to Italy for further musical study. Young Rameau did not take very well to Italian ways, and a few years later he returned to France, where he taught music and played the organ in Avignon. This was followed by a position as organist in Clermont-Ferrand, where he remained for four years. During the next ten years he held posts in Paris and in Lyons, then returned to Clermont-Ferrand to stay until 1722, when he moved permanently to Paris. While he was in Clermont-Ferrand he wrote one of the most important texts in the history of music, the *Traité de l'harmonie* (Treatise on Harmony). The publication of that work brought him considerable attention, because it established for the first time the function of harmony in the composition of music. He soon became one of the most popular teachers of harpsichord and musical theory in Paris. He became interested in writing opera when he was in his forties, and he was fortunate enough to win the friendship and support of some wealthy and influential people who saw to it that his talent was recognized and rewarded. Rameau lived to see many of his operas produced with great splendor at the royal court. In addition to thirty-seven stage works, most of them operas, he wrote five motets, eight cantatas for solo voice, five concertos, and many pieces for the harpsichord.

RANGE. (See *Compass.*)

RANZ DES VACHES (rahns day VASH). A French phrase meaning "song of the cowherds." A *ranz des vaches* is a Swiss melody sung or played on an alphorn* by the herdsmen to call the cows from the mountain meadows. There are a number of such melodies. Liszt* used a *ranz des vaches* in his piano piece, *Vallée d'Obermann*; Beethoven* used another version in his

Symphony No. 6 (the Pastorale); and Rossini* used still another in the overture to *William Tell*.

RATTLE. A percussion instrument with no definite pitch. One kind of rattle consists of a sort of cogwheel with strips of wood or metal that strike against the cogs when the wheel revolves. Another is a gourd (real or made of wood, plastic, or some other material) with pebbles or beans inside which rattle when the gourd is shaken.

RAVEL (rah VELL), **Maurice.** French composer, born in Ciboure on March 7, 1875; died in Paris on December 28, 1937.

Ravel began to take piano lessons when he was seven years old. Two years later he was studying harmony, and he was just fourteen when he was admitted to the Paris Conservatory. His most prominent teacher there was Fauré.* Ravel proved to be a talented student who showed great originality in his works. In fact, when two of his works were performed for the first time in public, some critics declared that he was a revolutionist and should not be tolerated. He continued to compose, however, and in spite of the critics the general public eventually came to consider him one of the greatest living French composers. Ravel always worked slowly and carefully on his compositions, and at times his composing was interrupted by other things, so in comparison with many other composers his output was small. His works, however, have gradually acquired a dominant place in the standard orchestra repertoire and are performed widely today. Ravel's works include two operas, four ballets (including the immensely popular *Daphnis and Chloe*), several works for orchestra, chamber music, piano solos and a piano duet, songs, and a number of folk-song accompaniments.

RE (ray). In the system of *movable do*,* the syllable name given to the second note of the major scale. In the *fixed do** system, the note *D*.

REBEC. A forerunner of the violin. It was a small, pear-shaped instrument with three or four strings, played with a bow, and popular during medieval times.

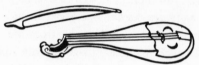

RECAPITULATION. (See *Sonata Form.*)

RECITAL. A performance by one or more soloists. The terms concert and recital are sometimes confused. A concert is given by a group of three or more musicians performing together. A recital is given by a pianist, an instrumentalist, or a singer. In the case of a singer or instrumentalist accompanied by a pianist, the performance is still called a recital.

RECITATIVE (res sih tah TEEV). A word taken from the Latin *recitare,* which means "to recite." It is a kind of speech-like type of singing used extensively in opera and oratorio. It usually precedes an aria or song, and is frequently accompanied only by chords played by orchestra, harpsichord, piano, or organ.

RECORDER. An early instrument of the flute family. It has a mouthpiece shaped like a beak and eight finger holes, one of them for the thumb. The player holds the instrument in a vertical position and blows into the mouthpiece. The modern recorder, which is modeled after those of the seventeenth and eighteenth centuries, usually consists of two jointed sections. It comes in six sizes, contrabass, bass, tenor, alto, soprano, and sopranino. It has a sweet and pleasing tone, and is relatively easy to play. For this reason it has become popular in recent years as an instrument for school use and for amateur music-making in the home.

REED. The vibrating piece of cane or metal, called a tongue, used in the mouthpiece of certain types of wind instruments, accordions, pipe organs, harmonicas, and so on. Instruments of the oboe* family are equipped with two reeds that vibrate against each other. The clarinet* and the saxophone* have single reeds that vibrate against the surface of the mouthpiece.

REEL. A lively dance, usually in 2/4 or 4/4 time, that originated in the British Isles. Two or more couples face each other and dance through rather intricate steps to eight-measure phrases. The Virginia Reel, popular during Colonial days in America, was a version of the Irish and Scottish reels. A characteristic of the reel is a fairly steady rhythm based on a bouncing eighth-note figuration:

REFRAIN. The section of a song, sometimes called the *chorus,* that is repeated after each verse. The refrain in music, as in poetry, goes back several centuries to the responses or antiphons* in early church music. The refrain was used also in early French songs such as the ballade* and rondeau.*

REGAL. A small, portable keyboard organ that was popular in the late Renaissance period. It was equipped with beating reeds of the type used in the clarinet. One type, called the *Bible-regal* could be folded shut like a book. The regal was widely used in churches and for plays such as the mystery and miracle plays of the period.

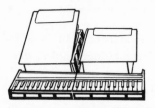

REGER (RAY ger), **Max.** German composer, born in Brand, Bavaria, on March 19, 1873; died in Leipzig on May 11, 1916.

At the age of thirteen Reger was already playing organ in the Catholic Church at Weiden, where his family had moved when he was a year old. By the time he was seventeen his parents realized that he was an unusually gifted musician and took him to study with Hugo Riemann. Riemann interested the boy in Bach* and Brahms,* two composers who influenced Reger's work in composition greatly. He became a master of contrapuntal writing, but at the same time developed a style of his own that in some ways resembled the works of Debussy* and the other impressionists. He held a number of positions of importance in the universities and conservatories of Europe, and he enjoyed a number of successful concert tours as a virtuoso pianist in Germany, Russia, Holland, Switzerland, and England. Reger wrote a great many works, most of them extremely complex. He never wrote an opera, and although he planned to write a symphony, he died before he was able to accomplish this. His compositions include choral works, ten orchestral works (one of which, his *V* music and pieces for solo instruments, a large number of piano pieces, four volumes of songs, and some thirty-six works for organ.

REGISTER. (1) Various ranges of the voice, as the head register, the middle register, and the chest register. (2) A set of organ pipes that is controlled by a single stop.* (See also *Organ*.)

REINECKE (RINE neck eh), **Carl.** German composer, pianist, and teacher, born in Altona on June 23, 1824; died in Leipzig on March 10, 1910.

Reinecke's father was a musician who began to train his son while he was still very young. The boy learned to play the piano so well that he performed in public when he was eleven and made a concert tour to Denmark and Sweden at the age of eighteen. He continued to concertize for the rest of his life, and, in addition, held a number of important positions as a professor of piano and composition and as a conductor of some of Europe's finest orchestras. He also found time to write a good deal of music, a number of books about music, and a two-volume autobiography. His compositions include four operas, an oratorio, three symphonies, nine overtures, four piano concertos, chamber music, and a great many piano pieces and songs.

RELATIVE MAJOR AND MINOR. The terms relative major and relative minor are used to indicate the relationship between keys that have the same key signature. For example, the key of A minor has the same key signature (no sharps or flats) as the key of C major. Every major key has a relative minor, and every minor key has a relative major. (See also *Keys*.)

REPEAT MARKS. The signs ‖: and :‖ indicate that the section of music between the two signs is to be repeated. If only the second of the two signs is used, the performer is to go back to the beginning of the piece or of that particular movement and repeat until he reaches the sign again.

REPRISE (re PREEZ). A French word meaning "a resumption." (1) The repetition of an earlier section of a composition (usually the first section), after an intervening section. (2) The repetition in a musical play of a song that has been sung earlier. (3) The same as *recapitulation* in sonata form.*

REQUIEM (RAY kwee yem) **Mass.** The Mass for the dead in the Roman Catholic liturgy. In plainsong* the complete Mass is made up of the *Introit,* "Requiem aeternam dona eis Domine" (Give them eternal rest, O Lord); the *Kyrie* (Lord, have mercy upon us); a Gradual; a Tract; the *Sequence*: "Dies Irae" (Day of Wrath); an Offertory; the *Sanctus* (Holy, Holy, Holy); the *Agnus Dei* (O Lamb of God); and a Communion. Famous composers—including Palestrina,* Mozart,* Verdi,* and Fauré* —have made elaborate settings of the Requiem Mass. Usually, however, some of the plainsong sections are omitted in the settings.

RESOLUTION. A term used in harmony and counterpoint to describe the movement of a dissonant chord (or tone) to a consonant, or more restful one. In the following example, the "dissonant" (dominant seventh) chord resolves to the tonic chord, and the tones F and B resolve to E and C:

RESONANCE. The reinforcement of musical tones by one or more vibrating mechanisms. On the piano, for example, the sounding board acts as a resonator, reinforcing the sound of all the strings. On the violin, the belly* acts as a resonator. The xylophone has metal cylinders directly beneath each metal bar that is struck. These cylinders amplify and cause continued resonance of each tone. (See also *Acoustics.*)

RESPIGHI (ray SPEE ghee), **Ottorino.** Italian composer, born in Bologna on July 9, 1879; died in Rome on April 18, 1936.

Respighi began his study of the violin and the viola at the Liceo Musicale of Bologna when he was twelve years old, and received his diploma in 1899. A year later he went to Russia as first violinist in the opera orchestra at St. Petersburg (now Leningrad). While he was there, he studied composition and orchestration with Rimsky-Korsakoff.* He later studied with Max Bruch* in Berlin. After a number of years devoted to playing viola in the Mugellini Quartet and touring as a concert violinist, he returned to Italy as the director of the Santa Cecilia Academy in Rome. He later resigned that position to teach composition. Except for occasional tours, he remained in Rome for the rest of his life, teaching and composing. His works include eight operas, three ballets, some fourteen orchestral works, chamber music, and a great many songs. He is probably best known in America for his two popular tone poems, *The Pines of Rome* and *The*

Fountains of Rome, and for his ballet *La Boutique Fantasque* (based on themes of Rossini).

REST. A silence or pause in the music occurring in one or more parts or voices. (For the signs used to indicate rests of various lengths see *Notation*).

RETROGRADE MOTION. A term used to describe the technique of writing a theme or melody in reverse order, that is in backward motion. It was especially popular with writers of the polyphonic and contrapuntal styles. (J. S. Bach used it, but rarely.) In modern times, Hindemith as well as writers of the twelve-tone* school of composition have used it effectively. In the following example, the second line is written in retrograde motion. It begins with the last note of the first line and ends with the first note.

RHAPSODY (RAP soh dee). A composition, somewhat in the style of a fantasy,* consisting of several sections that are rather loosely connected with each other. Liszt was one of the first composers to use the term as the title of a musical composition. He wrote fifteen pieces that he called *Hungarian Rhapsodies,* each one using several Hungarian Gypsy tunes. Other composers of the nineteenth and early twentieth centuries who wrote *Rhapsodies* of more or less the same character are Brahms (*Rhapsodies,* Op. 79, for piano), Enesco (*Rumanian Rhapsodies* for orchestra), Ravel (*Rapsodie espagnole* for orchestra). An exception, so far as style is concerned, is Brahms's *Alto Rhapsody,* a tightly constructed work for contralto solo, chorus, and orchestra.

RHEINBERGER (RINE bairr ger), **Joseph.** German composer, organist, and teacher, born in Vaduz, Liechtenstein, on March 17, 1839; died in Munich on November 25, 1901.

Rheinberger was a true child prodigy. He began lessons on the piano and organ and the study of theory when he was only five years old. By the time he was seven he was already the organist at the parish church in Vaduz. When he was eight, his first composition, a Mass, was performed. This aroused a great deal of interest in the boy, and he was given free tuition to live and study in Feldkirch when he was ten years old. During his two years there he walked ten miles every Sunday to Vaduz so he could keep his post as organist. He entered the Munich Conservatory when he was twelve, and when he left three years later he began a career of teaching that lasted for the rest of his life. He held a number of high posts, including that of Director of Court Church Music in Munich. Rheinberger's fame today rests chiefly on his numerous works for the organ, especially his twenty sonatas for that instrument. In addition to these and various other organ compositions, he composed four operas, incidental music for two plays, fourteen Masses, and an unusually long list of other choral music and part songs, a great many pieces for piano, songs, chamber music, orchestral works, and so on.

RHYTHM. Generally speaking, rhythm has to do with the lengths of tones and the way in which they are accented. Musical time is divided into regular intervals or pulses, which, when organized into measures* are called beats.* A waltz in 3/4 time has a steady beat of 1-2-3, 1-2-3; a march in 4/4 time has a steady beat of 1-2-3-4, 1-2-3-4. However, within the measures of a waltz or a march, notes of different values may be arranged according to any number of different rhythmic patterns. But no matter what the pattern within each measure, the measure itself retains the regular beats of the basic meter. Even when the length of time taken to play the notes in a measure (or group of measures) is changed by some such direction as *accelerando* (go faster) or *ritardando* (go slower), the basic beat of the measure is rarely more than slightly altered. There are innumerable possibilities for arranging notes into rhythmic patterns. The following examples show a few of them.

RHYTHM BAND. A group of players who perform together on percussion instruments of various kinds—drums, triangles, blocks, and so on.

Rhythm bands are popular in the lower grades of elementary schools for providing a rhythmic accompaniment for singing, dancing, marching, and games. They are especially good for learning about the different kinds of rhythm* and time* that are important in music.

RICERCAR (ree chair KAHR). An Italian word meaning "to search out." The ricercar was a type of contrapuntal* composition of the sixteenth and seventeenth centuries, usually written in imitative style. Most ricercars were written as studies for instrumental ensembles, although there were organ ricercars and vocal ricercars as well.

RIEGGER, Wallingford. American composer, born in Albany, Georgia, on April 29, 1885; died in New York City on April 2, 1961.

Riegger's family was musical, and the boy received his earliest musical training at home. When he was fifteen, the family moved to New York, where he began his formal study at the Institute of Musical Art. In 1907 he went to Berlin for further study at the Hochschule (highschool for music), and from 1915 to 1917 he conducted opera and a symphony orchestra in Germany. After his return to the United States, he held a series of teaching appointments in colleges and conservatories, and was awarded two important prizes for compositions: the Paderewski prize for his piano trio, and the Coolidge prize for his version of Keats's *La Belle Dame sans Merci.* He composed a number of works for such outstanding American dancers as Martha Graham, Charles Weidman, and Doris Humphries, and wrote five important choral works, three symphonies, several shorter orchestral works, chamber music, and a composition for organ and orchestra.

RIGADOON. The English spelling of the French word *Rigaudon,* a lively dance in 2/2 or 4/4 time that originated in Provence, a region in southern France, in the early part of the seventeenth century. It was usually in four parts, and was performed with a kind of jumping step. It became popular at the court of Louis XIII, and a little later in England. Towards the end of the seventeenth century it was used in the suite* and occasionally in the ballet* of the French opera.

RIMSKY-KORSAKOV (RIM skee KOR sah koff), **Nikolai.** Russian composer, born in Tikhvin on March 18, 1844; died in St. Petersburg (now Leningrad) on June 21, 1908.

Rimsky-Korsakov was born into a cultured and aristocratic family of Czarist Russia. He began taking piano lessons when he was six, and even attempted to write music when he was nine. However, his family did not feel that a career as a musician was what they wanted for their son, so they sent him to the Naval College in St. Petersburg. From that time until he retired from the service at the age of twenty-nine, he was connected in various ways with the Russian naval forces. Even so, he managed in the meantime to develop himself as a serious composer. He wrote a considerable amount of music (including a symphony while he was at sea), and kept fairly active in the musical life of Russia. Soon after his arrival in St. Petersburg he became associated with Balakirev,* and then with the group of Russian composers known as "The Five."* In 1871, two years before he resigned his post as a reserve officer, he was appointed professor of composition and orchestration at the St. Petersburg Conservatory. With the exception of a short period in 1905, when he was dismissed because of his sympathy with students who took part in the revolution of that year, he continued to teach at the Conservatory until his death.

Rimsky-Korsakov's more important works include fifteen operas, fifteen choral works, some fifteen orchestral works, including three symphonies, piano solos, concertos, chamber music, and songs. He is also noted for his textbook on orchestration which for years was considered a standard work in many schools.

RINFORZANDO (reen for TSAHN doh). An Italian word meaning "reinforce." It is a direction to increase the volume, or loudness, usually for a brief time. It is abbreviated as *rf., rinf.,* or *rfz.*

RITARDANDO (ree tar DAHN doh). An Italian word meaning "delay" or "retard." Ritardando indicates that the music is to become gradually slower. It is abbreviated as *rit.,* or *ritard.,* and has the same meaning as *rallentando.**

RITENUTO (ree tay NOO toh). An Italian word meaning "held back." It is a direction to hold back the speed. Although sometimes taken to mean the same as *ritardando,* many musicians think of *ritenuto* as a more precise and perhaps quicker process of slowing down.

ROCOCO (roh COH coh). A term borrowed from art history to indicate a period of music history, approximately from 1710 to 1775, when a kind of elegant and luxurious type of decoration was stylish. During that period, which bridged over from the Baroque* period to the Classical period, music, too, was characterized by a lightness and frivolity quite different from the seriousness of the Baroque. Some composers whose music is most typical of the Rococo style, sometimes called *style galant,* are Couperin,* and Telemann.* To a certain extent C. P. E. Bach,* Haydn,* and Mozart* in their earlier works, employed the style.

RODGERS, Richard. American composer, born in New York on June 28, 1902.

Rodgers studied first at Columbia University, then at the Institute of Musical Art in New York City. He had a remarkable gift for melody, and for eighteen years collaborated with Lorenz Hart in writing a large number of successful musical comedies. These include such hit shows as *On Your Toes, The Boys from Syracuse,* and *Pal Joey.* After Hart's death, Rodgers formed an equally successful partnership with Oscar Hammerstein. Together they wrote the enormously successful musical plays *Oklahoma, Carousel, South Pacific, The King and I, The Sound of Music,* and *Flower Drum Song,* as well as other shows. *South Pacific* won the Pulitzer Prize in drama for the authors in 1950.

ROGERS, Bernard. American composer, born in New York on February 4, 1893.

At first Rogers was interested in architecture, but he later turned to music. He studied at the Institute of Musical Art in New York, then with Ernest Bloch* in Cleveland. He won a Guggenheim Fellowship when he was twenty-four years old, making it possible for him to go to Europe for further study, first with Nadia Boulanger* in Paris, and then with Frank Bridge in London. Two years later he joined the staff of the Eastman School of Music in Rochester, New York. There he has remained as a teacher of composition and orchestration. His works include two operas, four choral works, four symphonies and several smaller orchestral works, a string quartet, three works for solo instruments and string orchestra, an oratorio, and a number of songs.

ROLL. An effect produced on the drum by alternating rapidly the strokes of the sticks. The effect is that of a continuous sound, something like a tremolo.*

ROMANCE. A rather short composition of a tender, sentimental nature without any definite form. Many Romances have been written for orchestra, for instruments with orchestra, and especially for voice. Some examples of pieces given the title *Romance* by great composers are Schumann's *Romance,* Op. 28, and Rubinstein's *Romance,* Op. 44, No. 1, both for piano; Beethoven's *Romance* for violin and orchestra, Op. 40; Brahms's *Romances from "Magelone"* for voice.

ROMANTIC PERIOD. A period that began near the first part of the nine-teenth century, when composers turned from the Classic* concept of music to a freer, more emotional kind of music. Some of the characteristics of Romantic music are: freedom from the strict forms of the great Classic writers, greater self-expression, use of more chromatic harmonies, employ-ment of visionary and even fantastic ideas, a concern for nationalism, development of fuller orchestral colors, and new rhythmic patterns. Some composers, as Beethoven and Schubert, stand at the crossroads between the Classical and Romantic eras. While most of their works bear a closer resemblance to the Classic, their middle and later works show strong Romantic tendencies. Some of the leading composers who can be definitely classified as Romantic are Chopin, Mendelssohn, Schumann, Berlioz, Liszt, Wagner, Brahms, Fauré, Dvořák, Smetana, and Tchaikovsky.

ROMBERG, Sigmund. Hungarian-American composer, born in Szeged, Hungary, on July 29, 1887; died in New York on November 9, 1951.

Romberg was interested in music and studied it to some extent while he was growing up. It was more or less a hobby with him, however, for he studied to be an engineer, specializing in the building of bridges. It was not until he came to the United States in 1909 that he switched to music as a career. He began by playing the piano in several orchestras, then in 1913 wrote the music for his first show, *Whirl of the World.* From that time on he devoted himself to writing operettas. In all, he wrote more than seventy, many of them becoming great hits. Among his most famous were *Blossom Time, The Student Prince, The Desert Song, The New Moon,* and *Up in Central Park.*

RONDO (RON doh). An Italian word meaning "round." The rondo is a musical form that developed from the French rondeau of the seventeenth century, and was often used by composers of the Classical period as the final movement of the sonata, the string quartet, the concerto, and the symphony. The rondo is characterized by the alternation of a principal theme, which recurs several times throughout the piece, and a section of independent material. Rondos have also been written as separate pieces. (See also *Form.*)

ROOT. The lowest note of a triad or chord. In the triad C-E-G, for example, the root is C. When the root tone is at the bottom, a chord is said to be in "root position." If any other note of the chord is at the bottom, the chord is in one of the inversions.* (See also *Chords.*)

ROREM, Ned. American composer, born in Richmond, Indiana, on October 23, 1923.

Rorem studied music in Chicago, and when he was nineteen won a scholarship for further study at the Curtis Institute of Music in Philadelphia. He later studied at the Juilliard School of Music in New York, and privately with Aaron Copland* and Virgil Thomson.* In 1951 he was awarded a Fulbright Fellowship which enabled him to study and live in Paris for four years. Since his return to the United States in 1955 he has lived and worked as a composer, mainly in New York City. His compositions include two operas, two symphonies, two piano concertos, concertos for various instruments, chamber music, and songs.

ROSSINI (roh SEE nee), **Gioacchino.** Italian composer, born in Pesaro on February 29, 1792; died in Paris on November 13, 1868.

When Rossini was only four years old, his father was sent to jail for political reasons and his mother took him to Bologna, where she found work as an opera singer. His father was a musician, and when he was released from jail he found work as a horn player in the orchestras of the opera houses where his wife was singing. When they traveled, they left their little son with a friend in Bologna, where he received his first musical training. Rossini quickly learned how to read music and to play the harpsichord* well enough to play accompaniments. By the time he was ten years old he was able to add to the family income by singing solos at church. At thirteen he was singing in the theatre, playing horn alongside his father, and doing some accompanying. He continued to study singing, took lessons in counterpoint,* and learned to play the cello. By the time he was fifteen he had already written some little songs, some pieces for horns, and even an opera. He continued to write music, and gradually began to make a name for himself as a composer. His first big success came in 1813 when his opera *Tancredi* was produced in Venice. Three years later the opera that is generally considered his masterpiece, *The Barber of Seville,* was presented in Rome. Although *The Barber* was not well received at first, it gradually found favor and has become one of the most popular operas ever written. After he wrote *The Barber,* Rossini became more and more famous. He was entertained by royalty in London, was given an appointment as Director of the Italian Theater in Paris, and eventually two honorary appointments that gave him a substantial income. In all, Rossini wrote forty operas. The best known are *The Barber of Seville, La Cenerentola, Semiramide, Le Comte Ory,* and *William Tell.* His other works include six woodwind quartets, cantatas, piano pieces, and songs.

ROUND. A popular type of canon,* which, because of its peculiar construction, can be repeated indefinitely. "Three Blind Mice" is a familiar example of a round.

RUBATO (roo BAH toh). An Italian word meaning "robbed." It is a musical term that is generally used to indicate a certain freedom in matters of tempo and rhythm. In singing or playing a rubato passage, the performer may "rob" certain notes of their proper length by playing them a little faster or add to their length by playing them a little slower. Or he may accent notes that would not normally be accented. Very often these liberties apply only to the melody, while the accompaniment is kept strictly to the normal beat. The slowing and quickening of the tempo (rubato) is especially noticeable in the kind of Viennese waltzes that Johann Strauss wrote. Some of Chopin's nocturnes and mazurkas call for rubato, as do the works of some even earlier composers.

RUBINSTEIN (ROO bin stine), **Anton.** Russian composer and pianist, born in Vykhvatinets on November 28, 1829; died in Peterhof on November 20, 1894.

Rubinstein began to take piano lessons with his mother. He showed exceptional talent, and soon went to Moscow to study. He gave his first public performances there when he was nine years old. His teacher took him to Paris when he was ten, and while he was there he performed for both Chopin and Liszt. From that time on he toured extensively, except for the periods when he taught or studied composition. He was only eighteen when the Grand Duchess of Russia appointed him Chamber Virtuoso. His fame both as a pianist and a composer spread throughout Europe and America. As a pianist he is said to have had only one rival, Liszt.* He had a marvelous technique and tremendous power, yet he played with great feeling. As a composer, he enjoyed great popularity during his lifetime, although his music is more German in style than Russian. As a teacher he made a great contribution. He founded the St. Petersburg Conservatory in 1862 and was its director from that time until 1867, and again from 1887 to 1890. He wrote many works, including some twenty operas and oratorios, nine choral works, six symphonies, ten smaller works for orchestra, five piano concertos and other works for solo instruments and orchestra, chamber music, a great many piano solos, duets, vocal solos, and vocal duets.

RUGGLES, Carl. American composer, born in Marion, Massachusetts, on March 11, 1876.

By the time Ruggles entered Harvard University he had already studied music for some time, and there he continued with Walter Spaulding and J. K. Paine,* both outstanding teachers. He founded the Winona Symphony Orchestra in Minneapolis in 1912, and for several years was its conductor. In 1937 he joined the faculty of the University of Miami, Florida, but by that time he had practically given up composing and had turned to painting. Although he had written a number of works, he did not allow many of them to be published or performed because he felt they were not good enough. Those that he did publish were atonal* and highly dissonant. They include a string suite, *Angel*; a choral work, *Vox clamans in deserto*; four orchestral works; and a composition for three pianos called *Polyphonic Composition*.

S

SACHS (ZAHX), **Hans.** German poet and musician, born in Nuremberg on November 5, 1494; died there on January 19, 1576.

Although Sachs was a shoemaker by trade, he was also the most famous of the Mastersingers.* He wrote a great many works, including some 4,000 poems, more than 200 dramatic poems, and a number of songs. Richard Wagner* immortalized him in his opera *Die Meistersinger von Nürnberg* (The Mastersingers of Nuremberg).

SACKBUT. English name for an instrument of the sixteenth and seventeenth centuries that was the ancestor of the modern trombone. The name is derived from an old French word, *saquier-boter,* which means "pull, push."

SAINT-SAENS (san SAHNS), **Camille.** French composer, organist, and pianist, born in Paris on October 9, 1835; died in Algiers, on December 16, 1921.

Saint-Saens received his first music lessons from his mother and from a great-aunt. By the time he was nine he had shown so much talent that his mother arranged for him to study piano and harmony with two well-known teachers. A year later he appeared in public as accompanist for a violinist who played the Beethoven violin sonatas. He was just twelve years old when he played his first piano recital, and fourteen when he was admitted to the Paris Conservatory. In the meantime he had already begun to compose, and at the age of eighteen he heard his own first symphony played. With the exception of four years spent as a professor of piano at the École Niedermeyer, he devoted the rest of his life to playing and composing. He enjoyed a successful career as a concert pianist, often playing his own works. All his life he worked to promote the music of young, unknown composers, and he fought valiantly for all that was modern and progressive in French music, even though his own music was quite conservative and "old-fashioned."

Saint-Saens wrote a large number of works. They include thirteen operas; incidental music for eight plays; a ballet; eleven religious works; about thirty secular choral works; eighteen works for orchestra, including three symphonies; twenty-four pieces for solo instruments and orchestra; nearly a hundred songs; and numerous other compositions. However, only a handful of his works are performed to any extent today. The most famous of these are the opera *Samson and Dalila,* which is performed frequently in many of the great opera houses of the world, and the suite, *Carnival of the Animals.*

SALTANDO (sahl TAHN doh). An Italian word that means "skipping" or "jumping." Saltando is a direction to players of bowed instruments to bounce the bow lightly on the strings.

SALTARELLO (sahl tah RELL oh). A word taken from the Italian *saltare,* which means "to jump." It is a lively dance that probably originated in the sixteenth century. It begins moderately and increases in speed until the end. The dancers constantly change steps and dance with a quite violent jumping motion. Mendelssohn wrote a saltarello as the final movement of his Symphony No. 4.

SALZEDO (sahl ZAY doh), **Carlos.** French-born American harpist, composer, and conductor, born in Arcachon on April 6, 1885.

Salzedo studied first at the Conservatory of Bordeaux, then attended the Paris Conservatory, graduating at the age of sixteen with first prizes in both harp and piano. After touring with great success in Europe and America, he settled in New York in 1909 and became first harpist of the Metropolitan Opera Orchestra. He helped to found the International Composers Guild, and has taught at the Juilliard School of Music and at the Curtis Institute in Philadelphia. In addition to many works for harp, he has written an important book on harp playing, *Modern Study of the Harp.*

SAMISEN (SHAM ee sen). A Japanese stringed instrument shaped something like a spade. It has three strings stretched over a skin belly and a long

neck. The strings are plucked with a plectrum.* The instrument is popular in Japan and corresponds somewhat to the guitar of Western countries.

SANCTUS (SAHNK toos). A Latin word meaning "holy." It is the name of the fourth part of the Mass in the Roman Catholic liturgy and one of the parts of the Communion Service in the Anglican and Episcopal churches. (See also *Mass.*)

SARABAND. A rather slow dance in 3/2 or 3/4 time that was popular in Spain during the sixteenth century, then spread to France and England. It became a standard part of the Baroque suite* along with the allemande,* courante,* and gigue.*

SARASATE (sah rah SAH tay), **Pablo.** Spanish violinist and composer, born in Pamplona on March 10, 1844; died in Biarritz on September 20, 1908.

Sarasate was highly gifted as a child. When he was ten years old he performed before Queen Isabella II of Spain. She was so delighted with his playing that she gave him a fine Stradivarius violin. When he was twelve he entered the Paris Conservatory, and three years later graduated with honors. He then toured Europe and North and South America with enormous success. Several well-known composers wrote violin works especially for him, and he himself wrote a great deal of music for his instrument, and made many transcriptions of Spanish dances. Among his best-known pieces for violin are *Zigeunerweisen, Jota Argonesa,* and his *Spanish Dances*

S.A.T.B. Abbreviation for *soprano, alto, tenor, and bass.* It is used most often in referring to part songs and choral music written for that combination of voices.

SATIE (sah TEE), **Erik.** French composer, born in Honfleur on May 17, 1866; died in Paris on July 1, 1925.

All his life Satie was a most unconventional person. He was extremely talented musically and was admitted to the Paris Conservatory when he was thirteen years old. However, he did not get along with his teachers and stayed for only a year. He continued to experiment with composition, however, and succeeded in having his first pieces for piano published in 1887. He enjoyed the friendship of artists and musicians and was attracted to the Bohemian atmospheres of Montmartre, where he worked part time as a cafe pianist. He was twenty-four when he met Debussy,* a composer who influenced young Satie greatly and who remained a close friend for most of Satie's life. He was forty years old when he decided to study music seriously once again. He entered the Schola Cantorum and there studied counterpoint under d'Indy* and Roussel. He was awarded a diploma, and from that time on he was taken more seriously as a composer. He wrote many works, but they did not appeal greatly to the public of his day, and are seldom played today. He did, however, exert a great deal of influence on other composers, then and later. Some of his devices and discoveries were utilized by such composers as Milhaud,* Stravinsky,* and Poulenc.*

SAUTILLÉ (soh tee YAY). A French word meaning "skipping" or "jumping about." Sautillé is a direction to players of stringed instruments to bounce the bow on the strings by using short strokes in rapid succession. (See also *Bowing*.)

SAXHORN. Any one of a family of valved brass instruments patented by Adolphe (real name Antoine Joseph) Sax of Paris in 1845. Saxhorns, which are rarely used except in military and brass bands, have conical bores and moderately flared bells. They range in size from the large contrabass in E-flat to the small soprano saxhorn in high E-flat. In France any instrument of the family is called a saxhorn. But in other countries they are called by such names as flügelhorn,* euphonium,* baritone,* bass saxhorn, saxtuba, and so on. (See also *Saxophone*.)

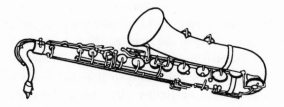

SAXOPHONE. Any one of a family of instruments invented by Adolphe (real name Antoine Joseph) Sax and patented by him in 1846. The saxophone is made of metal, has a single reed, and a conical bore. There are six kinds: sopranino in E-flat, soprano in B-flat, alto in E-flat, tenor in B-flat, baritone in E-flat, and bass in B-flat. Saxophones are used mainly in dance bands and in military and brass bands, although occasionally they are called for in symphonic or operatic scores, most often by French composers.

SCALE. A definite arrangement of notes in ascending and descending order. There are many different kinds of scales that are used in musical composition in many different ways. Certain scales are used also as exercises to develop facility in playing the piano and other instruments and in singing. (For examples of scales, see the individual entries: *Major-Minor, Chromatic, Pentatonic, Whole-Tone*. See also *Modes*.)

SCARLATTI (skar LAH tee), **Alessandro.** Italian composer, born in Palermo on May 2, 1660; died in Naples on October 24, 1725.

Alessandro Scarlatti is remembered today chiefly for his influence on the development of opera, having written some 115. He also wrote 150 oratorios, around 600 cantatas, church music, chamber music, and many pieces for piano.

SCARLATTI (skar LAH tee), **Domenico.** Italian composer, born in Naples on October 26, 1685; died in Madrid, Spain, on July 23, 1757.

Domenico was the son of the famous opera composer, Alessandro Scarlatti. He took his first music lessons with his father, and later studied with Gasparini and Pasquini. He was sixteen years old when he became organist in the same royal chapel where his father was choir master. Two years later his first two operas were produced in Naples. He wrote eight operas for the private theater of the Queen of Poland in Rome, where he served also as music director of St. Peter's. In 1720 he was named master of the Royal Chapel in Lisbon, Portugal, where one of his pupils was the Princess Maria Barbara. When she married the heir to the Spanish throne in 1729, she took Domenico with her to Madrid. There he remained for the rest of his life, with only brief trips to Italy to see his father, and on one occasion to bring back an Italian wife. When Maria Barbara became Queen of Spain in 1746 she named Domenico her *maestro de camara* (that is, head musician of the court). And when he died, leaving his family in bad financial shape, the Queen settled a pension on his wife and children. Domenico Scarlatti is remembered today largely for his remarkable harpsichord works, of which there are nearly six hundred. These sonatas are excellent not only for developing technical facility in piano and harpsichord students, but also because they are in most cases beautiful enough to be used as recital pieces. In addition to his operas and keyboard works, Scarlatti wrote several cantatas, oratorios, arias, Masses, a *Stabat Mater,* and other church music.

SCHARWENKA (shar VEN kah), **Ludwig Philipp.** German-Polish composer, born in Szamotuly on February 16, 1847; died in Bad Nauheim on July 16, 1917.

Scharwenka was very talented as a child, but he had little opportunity to develop his talent until he moved to Berlin and entered Kullak's Academy when he was almost eighteen years old. He did so well there, however, that he was given an appointment on the school's staff as an instructor in theory when he graduated. When his brother Xaver, a well-known pianist and composer, opened his own conservatory in 1881, Scharwenka went there to teach composition. And when his brother emigrated to the United States ten years later, he became Director. He wrote a great many works including an opera, two symphonies, numerous works for orchestra, violin pieces and concertos, chamber music, songs, and many sonatas and pieces for piano.

SCHELLING, Ernest. American pianist, composer, and conductor, born in Belvidere, New Jersey, on July 26, 1876; died in New York on December 8, 1939.

Schelling was a child prodigy who played his first public recital in Philadelphia at the age of four-and-a-half. He was still a child when he was sent to Paris, France, to study with Mathias. He later studied with Moszkowski,* Leschetizky, Huber, Barth, and Paderewski.* He was just sixteen when he started a three-year concert tour that took him throughout Europe and South America. In 1905 he returned to America, where he remained for the rest of his life.

Schelling became noted for his conducting of symphony concerts for children. His compositions include a symphony, a violin concerto, a suite for piano and orchestra, several shorter orchestral works, and piano solos.

SCHERZO (SKEHRT soh). An Italian word meaning "joke." The title was first used in the seventeenth century in Italy for some instrumental compositions and songs. After about 1750 it was used more and more often as a movement in a suite,* sonata,* or symphony.* In many cases the scherzo takes the place of the minuet.* It is generally in fast 3/4 or 3/8 time. Some composers, including Chopin, have written scherzos as separate pieces.

SCHOENBERG (SHERN bairg), **Arnold.** Austrian (naturalized American) composer, born in Vienna on September 13, 1874; died in Los Angeles, California, on July 13, 1951.

Schoenberg began to study the violin when he was eight years old. He had very little formal training in music, but he began to compose while he was still young. He studied counterpoint for a while with Alexander von Zemlinsky, and the two became good friends. In fact, Schoenberg married Zemlinsky's sister Mathilde. After his father's death, Schoenberg was forced to make a living by working in a bank; but in his spare time he continued to compose, and by 1900 his works had already begun to bring him some attention. He moved to Berlin, hoping to find more congenial work, but two years later he returned to Vienna and launched on a career of teaching and composing. Two of his most famous pupils were Alban Berg* and Anton Webern.* Gradually, Schoenberg began to develop a new style in music writing. He depended less and less on the traditional use of tonality (writing in definite keys), and eventually presented the world with twelve-tone* music. World War I interrupted his work, but after the armistice he took up teaching again and founded in Vienna an organization devoted to the performance of modern and contemporary works. His own works began to attract considerable attention and were given performances in a number of important musical centers. Because of his Jewish ancestry, he was forced by the Nazis to leave Germany, where he had been made a professor in the Prussian Academy of Fine Arts, and in 1933 he went first to Paris, then to the United States. He settled in California, became an American citizen in 1941, and taught and composed until the end of his life. Among his most important works are: *Erwartung,* a monodrama for solo voice and orchestra; *Gurrelieder,* a big choral work for solo voices and orchestra; *Transfigured Night,* for string orchestra; *Pelleas and Melisande,* a symphonic poem; *Ode to Napoleon,* for speaker, string orchestra, and piano; *Pierrot lunaire,* calling for "speech-song" and chamber instruments; a violin concerto; and a piano concerto. He also wrote two chamber symphonies, four string quartets, songs, and piano pieces. His opera *Moses and Aron* was unfinished at his death, but the two completed acts have been performed.

SCHOTTISCHE (SHOT ish eh). A German word meaning "Scottish." The schottische is a round dance something like the polka.* It was popular during the nineteenth century in England, where it was called "German Polka."

SCHUBERT (SHOO bert), **Franz.** Austrian composer, born in Vienna on January 31, 1797; died there on November 19, 1828.

Schubert was the son of a schoolmaster who was also an amateur musician. He taught his son violin and an older brother Ignaz gave him piano lessons. He soon learned all that his father and his brother could teach him, and was then sent to Holzer, the parish organist, for lessons. Holzer soon found that he had a young genius on his hands. The boy seemed to know everything before he had a chance to teach him. In 1808, at the age of eleven, he became a member of the choir in the chapel of the Imperial Court, where he remained for five years, living at the Imperial School, studying music and other subjects, and singing in the choir. He also played first violin in the school orchestra. When his voice broke, he left the school, took a course in teacher-training, and began to teach in his father's school. During this time he proceeded to compose at a rapid rate. Even before he left the choir school he had composed a symphony, and during the two years that he was teaching he wrote a Mass and no less than 115 songs, sometimes as many as eight in a single day. With the exception of two summers when he served as a music teacher in the family of Count Esterházy at Zelesz, Hungary, Schubert spent his entire life in Vienna. His friends and his brother helped him as much as they could, and occasionally he was lucky enough to make a small sum of money from the publication of his songs. But most of the time he suffered greatly from poverty. His attempts to find dignified work almost always came to nothing, his teaching brought him very little, and his publishers cheated him. When he died at the early age of thirty-one, all his possessions were valued at only about $7.00. In spite of his misery, he managed to write an enormous number of works. Although his formal training was severely limited, he is generally considered the greatest song writer of all times. A total of 634 of his songs have been preserved, and it is probable that many were lost or destroyed. He set his songs to the finest German poetry of his time, and the accompaniments he wrote for them are as beautiful and artistically composed as the songs themselves. In addition to songs, he wrote several operatic works; thirty-four religious works, including seven Masses; a large number of secular choral works; about twenty-five works for orchestra, including the great C major symphony and the "Unfinished" symphony; fifteen string quartets and numerous other chamber works; eight pieces for violin and piano; many sonatas and other works for piano, and a number of piano duets.

SCHULLER, Gunther. American composer and horn player, born in New York City on November 22, 1925.

Schuller's father was a violinist, and Gunther was exposed to a great deal of music as a young child. He did not become especially interested in music, however, until he became a choir boy at St. Thomas' Church when he was twelve years old. He first studied flute at the Choir School, but when he was fourteen he switched to the French horn and became so proficient on that instrument that he was soon playing professionally. In 1943 he joined the Cincinnati Symphony Orchestra as solo horn player, and in 1945 played his own *Horn Concerto* with the orchestra. Although Schuller had written a number of compositions more or less in traditional form, he became interested in the 12-tone technique about 1945, and since then has written works derived partly from that technique but reflecting his own individual style as well. Schuller has been active also in jazz circles, playing in a jazz combo and teaching jazz. Among his more important works are: *Concerto* for Cello and Orchestra; *Contours,* for orchestra; an orchestral piece called *Atonal Jazz Study*; *Suite for Chamber Orchestra*; *Concertina* for Jazz Quartet; a string quartet and other chamber works; pieces for voice; *12 by 11* for chamber orchestra and jazz improvisation; and a work for dancer, violin, piano, and percussion called *Symbiosis*.

SCHUMAN, William. American composer, born in New York on August 4, 1910.

After attending the Malkin Conservatory in New York, Schuman studied at Columbia University, earning the Bachelor's and then the Master's degrees. In 1935 he went to Salzburg, Austria, where he attended the Mozarteum. Returning to the United States, he began his long and eminent career as a teacher and administrator. He has taught at Sarah Lawrence College and Columbia University, was President of the Juilliard School of Music from 1945 to 1963, and since then has been Director of the

Lincoln Center for the Performing Arts in New York. Among the many awards and prizes he has won are: Guggenheim Fellowships in 1939 and 1940; first award of the Critics Circle of New York for his Symphony No. 3 in 1942; Pulitzer Prize for *A Free Song* in 1943; Koussevitsky Music Foundation Award; Metropolitan Opera grant; composition award from the American Academy of Arts and Letters. His compositions, which have been performed by the leading musical organizations in America, include: an opera, *The Mighty Casey*; three ballets; several choral works; six symphonies and other works for orchestra; a piano concerto; a violin concerto; three string quartets; and chamber music.

SCHUMANN, Robert. German composer, born in Zwickau on June 8, 1810; died in Endenich, near Bonn, on July 29, 1856.

Schumann's first piano lessons were with the organist of the Marienkirche in Zwickau. His father was an editor and book dealer, and he encouraged his son along literary as well as musical lines. After graduating from the *gymnasium* (grammar school) in Zwickau, he was sent to the Leipzig University to study law. From Leipzig he went to Heidelberg, attracted by a Professor Thibaut who not only taught law but happened also to be a fine musician. Schumann began to devote himself more seriously to the study of music, and in 1830 he returned to Leipzig to study piano with Freidrich Wieck, whose daughter Clara he married ten years later. Schumann worked hard at developing his piano-playing technique, with the idea of becoming a piano virtuoso. However, in working with a device of his own to strengthen the fourth finger of his right hand, he injured the hand so badly that he had to give up all thought of becoming a concert pianist. From that time on he devoted himself to composition and literary work. With three friends he founded an important magazine devoted to music, *Neue Zeitschrift für Musik,* and for a number of years was its editor. Schumann was thirty years old when he married Clara Wieck, a fine pianist who became the most celebrated interpreter of his compositions for piano. Up to that time he had written only for the piano. Now he began to write songs, and in the year 1840 alone wrote some 120. In 1843, at the request of Mendelssohn,* he was named instructor in piano, composition, and score-reading at the new Leipzig Conservatory. A year later he accompanied his wife on a highly successful concert tour of Russia, then moved to Dresden. In 1850 they moved to Düsseldorf, where he became town musical director. Three years later he had to resign from that post because of increasing insanity. Not long afterward he tried to end his life by jumping into the Rhine River. He was rescued, but had to be placed in an asylum at Endenich. There he spent his remaining days, never regaining his sanity.

Schumann's works include: an opera, *Genoveva*; some choral works with orchestra; four symphonies and other orchestral works; a piano concerto, which has become one of the most popular ever written; chamber music, of which his piano quintet is outstanding; an enormous number of piano solos; a great many vocal duets, trios, quartets, and various part-songs; and finally, his songs, which fill three volumes and include several great cycles and groups. Among these are his most famous song cycles, *Dichterliebe, Frauen-Liebe und Leben, Liederkreis*, Op. 24 and 39, and *Myrten*.

SCHÜTZ, Heinrich. German composer, born in Köstritz on October 8, 1585; died in Dresden on November 6, 1672.

When Schütz was fourteen years old he became a chorister at the Court Chapel in Cassel. There he was given a good general education as well as excellent training in music, and in 1607 he entered Marburg University to study law. The Landgrave of the Court became impressed with the boy's musical talent and made it possible for him to go to Venice, where he studied with the great Giovanni Gabrieli.* During his stay then and at later dates Schütz became deeply interested in Italian music. In fact, his first published compositions were Italian madrigals. In 1613 he became Court Organist in Cassel, and four years later was made *Kapellmeister** to the Electoral Court in Dresden. With the exception of several lengthy visits to Copenhagen, and a short return to Venice, Schütz spent most of the remaining years of his life in Dresden, where he worked as Court Composer. His many works, in addition to the Italian madrigals, include the first German opera, *Daphne*; a number of "Sacred Symphonies," and other compositions for voices and instruments; four Passions, and a Christmas Oratorio. Schütz's fame rests largely on the great influence he brought to bear on German music through his introduction of Italian musical ideas.

SCORDATURA (skorr dah TOO rah). An Italian word meaning "mis-tuned." It refers to the tuning of stringed instruments in some way other than normal. It was used often in the seventeenth century for the lute,* lute music indicating at the beginning just how the instrument should be tuned for playing a particular composition. *Scordatura* was used sometimes for the violin and the cello. The purpose usually was to make it easier to play in certain keys. Modern composers have sometimes indicated *scordatura* to obtain certain effects. An example is Mahler's Symphony No. 4 in which the solo violinist is required to tune his violin up one whole tone to achieve an "unearthly" sound of a dance of death.

SCORE. Notes written on a number of staffs* in such a way that all the notes sung or played at the same time are aligned vertically, with the bar lines running through all the staffs, or through the staffs that are used for related groups of instruments (sometimes called *choirs*). The three most commonly used types of scores are (1) the full score, used by the conductor, and showing all of the voice and instrumental parts, (2) the vocal score, which shows all of the voice parts but with the orchestral parts transcribed for piano, (3) the piano score, in which the entire orchestral or choral composition has been transcribed or arranged for the piano.

In the case of most large works for orchestras and choruses, the general practice is for each player or singer to have a sheet of music with his own part only, and for the conductor to have a full score that shows all the parts.

SCOTT, Cyril. English composer, born in Oxton, Cheshire, on September 27, 1879.

By the time Scott was seven years old he had already learned how to write musical notes and had made some attempts at composing. His family recognized his unusual talent and sent him to Hoch's Conservatory at Frankfurt-am-Main in Germany when he was twelve. He returned to England and studied for a while in Liverpool, but then returned once again to Frankfurt. He was just nineteen when he began his career of teaching and composing in Liverpool. Soon major works of his were heard in England and on the Continent and he became something of a celebrity. He toured the United States as a pianist and lecturer in 1921. For a long time he had been interested in Oriental philosophy and theosophy, and this interest influenced his works. He developed a highly personalized style, a kind of mysticism in his works that gave them a certain exotic feeling. Among his compositions are three operas, a ballet, some choral music, several orchestral pieces and concertos, and long lists of piano solos and songs.

SCRIABIN (skree YAH bin), **Alexander.** Russian composer and pianist, born in Moscow on January 6, 1872; died there on April 27, 1915.

Scriabin's mother died when he was a very young child, and he received his first music lessons from an aunt. He then studied piano and composition with private teachers, and when he was sixteen he entered the Moscow Conservatory. He graduated with a gold medal in piano. Except for five years when he taught piano at the Conservatory, he devoted his life to composing and concertizing. He toured widely and composed many of his works while he was in foreign countries. Scriabin developed a style that was uniquely his own. His works created a sensation during his lifetime, but they are seldom performed today. They include three symphonies, other works for orchestra, a piano concerto, and numerous pieces for piano.

SECOND. (1) Any interval made up of notes that have adjacent letter names, as C to D, A to B, F to G, and so on. A *minor second* consists of a half step, as D to E-flat or E to F; a *major second* consists of a whole step, as C to D or E to F-sharp; an augmented second consists of a whole plus a half step, as C to D-sharp, E-flat to F-sharp, or B to C double-sharp. (2) When used as an adjective, second usually refers to an instrument or voice that is pitched lower or plays or sings a lower part, as second violin, second tenor, etc. The word may also mean that the players or singers called second do not have quite as high a rank in the organization as the firsts.

SECONDO (seh KON doh). An Italian word meaning "second." In piano duet music, it means the lower of the two parts.

SEGNO (SAYN yoh). An Italian word meaning "sign." The expression *dal segno* indicates that the performer is to go back to the sign (usually 𝄋) and repeat from there. The abbreviation for *dal segno* is D. S.

SEGUE (SAY gway). An Italian word meaning "follows." It indicates that the performer is to begin the following movement or section of a piece without a pause.

SEGUIDILLA (say gee DEEL yah). A Spanish dance in fast 3/4 or 3/8 time. It is often accompanied by guitars and castanets, and the players sing *coplas* (couplets), which are verses of four short lines. Examples of seguidillas based on the folk dance are De Falla's *Sequidilla Murciana,* transcribed for voice and piano in his *Siete Canciones Populares* (Seven Popular Songs), and the seguidilla in the first act of Bizet's *Carmen*.

SEMIBREVE. The English name for the whole note (o). The semibreve rest is the same as the whole rest (▬).

SEMIQUAVER. The English name for the sixteenth note (♪). The semiquaver rest is the same as the sixteenth rest (♯).

SEMITONE. Same as half-tone. (See *Intervals*.)

SEMPRE (SEM pray). An Italian word meaning "always" or "continuing." It is used with other terms, as *sempre piano,* (to continue softly), *sempre forte,* (continue playing loud), and so on.

SENZA (SENT sah). An Italian word meaning "without." It occurs in such phrases as *senza rall,* (without slowing down), *senza sordini* (without the mute), and so on.

SEPTET. A musical work for seven voices or seven instruments. Beethoven wrote a Septet, Op. 20, for violin, viola, cello, double bass, clarinet, bassoon, and horn. Ravel,* Saint-Saens,* and Schoenberg* have written septets for various combinations of instruments. A famous vocal septet occurs at the end of the second act finale in Mozart's *The Marriage of Figaro*. It calls for three sopranos, a tenor, two baritones, and a bass.

SEQUENCE. A musical phrase that is repeated at a higher or lower pitch level. If the repeated phrase consists of melody alone, it is called a *melodic sequence*. If the repeated phrase consists of the melody and its harmony, it is called a *harmonic sequence*. If the repeated phrase is made up of intervals that are exactly the same as the original, it is a *real sequence*. If the intervals are altered slightly, so as to remain in the same key, it is called a *tonal sequence*.

SERENADE. Properly speaking, a serenade is music to be played or sung in the evening, as a serenade sung by a young man to his sweetheart as he stands beneath her window. An example of this type of serenade is the song "Deh vieni alla finestra" from Mozart's *Don Giovanni*. However, the title *Serenade* has been used for many different kinds of musical compositions, usually of a rather light and romantic type. Mozart, Beethoven, and Brahms all wrote serenades, mostly for small orchestras or chamber groups.

SERIAL MUSIC. (See *Twelve-Tone System.*)

SERPENT. An obsolete instrument used in churches and in military bands up to about 1850. It belonged to the cornet* family, was made of wood, and was played by blowing through a mouthpiece of ivory or horn. Its name derived from its serpent-like shape.

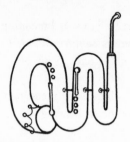

SESSIONS, Roger. American composer and educator, born in Brooklyn, New York, on December 28, 1896.

Sessions began to study music when he was very young, and by the time he was thirteen he had already written an opera. He entered Harvard University when he was fourteen, graduated with a Bachelor of Arts degree in 1915, then went to Yale University, where he studied with Horatio Parker. After earning a Bachelor of Music degree in 1917, he accepted a teaching appointment at Smith College and continued his music study with Ernest Bloch.* In 1921 he was made assistant to Bloch in the Cleveland Institute of Music. Between 1925 and 1933 he studied and worked in Europe, and when he returned to the United States he again became a teacher; first, at the University of California, and since 1952 at Princeton University.

Sessions' music is advanced in style, atonal, relatively contrapuntal, and difficult to perform. For this reason, it is not often heard. His works include an opera, *The Trial of Lucullus*; four symphonies; two piano sonatas; two string quartets; a piano concerto; and a violin concerto.

SEVENTH. An interval consisting of the lowest and highest of any seven consecutive notes in the diatonic scale. The following examples show the three sevenths possible when the lowest note is C. (See also *Intervals, Chords, Harmony.*)

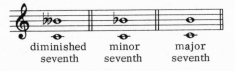

diminished   minor   major
seventh   seventh   seventh

SEXTET. A musical work for six voices or for six instruments. String sextets have been written by many composers, including Brahms, Dvořák, Schoenberg, and Tchaikovsky. The usual combination in a string sextet is two violins, two violas, and two cellos, as in Brahms' Sextet, Op. 36. Beethoven wrote a wind sextet, Op. 71, for two clarinets, two bassoons, and two horns. Probably the most famous sextet for voices is the "Sextet" from Donizetti's opera, *Lucia di Lammermoor.*

SEXTUPLET. A group of six notes to be played in the time of four notes. They may be written in any one of these ways:

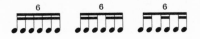

SFORZANDO (sfort SAHN doh). An Italian word meaning "forceful." A note or chord marked *sforzando* should be strongly accented. It is usually abbreviated *sf* or *sfz*. If the *sf* is followed by *p* (piano), the strongly accented note or chord should be followed by a sudden softening of the tones.

SHAKE. The old English name for the trill.*

SHANTY. (Sometimes spelled *chanty* or *chantey*.) The name given to sea songs, usually the work songs of English and American sailors. Sea shantys were almost always sung while the sailors were doing heavy work, seldom just for pleasure. Two famous shantys are *Blow the Man Down* and *Shenandoah.* Some collections of sea shantys date back to Elizabethan times.

SHARP. (1) The sign (♯) placed before a note to indicate that the note is to be raised by one half-step. If the sign is in the key signature,* every note on that pitch in any octave throughout the piece is to be raised a half step, unless another sign cancels or changes it. If the sign is before a single note, only that note and repetitions of the note (on the same line or space) within the measure are to be raised a half step. A double sharp (**✗**) indicates a note should be raised two half steps (one whole step). (2) The term is also used to describe a tone that is above its correct pitch, or a kind of singing or playing of an instrument that is consistently above normal pitch.

SHOFAR. (Sometimes spelled *shophar.*) An instrument made of a ram's horn. The shofar has been used for over three thousand years in Jewish synagogues to sound the beginning of the New Year. When blown into, the instrument produces two notes about a fifth* apart.

SHOSTAKOVICH (shaw sta KOH vitch), **Dmitri.** Russian composer, born in St. Petersburg (now Leningrad) on September 25, 1906.

Shostakovich showed a good deal of talent for composition while he was still very young. He wrote a scherzo* for orchestra when he was thirteen, and upon his graduation from the Leningrad Conservatory at the age of nineteen he wrote his first symphony, which was performed in Leningrad a year later. The symphony became an immediate success in Russia, and soon in other countries as well. Shostakovich's works include two operas, a ballet, twelve symphonies, a piano concerto, twenty-four preludes for piano, twenty-four preludes and fugues for piano, a cello sonata, a piano quintet, and three string quartets. He has also written a good deal of incidental music for plays and music for films.

SI. (See *Ti.*)

SIBELIUS (see BAY lee us), **Jean.** Finnish composer, born in Tavastehus on December 8, 1865; died in Järvenpää on September 20, 1957.

Sibelius, a son of an army surgeon, started piano lessons when he was nine, and violin lessons when he was fourteen. He entered the University of Helsinki with the idea of studying law, but he soon decided that music was the field in which he was most interested. After only one semester he transferred to the Conservatory, where he studied violin and composition.

He made rapid progress and exhibited such talent for composition that he was soon awarded a grant from the Finnish Government to study in Berlin and Vienna. Although he was only twenty-eight when he returned to Finland, he already had composed a number of large works and was recognized as an outstanding composer. In appreciation of his great talent, and to enable him to devote full time to composing, the Finnish Government gave him a life-time pension. Sibelius, in turn, showed his love of his country by immortalizing in music the folklore and scenes of Finland. His works include an unpublished opera; incidental music to eleven plays; fifteen choral works with orchestra; some twenty-five works for unaccompanied chorus; seven symphonies; ten tone poems, of which *En Saga, The Swan of Tuonela,* and *Finlandia* are probably the most famous; five orchestral suites; a violin concerto and other pieces for violin and orchestra; chamber music; piano solos; and numerous songs.

SICILIANO (see chee LYAH noh). An Italian word meaning "Sicilian." A siciliano is a type of dance and song that originated in Sicily. It is written in 6/8 or 12/8 time and moves along at a smooth and graceful, rather moderate speed. It was used frequently as the slow movement in Baroque suites and sonatas. J. S. Bach, for example, used it in his Violin Sonata in G-minor. Handel used the siciliano often in his operas as vocal pieces and orchestral interludes.

SIDE DRUM. (See *Snare Drum.*)

SIGHT-READING. The ability to perform a musical composition at first sight, without any previous study. Sight-reading of piano music is probably the most difficult, since the material is apt to be more complex than for other instruments or the voice. But for any musician the ability to sight-read quickly and accurately is a valuable skill, and it is indispensable for those who want to make a professional career of music.

SIGNATURE. There are two kinds of signatures used in conventional Western music: (1) The key-signature, which indicates the key, or tonality, of a composition by means of a certain number of sharps or flats which appear at the beginning of every staff. (2) The time signature, which indicates the number of beats in a measure as well as the kind of note that receives the basic beat. The time signature appears only at the beginning of a piece or of a movement, or wherever there is a change in the time.

SIMILE (SEE mee lay). An Italian word meaning "like." It indicates that a phrase or other section of music should be performed in the same way as a similar phrase or section that precedes it.

SINDING, Christian. Norwegian composer, born in Kongsberg on January 11, 1856; died in Oslo on December 3, 1941.

Sinding studied first in Christiania, Norway, then went to Leipzig to study with Reinicke* and others at the Conservatory. After a brief return to his native land, during which time a number of his works were performed, he returned to Germany for two more years of study, this time on a scholarship granted him by the Norwegian Government. After his return to Norway he settled in Christiania and devoted himself to composition. Except for one year, when he taught at the Eastman School of Music in Rochester, New York, he did not leave Norway again. In appreciation of his talent, and especially for his works that reflected strongly the romanticism of Scandinavian countries, the Government awarded him a lifetime pension. His compositions include an opera, three symphonies, a violin concerto, a piano concerto, a string quartet, choruses, songs, and many piano pieces. He is well-known to piano students for his popular *Rustle of Spring*.

SINFONIA. An Italian word meaning "symphony." The word has been used as the title for numerous works, such as an instrumental piece in an opera, oratorio, or other vocal work with orchestral accompaniment. J. S. Bach* used the word *Sinfonia* as a title for his three-part inventions. It has also been used as a title for various movements in larger works of the Baroque period, especially for overtures.

SINFONIETTA (sin foh nee ET tah). An Italian word meaning "little symphony." The term is used to describe a short symphony or a piece written especially for a small orchestra.

SINGSPIEL (ZING shpeel). A German word meaning "a play with singing." A type of German entertainment popular in the eighteenth century, the *singspiel* resembled the English ballad opera;* in fact the earliest were based on German translations of the English librettos. They usually consisted of comic plots with spoken dialogue interspersed with songs. In 1778 the Emperor Joseph II established a special company in Vienna for the performance of *Singspiele,* and for that company Mozart was commissioned to write *Die Entführung aus dem Serail* (The Abduction from the Harem).

SIX, THE. (In French, *Les Six.*) The name given to a group of six young composers who gathered together toward the end of World War I under the leadership of Jean Cocteau and Erik Satie* in France. They were Honegger,* Durey, Auric, Milhaud,* Poulenc,* and Tailleferre. These composers were interested in each others' works, and each tried to help the others. However, as a group they were not particularly close musically. Each one developed his or her music along quite independent lines.

SIX-FOUR CHORD. The common name for the second inversion of the tonic triad. The tonic triad in C is C-E-G; the second inversion would be G-C-E. The name "six-four" derives from the fact that the interval from G to E is a sixth, and the interval from G to C is a fourth. (See also *Intervals* and *Chords.*)

SIXTEENTH NOTE. A note (♪) that has one-sixteenth the value of a whole note. In other words, 16 sixteenth notes equal one whole note. The corresponding rest looks like this: (𝄿).

SIXTH. An interval consisting of the lowest and highest of any six consecutive notes in the diatonic scale. The following examples show the four sixths possible when the lowest note is C. (See also *Intervals, Chords, Harmony.*)

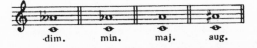

SLIDE. (1) In violin playing, the movement of a finger on a string from one position to another in such a way as to achieve a legato effect. (2) A device on trombones and some trumpets to lengthen or shorten the column of air inside the instrument. (See also *Trombone.*)

SLIDE TROMBONE. (See *Trombone.*)

SLUR. A curved line over or under two or more notes which is used to indicate that the notes should be connected smoothly. In music for stringed instruments, it indicates that all the notes should be played with one stroke of the bow. A slur over notes with staccato marks (dots under or over the notes) indicates that those notes should be played *mezzo staccato*; that is, not as short as *staccato,* yet not *legato.*

SMETANA (SMET tah nah), **Bedřich.** Czech composer, born in Litomyschl (Bohemia) on March 2, 1824; died in Prague on May 12, 1884.

Smetana's father was an amateur violinist, and he started his son's music lessons while he was a small child. By the age of five he played violin in a string quartet, and when he was six he made his debut as a pianist. He had very little systematic training, but he worked so diligently that by the time he was sixteen he was much sought after as a concert pianist. Nevertheless, he had a hard time financially, and without the aid of a number of friends he would not have been able to go on with his musical studies. Among those who encouraged him were Liszt* and Clara Schumann, both having heard him play while visiting Prague. When he was finally offered an excellent job, as conductor of the Philharmonic Society of Göteborg in Sweden, he accepted it immediately. He stayed there for five years, then resigned and returned to his native country to help in establishing a National Opera. In the course of time he composed eight operas, all having a patriotic or nationalistic Czech theme. The second of these, *The Bartered Bride,* is today one of the most popular musical works ever to come out of Czechoslovakia. Smetana directed the Prague National Opera until suddenly, when he was fifty years old, he became completely deaf. He continued to compose, however, and wrote some of his best instrumental works, including the celebrated symphonic poem *The Moldau.* In addition to his operas, Smetana wrote several other tone poems, choral works, chamber music, piano pieces, and songs.

SNARE DRUM. (Also called *side drum.*) A small drum used in the orchestra, military band, dance band, and so on. It is called a snare drum because it has strings of gut or wire (snares) stretched over the lower head. These cause a rattling effect when the player strikes the top with drumsticks. The snares can be detached if the music so indicates. (See also *Drums.*)

SOL. In the system of *movable do,** the syllable name given to the fifth note of the major scale. In the *fixed do** system, the note G.

SOLFEGE (sol FEZH). (Sometimes called *solfeggio.*) A system of ear training which consists of exercises of many kinds in which the notes are sung according to pitch names. (See *Solmization.*) It is sometimes applied to the entire study of the fundamentals of music: rhythm, harmony, pitches, intervals, and so on.

SOLMIZATION. A system in which the different degrees of the scale are identified by syllable names: do (or ut), re, me, fa, sol (or so), la, ti (or si). The system was invented by Guido Arezzo* in the eleventh century, who used the six syllables ut through la as a training device for singers. The syllable si was added later to complete the scale. In America, ut and si have been replaced by do and ti.

Solmization may be used in one of two ways: In the system called *movable do,* the syllables do-re-mi-fa-so-la-ti are given to the ascending degrees of the scale, no matter whether the scale begins on the key note C, the key note G, or any other key note. In the system called *fixed do,* C is always do, D is always re, E is always mi, and so on.

SOLO. An Italian word meaning "alone." A solo is a piece of music written for one voice or one instrument. This is not strictly true, of course, because most solos for voice or instruments, other than keyboard instruments, are accompanied.

SOLOVOX. An electronic instrument* that has a three-octave keyboard attached to the upper end of a piano keyboard. It produces a variety of electronic sounds by means of vacuum tube oscillators. The player usually plays the melody on the electronic device while accompanying himself with the left hand on the piano keyboard.

SONATA (soh NAH tah). An Italian word meaning "sounded." Although the term sonata was used for instrumental compositions as early as 1615, the sonata did not take on its Classical form until about 1750. The Classical sonata usually has four movements: the first is rapid; the second is usually slow; the third movement is generally a minuet* or in later music a scherzo;* the final movement is fast. The first and last movements are in the same key, whereas the slow movement is in a different key. The minuet or scherzo is usually in the same key as the first and last movements, or in a closely related key. The sonatas of Mozart* and Beethoven,* who are generally considered the two greatest exponents of the sonata, follow this pattern quite closely. In the course of time, however, there were changes and variations. Some later sonatas have more, some fewer, than four movements. A few, such as Liszt's Piano Sonata, consist of only one long movement. The term sonata usually applies to a composition written for one instrument, such as the piano, or for two instruments, such as the violin with the piano. A sonata for three instruments is usually called a trio;* one for four instruments is called a quartet,* and so on. A sonata written for a full orchestra, is called a symphony.*

SONATA FORM. A term used in two different ways: (1) It refers to the division into separate movements of the sonata, the symphony, and the trio, quartet, quintet, and so on, written usually for instrumental groups. (See also *Sonata.*) (2) It refers to the form of the first movement and occasionally to others, of compositions such as the symphony, the quartet, the sonata, and so on, that are written in separate movements. The three main sections of the first movement are (a) the exposition,* (b) the development,* and (c) the recapitulation.* In addition to these three main sections, there often is an introduction,* which comes before the exposition, and a coda,* which comes at the very end of the movement.

The *exposition* consists of a principal or main theme* in the original key, or tonic. Next comes a modulating bridge passage leading to the second theme, which is usually in the dominant* of the main key. For example, if the work is in the key of C major, the main theme will be stated in that key, and the second theme will be in the key of G, the dominant. The *development* section makes use of the themes of the *exposition* in a variety of ways. There may be modulations* to different keys, great variety in rhythmic patterns, and a general expansion of the original themes. The *recapitulation* brings a return of the original subject, followed by the second subject. But this time the second subject is in the original key, so that the movement closes in a satisfactory way.

If the first movement is in a minor key, then the second subject in the exposition is usually in the relative major rather than the dominant. For example, if the first movement of a sonata is in the key of A minor, then the first subject would be stated in A minor, and the second subject would be in C major.

SONATINA. An Italian word meaning "little sonata." A sonatina is exactly that: a short and usually simpler version of the sonata. Among the composers who wrote sonatinas are Clementi,* Dussek, and Kuhlau. Sonatinas are especially useful as practice material and performance by beginning piano students. A modern example of a sonatina is Ravel's *Sonatine* for piano, a quite difficult work in three movements.

SONG. A composition for a solo singer, usually with piano accompaniment. Songs have existed from earliest times and have been a part of the culture of nearly all levels of society in nearly all civilizations. The earliest notated songs are found in Latin manuscripts of the tenth century. During Medieval days, beginning about 1100, the troubadours* and a little later the trouvères* of France provided some of the earliest songs. These were written by poet-musicians and sung by the troubadours and trouvères, often to an accompaniment played by a fiddler, called a *jongleur*. In Germany a similar type of poet-musician, called Minnesinger,* flourished from about the same time until the fifteenth century, when they were followed by the Meistersinger.* Following this colorful period of the early Middle Ages, composers became more and more interested in writing songs, and from that time until the beginning of the Renaissance the song was one of the most popular and important forms of music. After about 1600 the song became less important as the opera and operatic aria became more prominent, and not until sometime in the late seventeenth century did composers again pay serious attention to song writing. The English songwriter, Purcell, and a number of German composers who preceded Bach became prominent as composers of songs, but it was almost a hundred years later that the modern song as we know it today became an important medium of musical expression, when Mozart wrote *Das Veilchen*. From that time until fairly recently practically every composer has considered song writing an important part of his craft.

SONG CYCLE. A group of songs by a single composer that are intended to be sung together so they form a unified whole. The songs are related in that they center around a story or a sequence of related ideas. Some examples of well-known song cycles are Beethoven's *An die ferne Geliebte* (To the Distant Beloved), Schubert's *Die schöne Müllerin* (The Beautiful Milleress) and *Winterreise* (Winter Journey), and Schumann's *Frauen-Liebe und leben* (Woman's Love and Life) and *Dichterliebe* (Poet's Love).

SONG FORM. A misleading term sometimes used for simple three-part (ternary*) form. It is misleading because it is seldom used in songs, exceptions being the old *da capo aria** and some modern songs that are essentially dance tunes.

SOPRANINO (soh prah NEE noh). An Italian word meaning "little soprano." The name is sometimes used for instruments that have a higher range than the soprano size, as sopranino recorder* and sopranino saxophone.*

SOPRANO. (1) The highest type of woman's or child's voice, with a normal range from Middle-C to the C two octaves above. The soprano voice may be *dramatic, coloratura,* or *lyric.* The dramatic soprano is a powerful voice capable of singing such "heavy" roles as Isolde in Wagner's *Tristan and Isolde.* The coloratura voice is extremely high and flexible, capable of singing roles in opera that require great agility, such as Lakmé, in the opera of that name by Delibes. The lyric soprano is less powerful than the dramatic soprano, and usually of a lower range than the coloratura, but smooth and of a quality suitable for singing such operatic roles as Mimi in Puccini's *La Bohème.* Child sopranos, boys or girls, are more limited in range and dynamic capabilities than women sopranos. (2) The name given certain instruments of high range, as the soprano saxophone,* soprano cornet,* and soprano recorder.*

SORDINO (sorr DEE noh). An Italian word meaning "mute." It refers to the mute* used on bowed stringed instruments, and usually occurs with other words, as *con sordino* (with the mute) or *senza sordino* (without the mute).

SOSTENUTO (soss ten NOO toh). An Italian word meaning "held" or "sustained." Sostenuto indicates that the section of music so marked should be performed smoothly.

SOTTO VOCE (SOH toh VOH chay). An Italian term meaning "under the voice." It indicates that the music should be so soft as to be almost whispered. The abbreviation for sotto voce is *s.v.*

SOUBRETTE (soo BRET). A French word meaning "maid" or "waitress." A kind of light soprano voice used most often in light opera, as for the role of Adele in Strauss's *Die Fledermaus* (The Bat).

SOUSA, John Philip. American composer and bandmaster, born in Washington, D.C. on November 6, 1854; died in Reading, Pennsylvania, on March 6, 1932.

Sousa began the study of violin when he was quite young, and by the time he was sixteen he was already playing in variety shows. Ten years later he was made Director of the U.S. Marine Corps Band. Under his leadership the Marine Band became one of the finest of military bands. In 1892 he organized his own band and began a long series of tours that took the organization to many parts of the United States and Europe, and in 1910–11 around the world. Sousa wrote songs, operettas, and orchestral suites, but he is most famous for his stirring marches, including *The Stars and Stripes Forever, Washington Post,* and *Hands Across the Sea.*

SOUSAPHONE. A kind of tuba with a large bell, shaped so it encircles the player's body. The lowest and largest of the brass instruments, it is named for John Philip Sousa, the bandmaster who suggested its design, which makes the instrument easier for a player to hold and play while marching. (See also *Helicon.*)

SOWERBY, Leo. American organist and composer, born in Grand Rapids, Michigan, on May 1, 1895.

Sowerby began to take piano lessons when he was seven years old, and harmony when he was eleven. He became intensely interested in the organ, and switched to that instrument when he was fourteen. After World War I, when he served as bandmaster in the U.S. Army, he began to study composition seriously, and in 1921 he became the first winner of the American

Prix de Rome.* Following his stay in Rome, he taught composition at the American Conservatory in Chicago, and later was appointed organist at St. James Episcopal Church there. His compositions include a number of frequently performed choral works, four symphonies, some shorter orchestral pieces, six concertos, chamber music, and a great many works for organ.

SPEAKS, Oley. American singer and composer of songs, born in Canal Winchester, Ohio, on June 28, 1874; died in New York City on August 27, 1948.

Speaks had an excellent baritone voice and enjoyed a long career as a singer, first as a church soloist and later as a concert artist. He was a talented composer of rather light songs and became famous with some that became popular favorites. Three of the best known are *On the Road to Mandalay, Sylvia,* and *The Prayer Perfect.*

SPICCATO (spee CAH toh). An Italian word meaning "distinct" or "clear." A term used to indicate a type of bowing of stringed instruments in which the bow plays rapid, detached notes with a bouncing movement.

SPINET. A type of harpsichord with one keyboard that was popular from about 1650 to 1800, especially in England. It was wing-shaped and equipped with one set of jacks.* The case was often ornately decorated. The term *spinet* is used today to describe a small, upright piano.

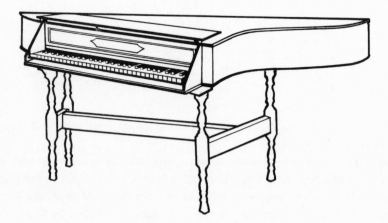

SPIRITUAL. A folk song with religious words. The earliest spirituals in America were the "white spirituals," sung by religious groups in the South from the earliest days of settlement. The Negro slaves imitated the spirituals of the white people to some extent, but changed them greatly. Through the years large numbers of both white and Negro spirituals have evolved. Soon after the Civil War a great many of the Negro spirituals were collected and published in a book called *Slave Songs of the U.S.* A short time later a group of trained singers, afterwards known as the Jubilee Singers, was organized at the Negro school in Nashville, Tennessee, that later became Fisk University. The singing of this choral society attracted attention to the spirituals and increased their popularity. Today the Negro spiritual is considered an important feature of American music and is included in the repertoires of choral societies, solo singers, and school music groups. Such spirituals as *Deep River, Nobody Knows the Trouble I've Seen,* and *Go Down, Moses* are familiar to almost everyone.

STABAT MATER (STAH baht MAH ter). The Latin name of a religious poem of the thirteenth century about the Virgin Mary's vigil at the Cross. Since 1727 it has been used in the liturgy of the Roman Catholic church. Many composers have written elaborate settings of the poem; among them Josquin,* Palestrina,* Pergolesi,* Haydn,* Schubert,* Rossini,* Dvořák,* and Verdi.*

STACCATO (stah CAH toh). An Italian word meaning "separate." Staccato indicates that the notes are to be played as short as possible, and detached from each other. It is indicated on the music by dots over or under the notes as:

STAFF. The parallel lines and spaces on which music is written. In modern notation the staff has five lines and four spaces, and can be extended by the use of ledger lines.* Clef* signs locate the pitches on the staffs.

STEEL GUITAR. An electrical instrument that sounds somewhat like a guitar, but otherwise has little resemblance to the conventional instrument. It has a body shaped like a box, with an amplifier connected to it. The strings are supported by the box-like body, and their tone is amplified electrically. The steel guitar is used mainly in dance orchestras.

STEP. The interval between two adjacent degrees of the scale* or staff.*

The smallest step is a half-step, as from C to C♯ or E to F. A whole step equals two half-steps, as from C to D or E to F♯.

STILL, William Grant. American Negro composer, born in Woodville, Mississippi, on May 11, 1895.

Still began his serious study of music in Little Rock, Arkansas, and continued at Wilberforce University. He attended Oberlin Conservatory and later studied composition with Chadwick* at the New England Conservatory. During World War I he served in the U.S. Navy, and after the war continued his music study with Varèse* in New York. After a number of years, during which he made his living by playing in jazz orchestras and making arrangements for such popular conductors as Paul Whiteman, he was awarded a series of prizes that made it possible for him to devote most of his time to composition. Still was the first American Negro to write a symphony and the first one to conduct a major symphony orchestra. In addition to his symphony, he has written a number of smaller works for orchestra, three operas, three ballets, choral works, chamber music, and considerable music for films and radio.

STOCKHAUSEN, Karlheinz. German composer, born in Mödrath, near Cologne, on August 22, 1928.

Stockhausen studied music first in Cologne, and later with Milhaud* in Paris. His compositions are largely atonal* with highly complex contrapuntal* effects and a wide range of tonal color. He uses rhythm in the freest way possible, and emphasizes percussion instruments in his works. Stockhausen was one of the first composers to experiment with electronic music. He has lectured widely in Europe and America, usually demonstrating with taped electronic compositions of his own. Besides his electronic compositions, Stockhausen has written several works for orchestra and pieces for various combinations of instruments.

STOP. A set of organ pipes that are all operated by one lever. The lever itself is also called a *stop*. On modern organs the stops are small ivory levers that can be easily raised or lowered by a finger.

STOPPING. A technique used by players of stringed instruments to raise the pitch. This is done by pressing a string against the fingerboard with a finger of the left hand. The closer the action is to the bridge of the instrument, the higher the pitch becomes. A stopped string is the opposite of an open string (a string that vibrates in its entire length without being stopped). (See also *Double Stop.*) (2) In horn playing, the placing of the hand into the bell. This changes the pitch and tone quality of the notes played.

STRADIVARI (strah dee VAHR ree), **Antonio.** Italian violin maker, born in Cremona in 1644; died there on December 18, 1737.

When Stradavari was about fourteen years old he became an apprentice in the workshop of a famous violin maker, Nicolo Amati.* He learned the craft so well that by the time he was twenty-two he was signing his own name to the instruments he made. He continued for some time to produce violins, violas, and cellos patterned on those of his master, Amati, but with great skill and fine workmanship. He eventually became his own master and to the end of his life produced instruments that have never been surpassed. After his death his two sons, Francesco and Omobono, continued his work. Most of the instruments made by the Stradivari family are today in museums and private collections, although a number of famous performers are fortunate enough to own some of these valuable violins, violas, and cellos.

STRAUSS, Johann (The Elder). Austrian composer and conductor, born in Vienna on March 14, 1804; died there on September 25, 1849.

Johann was determined to have a career as a musician. His parents were opposed to this idea, and only after he had run away from home did they give their consent. He had studied violin and harmony, and by the time he was fifteen was playing in a dance orchestra. He was still in his early twenties when he organized his own orchestra and began to write the waltzes that were to make him famous. He made extensive tours throughout western Europe with his orchestra, and finally in 1845 was made conductor of court balls in Vienna. Altogether, he wrote more than 150 waltzes in addition to other dance forms, such as galops* and quadrilles.*

STRAUSS, Johann (The Younger). Austrian composer and conductor, born in Vienna on October 25, 1825; died there on June 3, 1899.

In many ways, the younger Johann Strauss's life followed the same pattern as his father's. His parents tried to discourage him from a career of music, but he would not listen to them. He managed to study violin and composition, and when he was nineteen years old he was already playing in a restaurant and conducting his own group of musicians. He had inherited his father's talent for composition and was soon writing a great deal of music. When his father died in 1849, the twenty-four-year-old Johann combined his own orchestra with his father's and began to tour extensively. In 1872 he visited the United States and conducted several concerts, mainly of his own music. By that time his waltzes and operettas had made him famous and he came to be known as "The Waltz King." He wrote sixteen operattas, including the popular *Die Fledermaus* (The Bat), and *Der Zigeunerbaron* (The Gypsy Baron). Two of his many waltzes that have become popular the world over are *The Beautiful Blue Danube* and *Tales from the Vienna Woods.*

STRAUSS, Richard. German composer, conductor, and pianist, born in Munich on June 11, 1864; died in Garmisch-Partenkirchen on September 8, 1949.

Richard Strauss showed signs of his musical genius at an extremely early age. He began to study music when he was four; by the time he was six he had composed a polka;* and before his tenth birthday he had written a *Festival March* for orchestra, his first Opus.* He continued to write music in many forms, and became well-known also as one of Europe's most outstanding conductors. Among the prominent conducting posts that he held were the Munich Opera, the Weimar Court Orchestra, the Philharmonic in Berlin, the Royal Opera in Berlin, and the Vienna Opera. As a composer, Strauss became famous in three fields: opera, the tone poem, and songs. Of his many operas, probably the best known and most frequently performed are *Salome, Elektra, Der Rosenkavalier, Ariadne auf Naxos, Arabella,* and *Capriccio.* His tone poems, which include such popular works as *Don Juan, Till Eulenspiegel,* and *Don Quixote,* are standard in the repertoire of most of the world's symphony orchestras. His many songs include such favorites as *Allerseelen, Zueignung, Morgan,* and *Ständchen.*

STRAVINSKY (strah VIN skee), **Igor.** Russian-born American composer, born in Oranienbaum on June 17, 1882.

Although his father was a famous opera singer, young Igor did not begin to study music seriously until he had completed law studies at the age of twenty-three. His composition teacher was Rimsky-Korsakov,* and under his tutelage Stravinsky developed rapidly into a first-rate composer. He was twenty-six when his first symphony was performed in St. Petersburg. A year later the performance of another of his orchestral works, *Scherzo fantastique,* attracted the attention of the famous ballet impressario

Diaghilev. Diaghilev asked him to write a ballet. This ballet, the now world-famous *Firebird,* was performed in Paris a year later. This was followed by another ballet, *Petrushka,* which was even more successful. Then came a work that created a great stir in musical circles because in it Stravinsky used a new style of composition. This was his ballet, *The Rite of Spring,* first performed in Paris in 1913 before an audience that protested vigorously against its harsh and unusual orchestral effects. Just a year later, however, it was received enthusiastically at a symphony concert conducted by Pierre Monteux.

World War I, followed by the Russian Revolution, brought to an end Stravinsky's association with Diaghilev and the pre-war world of ballet. He spent the war years with his family in Switzerland, then moved to Paris, where he remained for nineteen years, experimenting with new musical forms and idioms. During those years he abandoned the large-scale works that demanded full orchestras, and composed works of smaller dimensions, using as models the classical* and Baroque* forms for some of them. In 1939 he was invited to lecture at Harvard University, and when World War II broke out in Europe he decided to stay in the United States. He settled in California, and in 1945 became an American citizen.

Stravinsky's later works, written after he was seventy, show an increasing interest in the serial* techniques of the twelve-tone* style of composition. One of these, *Sacred Song to Honor the Name of St. Mark* received its premiere at St. Mark's in Venice in 1956. Others of this period are the ballet *Agon; Movements* for piano and orchestra; and *The Flood.*

Besides these works, Stravinsky's compositions include eleven ballets; three operas; an opera-oratorio, *Oedipus Rex;* a musical drama, *Persephone;* three symphonies; concertos and other works for instruments and orchestra; songs; chamber music; and piano pieces.

STRETTO (STRET toh). An Italian word meaning "narrow" or "close together." (1) Stretto refers to the entries of the subject* and answer* in fugues* as these entries become so close together that they overlap. (2) It is also a direction for the music to become faster toward the end of a composition.

STRING. (1) Thin strands of wire or gut used in a variety of musical instruments. Wire is used for the strings of the piano,* harpsichord,* harp,* etc. Gut, usually from sheep, is used for the strings of members of the violin family,* the ukelele,* mandolin,* etc. (2) Refers to an instrument that is played on strings, particularly members of the violin family. (The double bass is sometimes called a string bass.)

STRINGENDO (streen JEN doh). An Italian word meaning "pressing" or "squeezing." The term indicates that the speed should be increased rapidly toward a climax in the piece.

STRING ORCHESTRA. An orchestra composed of violins, violas, cellos, and double basses, often with the addition of harp and piano.

STRING QUARTET. (See *Quartet.*)

STRING QUINTET. (See *Quintet.*)

STRING TRIO. (See *Trio.*)

STROPHIC. A term applied to songs in which all the stanzas are sung to the same music. Hymns and folk songs are examples of songs that are usually strophic.

SUBDOMINANT. The fourth degree of the scale. The prefix *sub* means *under,* so subdominant means "under the dominant" (the fifth degree of the scale). The subdominant in the key of C-major is F; in the key of A major, C-sharp, and so on.

SUBITO (SOO bee toh). An Italian word meaning "suddenly." It is used with other terms, as *piano subito* (suddenly soft), or *subito forte* (suddenly loud), or *attacca subito* (begin the next movement suddenly, without a break).

SUBJECT. A theme* or melody that is predominant in a composition, as the subject of a fugue.*

SUBMEDIANT. The sixth degree of the scale. The submediant in the key of C-major is A; in the key of A-major, F-sharp; and so on.

SUBTONIC. (Also called *Leading Note.**) The seventh degree of the scale. The subtonic in the key of C-major is B; in the key of A-major, G-sharp; and so on.

SUITE (sweet). A musical form that became important during the Baroque* period. It consisted of several movements, all in dance forms. Some of the dances included in the Baroque suite were: allemande,* courante,* sarabande,* minuet,* bourée,* gavotte,* passepied,* polonaise,* rigaudon,* and gigue.* The Baroque suite became one of the most prominent instrumental forms of the seventeenth and eighteenth centuries. Among the most important composers of the Baroque suite were J. S. Bach,* Handel,* and Purcell.*

During the nineteenth and twentieth centuries the name suite has been used for collections of short movements taken from opera, ballet, or film scores, or music written for plays, or sometimes consisting of completely original material. Examples of the more modern suite are Tchaikovsky's *The Nutcracker* suite, Bizet's *L'Arlésienne* suites, Grieg's *Peer Gynt* suite, Ravel's *Daphnis et Chloe* suites, and Sibelius's *Suite champêtre* for strings.

SULLIVAN, Arthur. English composer, born in London on May 13, 1842; died there on November 22, 1900.

As a child, Arthur obtained excellent musical instruction from his father, who was a professor of brass band at the Royal Military School of Music. When he was twelve years old he became a choral singer in the Chapel Royal, and two years later he was awarded the Mendelssohn Scholarship at the Royal Academy of Music. This award made it possible for him to study at the Leipzig Conservatory in Germany. There he studied under a number of excellent teachers. Upon his return to England he immediately became well-known, when his music to Shakespeare's *Tempest* was performed. He was only twenty-four when he was made a professor of composition at the Royal Academy of Music. He wrote a number of works, including a symphony, but his greatest fame lies in the large number of comic operas he wrote to librettos by W. S. Gilbert. For about twenty years the two worked together and produced some of the most charming and enduring operettas the world has ever known. These include *H.M.S. Pinafore, The Mikado, The Pirates of Penzance, Ruddigore,* and *Trial by Jury.* Besides the operettas, Sullivan wrote an opera, *Ivanhoe,* incidental music for plays, ballets, choral works, and a great many hymns and solo songs, including the well-known hymn, *Onward Christian Soldiers,* and the popular song *The Lost Chord.*

SUPERTONIC. The second degree of the scale. The prefix *super* means "over," so supertonic means "over the tonic" (the tonic being the first degree of the scale). The supertonic in the key of C-major is D; in the key of A-major it is B; and so on.

SUPPÉ (soo PAY), **Franz von.** Austrian composer, born in Spalato (now Split) on April 18, 1819; died in Vienna on May 21, 1895.

Suppé was christened with one of the longest names in musical history: Francesco Ezechiele Ermengildo Cavaliere Suppé-Demelli, but he preferred to call himself simply Franz Von Suppé. He became interested in music at a very early age, and by the time he was fifteen he had composed a Mass. His father sent him to the University of Padua in Italy, but he preferred music and spent most of his time learning to compose. When his father died, Franz joined his mother in Vienna, and after some study there he began a long career of composing and conducting. Although he wrote a great many works, including thirty-one operettas, he is remembered today mainly for the overtures to his stage works, *Poet and Peasant* and *Light Cavalry.*

SUSPENSION. A term used in harmony to describe a note in a chord that is held while another note that forms a discord with it is sounded. The discord is usually resolved* when the held note falls to a note that is in harmony with the discordant note, as in the following example:

SUSTAINING PEDAL. (See *Piano.*)

SWEELINCK (SVAY link), **Jan Pieterszoon.** Dutch organist and composer, born in Deventer or Amsterdam in 1562 (the exact date and place are not known); died in Amsterdam on October 16, 1621.

Little is known about Sweelinck's early life until 1580, when, at the age of eighteen, he succeeded his father in the important post of organist at Amsterdam's Old Church. He became celebrated as an organist and teacher, many of his pupils becoming the leading organists of northern Germany. Sweelinck wrote a great many vocal works, only a few of which were published during his lifetime. His works for organ were remarkable in that they foreshadowed the later development of the fugue.*

SWELL. A device used on the organ and certain kinds of harpsichords to increase the volume of sound. The swell on the organ consists of a box built around a *rank* (a set of organ pipes belonging to one stop.*) The box has shutters that are opened by means of a foot pedal to increase the sound. (See also *Organ.*)

SYMPHONIC POEM. A large work for orchestra, often as long as a symphony,* but lacking the form of the true symphony. The symphonic poem is usually an interpretation of some extra-musical subject, such as a work of literature, a painting, an event in history, or even a geographic location. Liszt was the first composer to use the term *symphonic poem* for a number of his works. Other examples are Smetana's *My Country,* Debussy's *La Mer* and *Ibéria,* Respighi's *Pines of Rome* and *Fountains of Rome,* Richard Strauss's *Domestic Symphony.* Berlioz' *Symphonie fantastique* is considered an ancestor of the symphonic poem.

SYMPHONY. (1) A large work for orchestra, written in sonata form.* Most symphonies have four movements; though some, like several of Haydn's early symphonies, have three movements; a few have two or only one movement; others may have more than four movements. Most symphonies are identified simply by the key and the order in which a particular composer wrote them. For example, Brahms's fourth symphony is titled Symphony No. 4 in E minor. A few have other names as well; for example, Beethoven's *Pastoral Symphony,* Mendelssohn's *Scottish Symphony,* and Dvořák's *Symphony From the New World.* (2) The term *symphony* is applied also to the kind of orchestra that is large enough to play symphonies.

SYNCOPATION. The shifting of accents to beats that are normally not accented. A syncopated rhythm can be notated in different ways: (1) by tying into the strong beat (♩ ♩ ♩|♩), (2) by using a rest on the strong beat (♪ ♩ ♪ ♩), (3) by accenting the weak beat (♪ ♪ ♪ ♪). Syncopation is one of the most important characteristics of modern American popular music, but it is also found in a great deal of serious music.

TABLATURE (TAB lah tyoor). A system of musical notation that was used in the sixteenth and seventeenth centuries for instruments such as the lute.* In that system, numbers and other symbols were used to indicate the position of the performer's fingers on the strings. Tablature is used today only for the ukelele, the zither, the guitar, and a few other instruments designed for people who have not had enough musical training to read regular notation.

TABOR. A small drum, popular in the Middle Ages. The performer used the fingers of one hand instead of sticks to beat the drum, while he played a three-holed pipe* with the other hand.

TACET. A Latin word meaning "is silent." The term is used in some choral works and in orchestral and chamber works to indicate that a particular voice part or instrument is silent for a considerable time, as for an entire movement* or section of a movement.

TALLIS, Thomas. English composer and organist, born about 1505 (the exact place and date are unknown); died in Greenwich on November 23, 1585.

One of the most influential composers of the sixteenth century, Tallis was joint organist with Byrd* of the Chapel Royal, and with Byrd was given the exclusive right to print music and music paper in the year 1575. The first works they published were thirty-four motets,* sixteen by Tallis and eighteen by Byrd. Tallis was a skillful writer of contrapuntal music. His most famous work, *Spem in alium,* was a motet in forty parts: it called for eight choirs of five voices each. Most of his works for the church were motets, but he also wrote two Masses, two Magnificats, two Lamentations, anthems, and Psalms. His secular* works include pieces for keyboard instruments, viols,* the lute,* and voices. Vaughan Williams* based his *Fantasia on a Theme of Tallis'* on one of his Psalm-tunes.

TALON (tah LOHN). A French word meaning "heel." The talon is the lower end, or "frog" of the violin bow. The direction *au talon* means that the end of the bow nearest the hand is to be used.

TAMBOURIN (tahn boo REN). An ancient French dance that was accompanied by a pipe* and tabor* (French, *tambourin*). The dance was in lively, 2/4 time. A number of French composers of the Baroque period, including Rameau,* wrote tambourins for the harpsichord.*

TAMBOURINE. A percussion instrument consisting of a piece of skin stretched over only one side of a shallow, circular hoop of wood. Loose metal plates, called *jingles,* are set into the wood. The tambourine is a very old instrument. The Romans used it and the Gypsies were especially fond of it. Many composers have written music for orchestra that calls for the tambourine. It is played either by being tapped with the fingers or by being shaken.

TAM-TAM. The same as *gong.**

TAMPON. A drumstick with two heads. It is held in the middle and used with a rapid alternating motion of the wrist to produce a roll on the bass drum.

TANGO. A South American dance that resembles the habanera.* About the time of World War I, the tango became popular as a ballroom dance in the United States, and soon after in Europe. Several serious composers used the tango in their works, including Hindemith,* Křenek,* and Stravinsky.* Albeniz* wrote a popular piano piece called *Tango in D*. The basic rhythm of the tango is: (♩. ♪♩ ♩).

TANTO (TAHN toh). An Italian word meaning "so much." It is used with other words in such expressions as *allegro ma non tanto* (fast, but not too much so).

TARANTELLA (tah rahn TELL lah). An ancient dance from southern Italy, mainly from the town of Taranto. It is in extremely fast 6/8 or 12/8 time, the music alternating between major and minor. There is a superstition in Italy that a person bitten by a large and poisonous spider called a tarantula will be cured of the poison by dancing the tarantella. Some examples of the dance in classical music are Rossini's *La Danza*, Chopin's *Tarantella in A-flat major,* and the tarantella in the finale of Mendelssohn's *Italian Symphony*.

TARDO (TAHR doh). An Italian word meaning "slow." Also, *tarda, tardamente* (slowly), *tardare* (to retard), and *tardantemente* (slowly).

TARTINI (tahr TEE nee), **Giuseppe.** Italian composer, teacher, and violinist, born in Pirano on April 8, 1692; died in Padua on February 26, 1770.

Tartini, who was to become the greatest violinist and violin teacher of his day, got off to a slow start in music. He began to study for the priesthood, switched to law, then to training to become an officer in the Army. All this time he studied some music and became more and more interested in a career as a musician. His career as a violinist and teacher was interrupted when he married against the wish of his wife's guardian, Cardinal Cornaro. The Cardinal ordered his arrest, his own family cut off all support, and he was forced to flee to a monastery in Assisi. The monks protected him, and while he remained there in hiding until 1715, he perfected his playing and also improved the violin bow. When at last he was pardoned he was already famous. He toured widely as a celebrated virtuoso, and finally returned to Padua to found a school. Violinists flocked to Padua to study with him. He wrote many concertos and sonatas for violin, as well as trio-sonatas, vocal works, and theoretical works, some of them having to do with the acoustics* of violin playing. One of his most famous sonatas is called *The Devil's Trill*. Tartini claimed that in a dream the devil came to him and played the music, and that when he awoke he remembered it and wrote it down.

TAYLOR, Deems. American music critic, lecturer, and composer, born in New York on December 22, 1885.

Taylor began the study of piano when he was eleven. He went on with his study of music and other subjects, and graduated from New York University in 1906. He was still a young man when he became music critic for the *New York Tribune*. Other publications for which he wrote were *Collier's*, the *New York World, Musical America,* and the *New York American*. His recognition as an important composer came with the early performances of his orchestral suite, *Through the Looking Glass*. This was followed two years later by a successful performance of his tone poem for orchestra, *Jurgen,* and in 1927 by the Metropolitan production of his opera, *The King's Henchman*. That opera proved to be so successful that the Metropolitan commissioned him to write another opera, *Peter Ibbetson,* which was produced in 1931. In addition to his music, Taylor has written some highly popular books about music. They include *Of Men and Music, The Well-Tempered Listener,* and *Music to My Ears.*

TCHAIKOVSKY (chy KAWF skee), **Peter Ilyich.** Russian composer, born in Votinsk on May 7, 1840; died in St. Petersburg (now Leningrad) on November 6, 1893.

Tchaikovsky's father was well-to-do, and young Peter had the advantage of a French governess who knew enough music to give him his first lessons when he was seven. When he was ten years old his family moved to St. Petersburg, and there he was able to study with competent teachers. He made a great deal of progress, but his family had no intention of allowing their son to become a professional musician. They sent him to a school that prepared young men to become lawyers, and when he was nineteen he became a clerk in the Ministry of Justice. He remained there for four years, continuing to study music on the side. During that time his mother died of cholera and his father lost his fortune, leaving young Peter dependent on his own resources. He continued his musical studies at the newly founded St. Petersburg Conservatory, and in 1865 he graduated with a silver medal for a cantata* he had composed. The following year he was made a professor of harmony at the Moscow Conservatory, where he taught until 1878, continuing at the same time to write a great many works. About that time a wealthy woman, Madam Von Meck, began to provide him with a generous income that made it possible for him to devote most of his time to composing. Although he never actually met her, he corresponded with her for some thirteen years. He travelled extensively, and even made a brief trip to the United States, where he conducted one of his own compositions at the opening of Carnegie Hall in New York City. He died in St. Petersburg during a cholera epidemic, after carelessly drinking water that had not been boiled.

Tchaikovsky wrote a great many works including eleven operas, of which *Eugene Onegin* and *The Queen of Spades* are the best known today; three ballets: *The Nutcracker, Swan Lake,* and *The Sleeping Beauty*; six symphonies, of which the sixth (*Pathétique*) is the most famous; other works for orchestra; chamber music; many well-known songs and piano pieces.

TCHEREPNIN (cherr EPP nin), **Nicolas.** Russian composer and pianist, born in St. Petersburg (now Leningrad), Russia, on May 14, 1873; died in Issy-les-Moulineaux, near Paris, France, on June 26, 1945.

Tcherepnin was educated to become a lawyer, but when he was twenty-two years old he gave up his law career and entered the St. Petersburg Conservatory, where he became a piano pupil of Rimsky-Korsakov.* He made excellent progress, and even before he left the Conservatory in 1898 he had made several appearances as a pianist and as a conductor. Between 1898 and 1908 he held several important conducting posts in Russia. He then went to Paris, where he served as conductor for the Diaghilev* Ballets. In 1914 he went back to Russia to become director of the Tiflis Conservatory; but when the Red Army occupied the Caucasus in 1921, he returned to Paris to make his permanent home.

Tcherepnin completed an unfinished opera composed by his old teacher, Rimsky-Korsakov, *Sorochintsy Fair*. His own works include operas, ballets, two symphonies and other works for orchestra, chamber music, a piano concerto, two Masses, and many songs and pieces for piano.

TELEMANN (TAY le mun), **George Philipp.** German composer, born in Magdeburg on March 14, 1681; died in Hamburg on June 25, 1767.

As a boy, Telemann had very little instruction in music. He had a good general education, and studied law at Leipzig University, but his later eminence as a musician was due to his self-study of music. The first of many important music posts he held during his lifetime was as organist at the New Church in Leipzig when he was twenty-three years old. He wrote an enormous number of works, including cantatas, Passions, oratorios and other church music; forty operas; a great many suites for orchestra; concertos; chamber music; organ fugues; and harpsichord pieces.

TEMPERAMENT. (See *Equal Temperament.*)

TEMPO. An Italian word meaning "time." The tempo of a piece is the rate of speed at which the music is to be performed. Some of the more common tempo indications are these:

largo—very slow and broad

lento—slow

adagio—slow, but not quite as slow as *lento*

andante—at a walking pace

moderato—moderate speed

allegretto—moderately fast

allegro—quite fast

presto—very fast

prestissimo—extremely fast

Tempo is often used with other terms, as:

a tempo—return to the original speed after some change.

tempo giusto—keep strict time.

tempo primo—the speed used at the beginning of the selection.

tempo rubato—changes of speed allowed.

TENOR. (1) The highest natural adult male voice. The tenor range is normally from the second B below Middle C to the G above Middle C. (2) The name given to certain instruments with ranges that more or less parallel that of the tenor voice, as tenor saxophone, tenor trombone. (3) In the music of the twelfth and thirteenth centuries, the part which contained the *cantus firmus** (the Gregorian melody), usually the lowest part.

TENOR CLEF. (See *Clef.*)

TENOR DRUM. A drum that is larger than a side drum or a snare drum, but smaller than a bass drum. It is used chiefly in military bands.

TENTH. (See *Intervals.*)

TENUTO (tay NOO toh). An Italian word meaning "held." *Tenuto* is a direction to hold individual notes or chords for their full value and to make a smooth connection between them. The abbreviation is *ten.*

TERNARY FORM. A musical form consisting of three distinct parts, often represented by the symbol ABA. The third part is a repetition, sometimes exactly the same and sometimes slightly different, of the first part. The *minuets* and *scherzos* of symphonies and sonatas are examples of works written in ternary form. So also are the *Nocturnes* of Chopin.*

TESSITURA (tess ee TOO rah). An Italian word meaning "weaving." Tessitura refers to the approximate range of the majority of the notes in a song or other vocal work—as a high tessitura, a low tessitura. It is also used in indicating the normal range of a particular voice, but it does not include the lowest or highest notes possible.

THEME. A phrase or short melody that constitutes one or more main ideas in a musical work. It is sometimes called the *subject,** although it may be longer than a subject. One or more themes may recur throughout a piece in one form or another, so it or they are the main material out of which the piece is built.

THEREMIN. An electronic instrument invented by a Russian scientist, Leo Theremin, around 1920. It consists of an upright box containing two oscillators and a loudspeaker, with two antennas fitted to the outside. It is played by passing the hands over or near the antennas, which produces single tones that can be varied in pitch and loudness.

THIRD. An interval that consists of three degrees of the diatonic scale, counting the top and bottom, as C-E (c-d-e). A major third consists of four half tones: C-E (c-c♯-d-d♯-e); a minor third consists of three half tones: C-E♭ (c-d♭-d-e♭). (See also *Intervals.*)

THIRTY-SECOND NOTE. A note (♪) that has one thirty-second the value of a whole note, one-fourth the value of a quarter note, and half the value of a sixteenth note. The corresponding rest looks like this: (⁊).

THOMAS (toh MAH), **Ambroise.** French composer, born in Metz on August 5, 1811; died in Paris on February 12, 1896.

Ambroise studied both the piano and the violin while he was a small child. He later entered the Paris Conservatory, where he did extremely well. He won the first prize in piano when he was eighteen, the harmony prize a year later, and the *Grand Prix de Rome* two years after that. He spent three years in Italy, then returned to Paris, where he wrote a great many operas. In 1852 he was appointed a teacher of composition at the Paris Conservatory, and in 1871 its Director. In addition to his many operas, which include the popular *Mignon,* Thomas wrote several ballets, chamber music, Masses, motets, songs, and pieces for the piano.

THOMPSON, Randall. American composer and music educator, born in New York City on April 21, 1899.

Thompson was educated at Harvard University and did private work with Bloch.* He was twice awarded a Guggenheim Fellowship and also received a fellowship at the American Academy in Rome. He has taught at a number of leading universities and music schools, including the Curtis Institute of Music in Philadelphia, where he was Director; Princeton University; and Harvard University. He has written a great many works that have been performed widely. They include a one-act opera, *Soloman and Balkis,* several large choral works; two symphonies; chamber music; piano solos; and songs.

THOMSON, Virgil. American music critic and composer, born in Kansas City, Missouri, on November 25, 1896.

After serving as a lieutenant in the Air Corps during World War I, Thomson attended Harvard University. He graduated in 1922, then went to Paris to study with the noted teacher, Nadia Boulanger.* When he returned to the United States he was appointed organist and choirmaster at King's Chapel in Boston. About that time he began his long career as a writer on musical topics. From 1925 to 1932 he again lived in Paris, where he became acquainted with the writer Gertrude Stein. She later provided the lyrics for two of his operas, *Four Saints in Three Acts* and *The Mother of Us All.* In addition to the operas, Thomson's compositions include a ballet, incidental music for several plays, music for five motion pictures, several choral works, two orchestral suites, two symphonies, a great deal of chamber music, and several songs. Thomson is perhaps even more widely known as a music critic than as a composer. From 1940 to 1954 he was the leading critic on the *New York Herald Tribune.* He has also written a number of books about music.

TI. (Sometimes called *Si.*) In the system of *movable do,** the syllable name given to the seventh note of the major scale. In the *fixed do** system, the note B.

TIE. A curved line joining two adjacent notes of the same pitch. It indicates that the second note should not be sounded, but that its value should be added to the value of the first note. For instance, in this example the note C is sounded once, but held for a total of four beats:

TIMBRE (TAN br). A French word meaning "bell." Timbre is used as a synonym for "tone quality" or tone color.*

TIME. The basic pattern of rhythm in a composition, or part of a composition. A piece may be in *three-four time* (3/4 time), which means that the basic rhythmical scheme is three quarter notes to the measure; it may be in *common time* (four quarter notes to a measure), *march time* (4/4 or 6/8), and so on.

TIME SIGNATURE. The pair of numbers at the beginning of a piece (or wherever there is a change of time within a piece) that shows the basic rhythmical pattern. The time signature 3/4, for example, shows that there are three beats to the measure and that a quarter note has a value of one beat. A time signature of 6/8 indicates that there are six beats to the measure, the eighth note having the value of one beat, and so on. The sign (𝄴) is often used as the time signature for 4/4. (See also *Duple Time* and *Triple Time.*)

TIMPANI. An Italian word meaning "kettledrums." A kettledrum is a large drum capable of producing definite pitches. It consists of a parchment-like skin stretched over the opening of a large copper bowl. By tightening

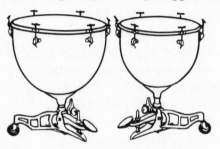

or loosening the skin, higher or lower notes can be played. On some types of kettledrums the skin is tightened or loosened by turning handles placed around the edge of the drum head. On others, pedals are used to adjust the skin. Most modern orchestras include three and sometimes more timpani, each tuned to a different note. The player holds a drumstick in each hand and strikes the drum heads in different ways to obtain different tone qualities. The sound ranges from delicate, soft tones to extremely loud ones.

TOCCATA (toh CAH tah). An Italian word meaning "touched." A toccata is an instrumental piece for one performer that is designed to show off the skill of the artist. It sometimes resembles a fantasy,* and sometimes a prelude.* J. S. Bach* wrote brilliant toccatas for both the organ and the clavier.* Other composers who have written toccatas that are often played on recitals by virtuoso artists are Schumann,* Debussy,* Prokofiev,* and Ravel.*

TOCH, Ernst. American (naturalized) composer, born in Vienna, Austria, on December 7, 1887.

Toch studied medicine and philosophy in Vienna, and taught himself music on the side, mainly by studying the works of Mozart and Bach. He was awarded a number of prizes for his compositions, including the Austrian State Prize for composition four times in succession. He later taught piano at the Hochschule für Music in Mannheim, and in 1921 was awarded the degree of Doctor of Philosophy. From 1929 to 1933 he taught piano and composition in Berlin, then when the Nazis came into power he moved to the United States. After two years as a teacher in New York, he moved to Hollywood where almost at once he began writing music for films. In addition to his film music, Toch's many compositions include operas, radio music, choral works, four symphonies and other works for orchestra, chamber music, violin pieces, piano solos, and songs.

TOM-TOM. An Oriental drum used in dance bands. It is played by beat-

ing the drum head with the fingers and the heel of the hand. The American Indians had a similar type of drum, also called *tom-tom*.

TONALITY. A different word for *key* as it pertains to music. Tonality gives the listener the feeling that the music is related to one particular major or minor key. It differs from *polytonality* (several different keys used simultaneously), and is the opposite of *atonality* (no key), both of which have been used by some writers of twentieth-century music.

TONE. A sound with a definite pitch. In England, the word *tone* is used in place of step,* as half-tone, whole-tone, and so on. It is used widely in describing such theoretical elements as whole-tone scale,* tone row,* twelve-tone* system, and so on.

TONE CLUSTER. A group of piano notes, all close together, played with the forearm, fist, or elbow to produce a highly dissonant sound. The term *tone cluster* was first used by an American composer, Henry Cowell,* when he introduced this method of playing. A typical tone cluster might be all the white keys from C to G, played by striking those keys all at one time with the fist.

TONE COLOR. The particular quality of the sound produced by different instruments and different voices. The tone color of two violins is never quite the same, nor is the tone color of two different voices. The tone color of a flute is completely different from the tone color of a recorder. A singer can change the tone color of his voice to achieve certain effects, and so can players of different instruments. The color of a tone can be made dark or bright, light or heavy, to suit the mood of the music.

TONE POEM. (See *Symphonic Poem.*)

TONE ROW. (See *Twelve-Tone Technique.*)

TONGUING. An important part of the technique used in playing wind instruments. It involves the use of the tongue to play faster or slower passages. From the slowest to the fastest, the motion of the tongue is called *single tonguing, double tonguing, triple tonguing,* and *flutter tonguing.*

TONIC. The first and most important degree in the scale. The tonic in the key of C is C, in the key of D it is D, and so on. It is the key note and the center of the tonality* of a composition written in that particular key.*

TORELLI (toh RELL lee), **Giuseppe.** Italian violinist and composer, born in Verona on April 22, 1658; died in Bologna on February 8, 1709.

Torelli was educated in Bologna and spent a good many years there as violinist and leader of a church orchestra. From 1697 to 1699 he was *Kapellmeister** to the Margrave of Brandenburg-Ansbach. He then visited Vienna, and finally returned to Bologna in 1701. He wrote a number of works for stringed instruments, and is credited with having contributed a great deal to the development of the *concerto grosso** along with his contemporary, Corelli.*

TRANSCRIBE. To arrange a piece of music so it can be performed by a different group of instruments or voices than it was originally written for. A transcription is usually more detailed than a simple arrangement.* Liszt, for example, made some elaborate transcriptions for piano of several Schubert* songs. Another example is Ravel's* transcriptions of his own piano pieces, *Alborada del Gracioso,* into a work for orchestra.

TRANSITION. A passage designed primarily to join two passages more important than itself, as two movements in a sonata.* (See also *Bridge.*)

TRANSPOSE. To perform or write out a composition in a key that is different from the original. Singers fairly often need to sing certain songs in lower or higher keys than the original, in which case the accompanist may need to transpose at sight. Many songs have been published in more than one key to suit different kinds of voices. In transposing any piece of music, it is essential that every note be changed to fit the new key.

TRANSPOSING INSTRUMENTS. Instruments for which the music is written in a key that is different from the instrument's actual pitch. For example, the clarinet in B-flat plays music that is written a whole tone higher than it sounds. This practice dates back to the eighteenth century when certain instruments had no valves* and could play only fundamental tones or overtones.* Other transposing instruments include the clarinet in A, the French horn in F, the trumpet in B-flat and A, the cornet in B-flat and A, and the English horn in F.

TRANSVERSE FLUTE. A name used to distinguish the ordinary flute, which is held crosswise, from the recorder* (also of the flute family), which is held downward.

TRAPS. Various instruments and devices used by drummers in dance bands for achieving different sound effects; for example, a kind of metal whisk-broom used to make a swishing sound.

TREBLE. (1) The highest parts in vocal or instrumental part writing. (2) A high voice, as soprano or child's high voice. (3) Certain instruments of high range, as the treble recorder, treble viol, etc.

TREBLE CLEF. Often called the G clef, the symbol is a modified letter G. It begins on the next-to-the-bottom line of the treble staff, indicating that the line is G: 🎼   The treble clef is used for notating all soprano parts and some alto parts; violin, occasionally viola; flute, piccolo, oboe, and certain transposing instruments* with a high range. Music for the tenor voice is usually notated in the treble clef, although it is actually sung an octave lower.

TRE CORDE (tray KOR day). An Italian term meaning "three strings." *Tre corde* is a direction to pianists to release the soft pedal. This causes the piano's action to shift so that all three strings are struck instead of the one (*una corde*) that is struck when the soft pedal is used.

TREMOLO (TRAY moh loh). An Italian word meaning "tremble." (1) In string playing, the tremolo is achieved by a very rapid back-and-forth motion of the bow on a single note; or, if it is a tremolo involving two notes, the fingers are used and the two notes are played alternately as rapidly as possible. The two different kinds of tremolo are notated in violin music like this:

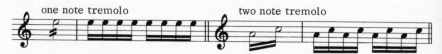

(2) On certain wind instruments a kind of tremolo is achieved by flutter tonguing.* (3) In music for the piano, the tremolo is the rapid alternation of the two notes in an octave. It is usually notated like this:

TREPAK (tray PAHK). An extremely fast Russian dance in 2/4 time that originated with the Cossacks. Mussorgsky* included a *trepak* in his cycle, *Songs and Dances of Death.*

TRIAD. A three-note chord. The most common triad consists of a principal note or root* plus the two notes a third and a fifth above, as C-E-G, the C-major triad, known also as the *common chord of C major.* Four possible triads on C are the following:

(See also *Chord.**)

TRIANGLE. A percussion instrument made of a round, steel rod, bent in the shape of a triangle. It is played by being struck with a small steel rod, and has a tinkling sound of no definite pitch.

TRILL. A musical ornament* that consists of the rapid alternate sounding of a given note and its neighbor above. A trill on a single note is indicated by the abbreviation *tr* above the note. A longer trill that extends over several tied notes has the abbreviation *tr* over the first note and a wavy line extending over all the remaining tied notes:

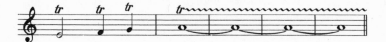

TRIO. (1) A composition for three instruments or three voices. A string trio is usually written for violin, viola, and cello; a piano trio for piano, violin, and cello. A vocal trio may be written for any number of different combinations of three voices. (2) Three performers who play or sing music written for trios. (3) The middle section of the minuet,* and many other dance forms, as well as of the scherzo* and the military march.*

TRIO SONATA. A sonata* written in three parts. The trio sonata of the Baroque* period usually consisted of two upper parts and a continuo* bass, but it was often performed by four instruments: two violins for the upper part, a cello for the middle part, and a harpsichord or organ for the continuo. Corelli,* Purcell,* and Handel* were three of many composers who wrote trio sonatas.

TRIPLE CONCERTO. A concerto written for three solo instruments and orchestra. An example is Beethoven's Concerto, Op. 56, for piano, violin, cello, and orchestra.

TRIPLE COUNTERPOINT. A variety of three-part counterpoint* in which the lower parts can be inverted; that is, the lower voices may be moved above the upper voice in a number of ways. An example of triple counterpoint can be found in Bach's Fugue in C♯-minor from *The Well-Tempered Clavier.** (See also *Counterpoint.*)

TRIPLE TIME. Time that can be divided into three primary beats, as 3/2, 3/4, 3/8.

TRIPLET. A group of three notes, or notes and rests, that are to be played in the time of two notes of the same value. The triplet is usually indicated by a slur and the numeral 3 above the triplet figure, as:

TRITONE. An interval that covers three whole tones, as C to F♯ (augmented fourth). It is identical with its inversion, F♯ to C (diminished fourth), and is equal to exactly half an octave.

TROMBONE. One of the earliest of brass wind instruments, the trombone has a cylindrical bore, a cup mouthpiece, and a flared bell. The most distinctive feature of the trombone is its slide, a mechanism that has the same function as the valves in other brass instruments. The trombone is capable of playing a chromatic range of about two and a half octaves. It comes in four sizes: alto, tenor, bass, and contrabass. Of these, the most common are the tenor (in B flat) and the bass (in G or F). The trombone was used mainly in church music until it became an established instrument of the symphony orchestra around the beginning of the nineteenth century. It is also used widely today in military and brass bands and in dance orchestras.

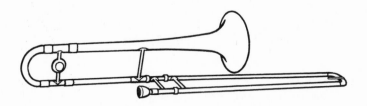

TROPPO (TROP poh). An Italian word meaning "too much." *Troppo* is used to modify other words, as *allegro non troppo* (not too fast) or *allegro ma non troppo* (fast, but not too fast).

TROUBADOURS. Poet-musicians of the Medieval period, popular in southern France. The troubadours were usually members of the nobility and they performed largely in court circles. Some 250 of their songs have been preserved.

TROUVÈRES (troo VER). Medieval poet-musicians of northern France, corresponding to the troubadours* of southern France. They were often of the nobility and performed mostly in court circles. About 1400 of their melodies have come down to us, most in the form of the ballade.* One of the most famous of the trouvères was Adam de la Hale,* who composed the musical play *Robin and Marion,* one of the most interesting stage works to survive from the Middle Ages.

TRUMPET. A brass wind instrument with a cup mouthpiece and a narrow cylindrical bore that widens into a flared bell. The trumpet is an ancient instrument and in its original form was much simpler than it is today. It was used in religious ceremonies and for military purposes in most of the ancient Mediterranean and Near Eastern civilizations. The modern trumpet can play any note in the scale, and its penetrating, brilliant tone quality has made it one of the most important instruments of the orchestra. It has three valves and is either a transposing instrument* in B-flat or a non-transposing instrument in C. It is used also in brass and military bands and in dance orchestras. A long, straight trumpet, known as a *fanfare trumpet,* is sometimes hung with a flag and used in groups for ceremonial occasions.

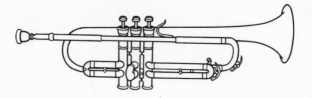

TUBA. A low-pitched brass wind instrument with a widely-flaring bell. It is equipped with four or five valves and has a cupped mouthpiece and conical bore. The most common tubas are the tenor tuba in B-flat, the bass tuba in E-flat, the bass tuba in F, and the double-bass tuba, an octave lower than the tenor tuba. The euphonium,* the helicon,* the Sousaphone,* and the baritone* are all closely related to the tuba. The tuba has a mellow tone and extremely low pitch. It has become an important instrument of the orchestra and is used also in various kinds of bands—usually in one of its related forms, as the Sousaphone or euphonium.

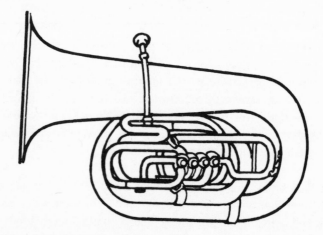

TUNE. (1) A melody, especially one that is easy to remember. (2) A term used in referring to pitch,* as "to sing in tune," to "tune a piano," and so on.

TUNING FORK. A steel fork with two prongs. When struck it gives a fundamental* pitch without upper partials.* It is used to give correct pitches to singers and also to check the pitch of certain instruments.

TURN. An ornament consisting of three, four, or five notes. It may be notated in full, or it may be indicated by the sign ∾ .

TUTTO (TOOT toh). (Also *tutti, tutte.*) An Italian word meaning "all." It is used with other words, as *tutte le corde* (all the strings), which means that the full power of the piano should be used following use of the soft pedal; *con tutta forza* (with all power), which means that the music should be performed with great volume and intensity; *tutti* (all) in orchestral music means that the entire orchestra is to play.

TWELFTH. (See *Intervals.*)

TWELVE-TONE SYSTEM. (Also called *twelve-tone technique,* and *serial technique.*) A system of musical composition devised by Arnold Schoenberg* between 1911 and 1923, that makes little or no use of traditional concepts of melody, harmony, and tonality. The composer devises from the twelve tones of the chromatic scale* a series or row of twelve tones in whatever order he wishes. Once he has selected a definite arrangement for his twelve tones, he must use that order faithfully throughout the entire composition, with a few variations: (1) he may change the octave position of any tone; (2) he may invert the row (turn it upside down); (3) he may use the row in retrograde (begin with the last note in the row and work back to the beginning); (4) the retrograde may also be inverted; (5) any of these alterations may be transposed* to any one of the twelve possible initial tones of the chromatic scale. This gives at least forty-eight variations. (6) He may also use the row vertically; i.e., he may use the row (or, usually, parts of it) simultaneously—to sound chords. The composer may make any variations in rhythm that he wishes.

Three composers, all pupils of Schoenberg, who have adopted the twelve-tone technique, or parts of it, in their own works are Alban Berg,* Anton Webern,* and Egon Wellesz. Some later composers have applied the organizational principles of the twelve-tone system to other aspects of their compositions, such as rhythm, dynamics, orchestration, etc.

U

UKULELE (yoo kuh LAY lee). (Sometimes spelled *ukelele*.) A small stringed instrument with a fretted neck and four strings. It was brought originally to the South Pacific islands by the Portuguese and became popular in the Hawaiian Islands. During the 1920's it was adopted widely in the United States, largely because it was easy to play and had a pleasant sound for accompanying group singing. A special notation for the ukulele resembles a form of ancient lute* tablature,* showing the position of the fingers on the frets. The strings are tuned to

UNA CORDA (OO nah COR dah). An Italian term meaning "one string." Una corda is a direction to pianists to use the soft pedal. This causes the action to shift so that only one string is struck by each hammer, thus producing a softer tone. The abbreviation for *una corda* is *u.c.* The direction to release the soft pedal is *tre corda** or *tutte* le corda*.

UNISON. (1) Singing or playing by several performers all on the same pitch is called "singing or playing in unison." Actually, as with men and women singing together, the pitch may be an octave apart. (2) The term is also used to describe the interval that has no pitch difference, that is, when the two notes are on the same line or space, as C-C.

UP-BEAT. (1) The note or notes that fall on the weak beat just before a

308

bar line, but that begin a phrase, as the first two notes in the following excerpt:

(2) The upward motion of the conductor's hand or baton to indicate a beat that begins a phrase and is notated immediately before a bar line.

UP BOW. The upward stroke of the bow in playing bowed stringed instruments. It is indicated on the music by the sign (V) directly above the notes that are to be played with an upward stroke. (See also *Bowing*.)

UT. In the original system of solmization,* the syllable name now replaced in America by *do*.* *Ut* is still used in Europe.

V

VALSE. The French word for waltz. Some famous compositions with the title *Valse* are Ravel's *La Valse* for orchestra, Tchaikovsky's *Valse,* Op. 39, No. 8, for piano, and Sibelius' *Valse triste* for orchestra.

VALVE. A device used in brass instruments, invented by Blühmel in 1813. The valve, which revolutionized the playing of brass instruments, consists of upright lengths of pipe set into the tubing. By depressing a piston with his fingers a player can connect the main tubing of the instrument with a "valve," thus diverting the current of air around additional lengths of the instrument's tubing. It is possible to use the valves singly or in combination to produce a complete chromatic scale. Before the invention of the valve, most brass instruments were able to produce only one harmonic series,* which left large gaps in the scale. Practically all of the brass instruments used today in orchestras and bands are equipped with valves. An exception is the trombone, which has a slide mechanism. (See also *Wind Instruments.*)

VAMP. An improvised introduction or accompaniment to a popular song. It usually consists of simple chords, played in a steady rhythm, and repeated over and over until the singer is ready to begin.

VARÈSE, Edgard. French composer, born in Paris on December 22, 1885.

As a child, Varèse was intensely interested in music, even writing an opera at the age of twelve. His parents, however, opposed his musical ambitions, and when he was nineteen he left home in order to study music seriously. He enrolled in the Schola Cantorum, where he studied with d'Indy,* and at the Paris Conservatory, where he worked with Widor.* His early works, written between 1904 and 1914 were largely impressionistic* and romantic in style. Then, in 1915 he came to America, settled in New York, and began to work out a completely new concept of musical composition. He became interested in sound for sound's sake, rhythm taking precedence over harmony, melody, and thematic development. Most of his later works make wide use of percussion,* as in his best-known composition *Ionization* which calls for thirteen players playing thirty-five instruments, all (except a piano and tubular gongs) of indefinite pitch. Varèse has experimented also with electronic music.* In *Deserts,* electronically treated sounds are used with wind instruments and percussion. *Poème Électronique,* composed for the 1958 Brussels Exposition, consisted of electronic music broadcast over four hundred loudspeakers.

VARIATIONS. An important musical form consisting of a theme,* which is presented first, followed by any number of variations of the theme. The original theme always is the basis for the variations that follow. These variations may be simple or extremely elaborate. The original theme may be an original one composed by the composer of the composition, or it may be "borrowed" from another composer. Some variations are independent compositions; others occur as a movement in a sonata or a symphony. Many great composers have written sets of variations. Some examples are J. S. Bach's *Goldberg Variations,* Beethoven's *Diabelli Variations,* Brahms's *Variations on a Theme of Handel,* and Elgar's *Enigma Variations.* The passacaglia* and chaconne,* both popular forms of the Baroque period are essentially variations.

VAUGHAN WILLIAMS, Ralph. English composer, born in Down Ampney, Gloucestershire, on October 12, 1872; died in London on August 26, 1958.

Vaughan Williams was educated at Charterhouse School in London and at Trinity College in Cambridge. He studied later with Max Bruch* in Berlin and with Ravel* in Paris. He became intensely interested in the folk music of England and English music of the Elizabethan and Tudor periods. These interests are reflected strongly in his own compositions, and although his music is highly individual and modern, his works show his deep regard for traditional English melodies and musical forms. In 1935 he was awarded the Order of Merit by King George V. He was greatly honored and re-spected during his lifetime, and lived to see the performance of most of his major works. These include nine symphonies and other works for orches-tra, choral works, five operas, two ballets, chamber music, music for motion pictures, church music, and an extensive list of solo songs and song cycles.

VERDI (VEHR dee), **Giuseppe.** Italian composer of opera, born in Le Roncole on October 10, 1813; died in Milan on January 27, 1901.

Verdi was born to a poor family. His father ran a humble inn in Le Roncole, and young Giuseppe's first education was given him by the parish priest. When he was ten, he began to attend school in Busseto, a town about four miles from his home. His first music lessons were given him by the organist in the church at Le Roncole, and before long he himself was given the job of organist. At that time he was still living in Busseto. In order to save wear and tear on his shoes, he walked the four miles on Sundays, and other days when he played the organ, in his bare feet, carry-ing his shoes. A wealthy merchant in Busseto, Antonio Barezzi, took an interest in the boy and made it possible for him to continue his study of music. He studied for four years at the municipal music school, then became an assistant to his teacher, Provesi. During this time he composed a great deal of music, played the organ, appeared as a pianist in concerts, and copied parts for the local Philharmonic Society's orchestra. Barezzi per-suaded Verdi's father to apply for a scholarship at the Milan Conservatory, and he himself promised to support the boy for a year. Verdi went to Milan in 1832, but failed the difficult entrance examination and was not admitted to the Conservatory. He remained in Milan, however, for study with Lavigna. For the next few years he travelled between Busseto and Milan, studying and holding down various posts in the two towns. In 1835 he was appointed *maestro di musica* to the commune of Busseto, after suc-cessfully completing an examination at Parma. Now he felt that his finan-cial situation was secure enough to enable him to take a wife, and on May 4, 1836, he married Margherita Barezzi, the eldest daughter of his benefactor. For the next three years he was busy with his duties at Busseto, but during that time his two young children died. By the time the second child died he had moved to Milan, where about a year later, his wife died. These tragedies affected him deeply and it was some time before he recov-ered sufficiently to resume his composing. For some time he had been interested in writing opera, and was fortunate enough to have his first opera *Oberto* produced at the La Scala in 1839. It was received quite favorably, but his second opera, *Un Giorno di regne,* produced a year later, was a failure. Merelli, the impressario* of the La Scala, had faith in Verdi in spite of that misfortune and promised him that if he would write another opera he would produce it. Verdi became interested in a libretto on a Biblical subject, *Nabucodonosor,* and in a fairly short time completed the opera *Nabucco.* When it was produced at the La Scala the following spring it became an immediate success. *Nabucco* brought fame to Verdi not only in Italy, but in other parts of Europe as well. From that time on, Verdi turned out one opera after another, most of them successful. He constantly improved and added to his technical skill, and many authorities believe that his last opera, *Falstaff,* written when he was nearly eighty years old, was his finest.

Altogether, Verdi wrote thirty operas, the best known of which are *Nabucco, Macbeth, Louisa Miller, Rigoletto, Il Trovatore, La Traviata, Simon Boccanegra, Un ballo in maschera, La forza del destino Don Carlos, Aida, Otello,* and *Falstaff.* In addition, he wrote a number of sacred choral works, including the great *Requiem* and *Stabat Mater,* several secular choral works, a string quartet, and twenty songs.

VERISMO (vay REEZ moh). An Italian word meaning "realism." *Verismo* is a term applied to a movement aimed at a more realistic representation of everyday life in opera. It originated in Italy in the late nineteenth century. Some of the best examples are Mascagni's* *Cavalleria rusticana,* Leoncavallo's* *Pagliacci,* Charpentier's* *Louise,* and Puccini's* *La Bohème.*

VESPERS. The evening service of the Roman Catholic church. It consists mainly of a series of Psalms, a hymn, and the Magnificat.* Monteverdi* and Mozart* both wrote elaborate settings of the vesper service for voices, orchestra, and organ.

VIBRAPHONE. A percussion instrument that resembles the xylophone.* It consists of metal bars arranged like the keys of the piano, with wooden resonators underneath. The resonators are constantly opened and closed electronically. When the bars are struck with felt- or wood-covered beaters, the resonators impart a vibrating effect to the tone. The instrument is used primarily in dance bands, but has been used by a few modern composers, as in the opera *Lulu* by Alben Berg* and the orchestral work, *Spring Symphony,* by Britten.*

VIBRATO (vee BRAH toh). An Italian word meaning "vibrated." A vibrato is a fast but very slight fluctuation in pitch. In playing bowed stringed instruments, the vibrato is necessary for artistic performance. The player gets a vibrato by pressing the finger firmly on the string and moving the wrist rapidly in and out. In singing, a slight, natural vibrato is essential to artistic quality (as opposed to the "straight tone" cultivated by some popular singers), but singers need to guard against developing too wide a vibrato that may become a tremolo.* The pipe organ has a stop* called *Voix Céleste* that produces a vibrato. A form of vibrato called *Bebung* is produced on the clavichord* by repeatedly pressing a key without releasing it.

VICTORIA (vit TOHRR yah), **Tomás Louis de.** Spanish composer, born in Avila about 1548; died in Madrid on August 27, 1611.

It is probable that Victoria was a chorister and student at the Cathedral in Avila. When he was about seventeen he went to Rome for study at the Collegium Germanicum, and four years later became organist at the Church of Santa Maria di Monserrato. Two years later he succeeded his former teacher, the great Palestrina,* as organist and choirmaster at the Collegium Germanicum. In 1575 he was ordained a priest, and about five years later became chaplain to the Empress of Spain. Victoria is famous for his expressive and ingenious use of polyphony* in his many Masses,* motets,* Magnificats,* and other works.

VIELLE (vyell). A forerunner of the violin, the vielle was a bowed stringed instrument of the Medieval period. (See also *Hurdy-Gurdy*.)

VIEUXTEMPS (vyer TAHN), **Henri.** Belgian violinist and composer, born in Verviers on February 17, 1820; died in Mustapha-lez-Alger, Algiers, on June 6, 1881.

Son of an instrument maker and amateur musician, Vieuxtemps had his first music lessons with his father. He studied later with Lecloux, an excellent teacher who developed in the boy enough technique and musicianship so he was able to play a concerto with orchestra in a public concert when he was only six years old. Just a year later he made a tour as a concert artist with his father and his teacher. De Bériot, a fine teacher, heard him and was so impressed that he took him to Paris to perform. Vieuxtemps remained there to study with De Bériot for two years. By 1833, when he was still only thirteen, he made an impressive tour throughout Germany and Austria, playing such difficult works as Beethoven's Violin Concerto. From that time on, he continued to study and to tour extensively, except for a period of five years when he was a professor at the St. Petersburg Conservatory in Russia and two years when he was on the faculty of the Brussels Conservatory in Belgium. In 1873 he suffered a stroke of paralysis that forced him to retire, and except for teaching a few private pupils, he spent the remainder of his life composing and traveling.

Vieuxtemps was one of the greatest violinists of all times. He played with an amazingly powerful tone, with perfect intonation; he had enormous skill with the bow, and was famous for his playing of rapid staccato passages. He wrote a great many works for violin, the best-known of which are his six concertos.

VILLA-LOBOS (VEE lah LOH bohs), **Heitor.** Brazilian composer, conductor, and music educator, born in Rio de Janeiro on March 5, 1887; died there on November 17, 1959.

Villa-Lobos learned to play the viola when he was six years old, and by the time he was eleven was a fair performer on the piano and clarinet. His father was his first teacher and encouraged him to continue with his study of music. His father died when he was twelve years old, however, and his mother, who did not want him to have a career in music, did everything she could to discourage him. He continued as best he could to study music anyway, but finally when he was sixteen he ran away from home in order to find a more congenial atmosphere. During this period he earned his living by playing in cafes and restaurants. He made four lengthy trips into the primitive interior of Brazil to collect folk materials and study folk music. These materials were incorporated to some extent into his own works, of which he was writing a great many. When he gave a concert of his compositions in Rio de Janeiro they created a sensation. In 1918 he met the great virtuoso pianist, Artur Rubinstein, and a lasting friendship grew up between them. Rubinstein became interested in the young composer and played his works in many parts of the world. As more and more of his compositions were performed, Villa-Lobos became more and more celebrated. In fact, he was the first South American composer to become world-famous. Some of the important positions he held were Director of Music Education in São Paulo, Superintendent of Music and Artistic Education in Rio de Janeiro, and Director of the National Conservatory, an institution that he himself founded. He wrote a great many works, including five operas; fourteen ballets on Brazilian subjects, nearly all for school children; nine works entitled *Bachianas Brasileiras*; thirteen works entitled *Choros*; eleven symphonies and other works for orchestra; chamber music; a great many piano solos and songs.

VIOL. A family of bowed stringed instruments that were widely used during the sixteenth and seventeenth centuries. After about 1700 they were superseded by instruments of the violin family, but have been revived in modern times for the purpose of playing music of the earlier period. Viols had flat backs, sloping shoulders, and six strings. The instruments were held on the knees or resting between them, and played with a bow that was held above the palm of the hand. They came in three sizes: treble, tenor, and bass. The bass viol was also called *viola da gamba* (leg viol).

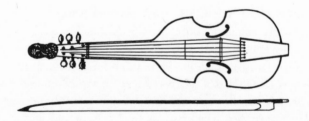

VIOLA. The second member of the violin family, the viola is one of the important instruments of the modern orchestra. It is one seventh larger in size than the violin and is tuned a fifth lower:

Its tone is more muted and has less brilliance and power than the tone of the violin, but it has a special quality of its own that has made it a favorite instrument with some composers. Hindemith* and Bartók,* for example, have written splendid concertos for the viola. (See also *Violin Family*.)

VIOLA DA GAMBA (vee OH la dah GAHM bah). (See *Viol*.)

VIOLA D'AMORE (vee OH la dah MOH ray). An instrument that was prominent in the seventeenth and eighteenth centuries. The name, which means "love viol," probably derives from the scroll, which often was carved in the shape of the blindfolded face of the god of love. The instrument was about the size and shape of the treble viol,* but it had an additional set of strings lying under the bowed strings. These extra strings produced a special kind of resonance.* The viola d'amore is still used occasionally for playing old music, and several modern composers, including Richard Strauss, Puccini, and Hindemith, have written music for it.

VIOLIN. The principal member of the family of modern bowed stringed instruments. The main parts of the violin are the body, consisting of the sounding board, back and side walls; the finger board,* terminating in the pegbox and scroll; the string holder, or tail piece; and the bridge. The four strings are tuned in fifths:

The modern violin dates from the sixteenth century, and oddly enough, it has not been altered or improved to any degree since its first appearance. In fact, its greatest period of perfection was from about 1600 to 1750. During that period the three greatest violin makers of all time, Amati,* Stradivari,* and Guarneri,* turned out violins so fine they have never been surpassed, and those that have survived to the present time are worth fabulous sums of money. (See also *Violin Family*.)

VIOLIN FAMILY. The family of modern stringed instruments that consists of the violin,* the viola,* the cello,* and the double bass.* (See individual entries for descriptions of those instruments.)

Violin   Viola

Cello   Double bass

VIOLONCELLO. (See *Cello*.)

VIOTTI (vee OT ee), **Giovanni Battista.** Italian violinist and composer, born in Fontanetto da Po on May 12, 1755; died in London on March 3, 1824.

Viotti's father, a blacksmith and amateur musician, bought his son a small violin and gave him lessons when he was a small boy. He proved to be remarkably gifted, and when he was thirteen years old the celebrated teacher Pugnani* accepted him as a pupil. Under Pugnani's guidance Viotti developed a virtuoso technique, and by the time he was twenty-five he was touring Europe as a concert violinist. Marie Antoinette appointed him to the position of court musician and manager of a royal opera theater, but the French Revolution interrupted his stay in Paris, and in 1792 he went to London to conduct Italian operas. When the French Monarchy was restored in France, he returned to Paris as Conductor of the Italian Opera there, but the times were difficult and he suffered financially as well as physically. He returned to London in 1822, but his health was broken, he was heavily in debt, and he lived only two years longer.

Viotti was one of the finest violinists of his day, and his influence as a teacher was far-reaching. He wrote a great many works, most of them for strings, including twenty-nine violin concertos. His Violin Concerto No. 22 in A minor is probably his best known work.

VIRGINAL. A keyboard instrument popular in the sixteenth and seventeenth centuries, especially in England. It resembled the harpsichord in that its strings were plucked, but it was smaller and had a different shape— usually oblong, with the keyboard running along one of the long sides, though some virginals were wing-shaped. Some important English composers of music for the virginal were William Byrd,* John Bull,* and Orlando Gibbons.* *The Fitzwilliam Virginal Book,* dating from about 1620, contains 297 pieces for the virginal.

VIRTUOSO (veer too OH soh). An Italian word meaning "virtuous." The term is used in music to describe a highly skilled performer who possesses great technical ability.

VIVACE (vee VAH chay). An Italian word meaning "vivacious, lively." Vivace indicates that the music should be performed in a lively manner. It is often used in the expression *allegro vivace* (fast and lively).

VIVALDI (vee VAHL dee), **Antonio.** Italian violinist and composer, born in Venice about 1675; died in Vienna, Austria, in July, 1741.

Almost nothing is known about Vivaldi's childhood except that his father, a violinist at the church of San Marco in Venice, was his first teacher. Vivaldi entered the priesthood, taking holy orders in 1703. That same year he became a teacher in the musical seminary of the Hospital of Pity in Venice. Six years later he was appointed *Maestro de' concerti* of the seminary, a post he kept for thirty-one years. During that time, however, he performed a great deal, wrote a large amount of music, and even travelled extensively. Although he was a priest, he never once said the Mass, because he suffered from asthma. He left several concertos* for the violin, including his most famous work, a set of four concertos called *The Four Seasons,* and some keyboard music. Many of his works were imitated by other composers, and some were utilized in transcriptions by J. S. Bach.*

VOCALISE. A composition without words used primarily as a vocal exercise by singers. It is sung on a single vowel sound, usually *ah.*

VOCE (VOH chay). An Italian word meaning "voice." The term is used in different ways, as *a due voci* (for two voices or parts); *colla voce* (with the voice, meaning that the accompanist must follow the singer rather than keep strict time); *mezza voce* (medium voice, fairly quietly); *sotto voce* (under the voice, very quietly).

VOICE. (1) The human voice when used as an instrument for producing music, as "a high voice," "tenor voice," "to study voice," and so on. (2) An individual part in a contrapuntal* composition, either for voices or for instruments. The term *voice* is used in reference to instrumental parts because the writing of instrumental part music was originally based on writing for voices. A fugue* in four-part counterpoint, such as Fugue I from Bach's *The Well-Tempered Clavier,* is a fugue in four voices.

W

WAGNER (VAHG nerr), **Richard.** German composer and author, born in Leipzig on May 22, 1813; died in Venice, Italy, on February 13, 1883.

Wagner was only six when his father died. His mother soon remarried, and the boy got along well with his stepfather, who was an actor and playwright. The theatre interested young Richard to the extent that at the age of fourteen he wrote a grand tragedy in the style of Shakespeare. He had begun his study of music when he was twelve, first on the piano, then on the violin. He did not do especially well with either, partly because he was eager to play music that was too difficult for him. For example, he attempted to read through such operatic scores as *Der Freischütz* almost as soon as he had learned his five-finger exercises, and he tried to learn how to compose by studying a textbook. Before long, however, he began to study harmony and composition with the Cantor of the famous Thomas School, and from then on he made better progress. When he was sixteen an overture he had written was performed at a Christmas concert. It was not a success, but this failure did not discourage him. He had become interested in opera, and when he was twenty years old his brother, who was stage manager of the opera theater in Würzburg, got him a position as chorus director. A year later he became conductor of the opera at Magdeburg. That appointment led to two others, first in Königsberg, then in Riga.

By this time, Wagner was twenty-six years old, and he decided to go to Paris for two reasons: first, he had already written an opera, *Rienzi,* and hoped to get it produced there; second, he wanted to hear the operas of Meyerbeer, all the rage then in Paris. He stayed in Paris for two years, leading a rather miserable existence. He was unable to get a performance of *Rienzi,* and was forced to support himself by arranging dance music, writing articles about music, and doing whatever he could to make a bare living. Even so, he suffered great poverty and at one time was confined in debtors' prison for nearly a month.

He was already twenty-eight years old when the news came than *Rienzi* was to be produced in Dresden, and he went there to direct rehearsals. The opera was a great success, and the management decided to produce another of his operas—one that he had composed while he was in Paris—*The Flying Dutchman.* This, too, was a success, and Wagner found himself appointed to an important position, Musical Director of the Saxon Court, and Conductor at the Dresden Opera. During the next six years he was responsible for many fine performances, including a performance of his own next opera, *Tannhäuser.* About this time he wrote *Lohengrin,* but he did not direct it at Dresden. Its first performance was under the direction of Liszt* at Weimar in 1850. Wagner himself did not hear a performance of *Lohengrin* until eleven years later.

In 1849 Wagner was forced to flee from Dresden to escape imprisonment for having been involved in a revolutionary political movement. At that time there were uprisings all over Europe, and Wagner had taken the side of the people who were demanding more freedom. He found refuge with Liszt in Weimar, but was forced to leave there and go to Switzerland. He settled in Zürich, where he wrote a number of books, most of them concerned with how he thought opera should be written. He also began work on his great cycle of four operas, *The Ring of the Nibelung,* as well as *Tristan and Isolde.* Except for visits to London, Paris, and Venice, Wagner stayed in Switzerland until 1861, when it finally was safe for him to return to Germany. He was now forty-seven years old, and when the newly-crowned King Ludwig II invited him to come to Munich to perform his operas he was only too happy to accept. There, however, he became involved in a scandal and lost favor with the nobles of the court. When asked by the King to leave the city he returned to Switzerland, this time to an island in the Lake of Lucerne, taking with him the woman with whom he had fallen in love, Cosima von Bülow, daughter of Liszt. She succeeded in obtaining a divorce from von Bülow, and in 1870 she and Wagner were married. During his stay in Lucerne, Wagner finished *The Ring,* wrote *The Mastersingers,* and did a great deal of work on his great religious music drama *Parsifal.* During that time, too, his only son, Siegfried, was born.

In 1872 Wagner received an offer from the city of Bayreuth in Germany to build a theatre for the production of his works alone. The theater, called *Festspielhaus* (Festival Theater) was designed by Wagner himself, and erected with the help of many individuals and musical societies who had become deeply devoted to Wagner's operas. Wagner built his own home in Bayreuth and by 1876 had realized his life-long dream: full performance of his cycle of four operas, *The Ring of the Nibelung,* prepared under his own supervision. The performances at Bayreuth were a great success, but very costly. However, people from all over the world continued to support the theater, and except for periods during World Wars I and II, the Bayreuth Festivals have been held almost continuously. When Wagner died in 1883, his widow, Cosima, took over the management of the performances. When she became too old, she turned over the responsibility to their son, Siegfried. When Siegfried died in 1930, his widow, Winifred, carried on. After World War II, when performances were again resumed, the two sons of Siegfried and Winifred, whose names are Wieland and Wolfgang Wagner, became the managers. So, today, the grandsons of Richard Wagner continue the long tradition of presenting Wagnerian opera in the great Festpielhaus that he himself inaugurated.

WALTON, William. English composer, born in Oldham on March 29, 1902.

Walton's first musical instruction was received from his father. Then, when he was ten years old, he entered the Christ Church Cathedral Choir School at Oxford. His teachers quickly recognized his strong musical talent and gave him a great deal of freedom to develop his creative ideas. When he was seventeen, he composed a piano quartet that showed tremendous promise, and from then on his development was rapid. He has written excellent music in many different forms, all of it showing great individuality. His works include a viola concerto, a violin concerto, a symphony, an outstanding oratorio called *Belshazzar's Feast,* film music, an opera called *Troilus and Cressida,* and many other things, including a *Te Deum* for the coronation of Queen Elizabeth II in 1953.

WALTZ. A ballroom dance in 3/4 time. The waltz became especially popular during the nineteenth century when the Viennese composers Johann Strauss* and his sons, Johann Jr. and Joseph, wrote their many beautiful waltzes, including *The Beautiful Blue Danube, Tales from the Vienna Woods,* and *The Emperor Waltz.* Schubert,* Weber,* Chopin,* and

Brahms* wrote sets of waltzes for piano, as have many other composers. The waltz is found in opera, as in Richard Strauss's *Der Rosenkavalier,* and occasionally as a movement in a symphony.

WEBER (VAY berr), **Carl Maria von.** German composer born in Eustin, near Lübeck, on November 18, 1786; died in London, England, on June 5, 1826.

Carl's father, who loved music, desired nothing more ardently than to have his son become a child prodigy like Mozart. But little Carl showed no talent. In fact, his brother Fritz, who was his first teacher, became exasperated with his little brother's lack of ability and felt that he would never become a musician. Carl was nine years old before he showed any signs of the great musical talent he actually possessed. He spent a great deal of time travelling with his father, who had his own dramatic company, and this constant first-hand experience with the theater gave the boy a background for the kind of music for which he was later to become famous: the opera.

When Carl was ten years old his family moved with their troup to Salzburg, and there Carl was taken to Michael Haydn, brother of the famous composer Joseph Haydn.* Haydn was quick to recognize the boy's special talents. He took him into his training school for choir boys and helped him with his musical studies. By the time he was thirteen, Carl had written several works, including an opera called *The Power of Love and Wine.* After a few more years of traveling about with his family, Weber, at the age of seventeen, was made *Kapellmeister* of the theatre at Breslau. This was the first of a number of posts that he held from time to time, interspersed with concert tours and a great deal of composing. His final post, which was to occupy the remaining years of his life, was the most important of all: that of conductor of the German Opera at Dresden. He completely reorganized the opera there, and instituted many reforms that raised the standard of German opera immensely. Weber had already written a great many works when the first production of his masterpiece, the opera *Der Freischütz,* was given on June 18, 1821, in Berlin. It was a great triumph and was acclaimed throughout Germany and Austria. Five years later, Weber went to London to begin preparations for the production of *Oberon,* an opera in English that he had written for the famous Covent Garden Opera. He himself conducted the first twelve performances, which were enormously successful. He did not live much longer to enjoy the fame that had finally come to him. He fell ill of a throat ailment that probably stemmed from a time in his youth when he had swallowed nitric acid, thinking it to be wine. In addition to *Der Freischütz* and *Oberon,* Weber wrote several other operas, including *Euryanthe* and *Abu Hassan*; incidental music to plays; two concertos for piano and orchestra; two concertos and one concertino for clarinet and orchestra; a bassoon concerto; many piano solos, including the well-known *Invitation to the Dance*; church music; several part-songs and canons; and well over one hundred songs with piano or guitar accompaniment.

WEBERN (VAY bern), **Anton.** Austrian composer, born in Vienna on December 3, 1883; died in Mittersill on September 15, 1945.

Webern was a student of the music historian, Guido Adler, and was awarded a Ph.D. from the University of Vienna when he was twenty-two years old. He was also a student of Schoenberg.

Webern became one of the most important exponents of the twelve-tone system* of composition, but adapted it to his own individual style. In addition to composing, he held various posts as conductor, and aided Schoenberg with the preparation of concerts for a society devoted to the performance of modern music. Through these performances as well as in his position as conductor of the Vienna Workers' Symphony Concerts, he did much to acquaint the public with the works of Schoenberg as well as those of other contemporary composers. From 1918 on he lived in semi-retirement, devoting himself largely to teaching and to composing. His death occurred accidentally when he was shot during the occupation of Austria at the close of World War II. His compositions include five choral works; five orchestral works; seven instrumental chamber works; seven vocal chamber works; some twenty songs and other compositions. Almost all of these works are in strict twelve-tone idiom.

WEILL, Kurt. German composer, born in Dessau on March 2, 1900; died in New York on April 3, 1950.

As a young student, Weill obtained an excellent musical education at the Berlin High School for Music, where he studied with Humperdinck* and Krasselt. He later studied with the eminent pianist and composer, Busoni,* a teacher who helped him enormously to develop his creative talent. By 1933 he had written several works, including *The Threepenny Opera,* that were to become famous both in Europe and the United States. By then the

Nazis had come to power, and Weill was forced to leave Germany. He spent two years in Paris and London, then in 1935 settled permanently in the United States. Weill wrote fifteen operas, several Broadway musical plays, incidental music for plays, film music, a few choral and orchestral works, and several songs. Two of his most popular works in addition to *The Threepenny Opera* are *Down in the Valley,* a folk opera, and *Lost in the Stars,* a musical play that enjoyed a long run on Broadway.

WELL-TEMPERED CLAVIER, THE. The title given by J. S. Bach* to two sets of preludes and fugues he composed for keyboard instruments. Each set consists of twenty-four pairs of preludes* and fugues* in all the major and minor keys, beginning with a prelude and a fugue in C major. The first set dates from 1722; the second from 1744. Bach wrote the *Well-tempered Clavier* to demonstrate the advantages of the new system of tuning keyboard instruments in *equal temperament,** that is, to show that the new system made it as easy to play in one key as in another, something that was not possible with the older system of tuning.

WHIP. A percussion instrument that consists of two pieces of wood fastened together in the form of a V. The player snaps the pieces together loudly to imitate the crack of a whip.

WHOLE NOTE. Among the notes commonly used in modern notation, the note that has the longest value, being equal to two half-notes or four quarter-notes. It has no stem: (o). The corresponding whole rest is this: (▬).

WHOLE TONE. The interval of one whole step in the diatonic scale. In the key of C-major, for example, the step from C to D is one whole tone. It is also the equivalent of two half steps, as E to F-sharp.

WHOLE-TONE SCALE. A scale made up entirely of whole steps instead of the patterns of whole and half steps that make up the major and minor scales. The whole-tone scale beginning on C would be: C-D-E-F♯-G♯-A♯-B♯(C). The only other possible whole tone scale might begin on D♭: D♭-E♭-F-G-A-B-C♯. Debussy is one of many composers who have made wide use of the whole-tone scale in their compositions.

WIDOR (vee DOR), **Charles Marie.** French organist and composer, born in Lyons on February 24, 1845; died in Paris on March 12, 1937.

Widor studied first with his father, who was a church organist in Lyon. He went later to Belgium for further study, and by the time he was twenty-five had become organist at the church of St. Sulpice in Paris. He soon began to distinguish himself as an organist and composer and was given first the post of organ professor at the Paris Conservatory and later that of professor of composition. He wrote a great many works, including concertos for various instruments and orchestra, two symphonies, operas, ballets, piano solos, and chamber music. However, he is best known today for his many fine organ works, including ten large ones called "symphonies," and a concerto for organ and orchestra.

WILLAERT (vill LEHRT), **Adrian.** Flemish composer, born in Bruges about 1490; died in Venice, Italy, on December 7, 1562.

Willaert was sent to Paris to study law, but soon switched to music theory. Some years later he travelled to Italy, and after serving in two royal courts was appointed Chapelmaster at St. Mark's in Venice. Inspired by the two great organs there, he initiated the practice of antiphonal* singing by two choirs. His works include Masses,* madrigals,* motets,* chansons,* and instrumental ricercars.* One of his many pupils in Venice was the famous Andrea Gabrieli.*

WIND INSTRUMENTS. Instruments of the modern orchestra that have air columns enclosed in some sort of pipe,* and which are made to sound by blowing into them or across them as in the case of the flute. The two main types are woodwinds* and brass.* (See also *Instruments* and *Orchestra.*)

WOLF (volf), **Hugo.** Austrian composer, born in Windischgraz (now Slovenjgradee, a town in Yugoslavia) on March 13, 1860; died in Vienna on February 22, 1903.

Wolf's father was a leather manufacturer and also an excellent amateur musician. He gave his son his first music lessons, and the boy did so well that he played violin in a "family" orchestra at a fancy-dress ball when he was only six years old. When Hugo was seven, a fire destroyed the family home and the workshops, and from that time on he knew great hardship and poverty. He did badly in his studies, neglecting his regular work for music, to which he was completely devoted. Furthermore, he suffered from a short temper, which made it difficult for him to work as a teacher. His fiery disposition even led to his being expelled from the Vienna Conservatory where he had finally been able to study seriously the technical aspects of music. In spite of his lack of self-control, Wolf had a certain charm that attracted the friendship and support of enough admirers to keep him from starving. He was constantly moving from one boarding house to another, and from one friendly family to another.

Through the influence of friends, Wolf found some employment as a music teacher in private homes, and for a while he even held the post of *Kapellmeister** at the theater in Salzburg. That employment came to a sudden end when he quarreled with the director. He returned to Vienna, and although he was again forced to live a hand-to-mouth existence, he enjoyed some rich musical and literary experiences. He attempted an opera, which he never finished, and wrote a few songs, but could find no publisher who would show an interest in his work.

In the spring of 1887, when Wolf was twenty-seven years old, his father died, bitterly disappointed that his son, from whom he had expected great things, seemed a complete failure. Then shortly afterward, Wolf seemed to hit his stride. He began to compose the many beautiful songs that were to make him famous as one of the greatest song writers of all time. In just over two years he composed more than one hundred and sixty songs that were well received. He again turned to opera, and finally, when he was thirty-three years old he heard his opera *Der Corregidor* performed in Mannheim. It was not a success, and Wolf returned to Vienna. He began work on another opera, but that, too, was never finished, for Wolf went completely mad and had to be committed to an asylum. Four and a half years later, after great suffering, he died.

Except for his one completed opera, a few orchestral and choral works, and some piano pieces, the great body of Wolf's compositions consists of songs. His most important songs can be grouped according to the poems he set to music: fifty-three by Goethe, fifty-five by Mörike, twenty by Eichendorff; plus forty-four in his *Spanish Song Book* and forty-six in his *Italian Song Book*.

WOODWINDS. The general family of wind instruments that include the flutes,* the oboes,* (the bassoon* is a member of the oboe family), the clarinets,* and the saxophones.* All consist basically of a tube, with holes, that encloses a column of air. The vibrating column of air is shortened or lengthened when the player opens or closes the holes with his fingers, thus varying the pitch of the notes played. Air is blown across the moutn opening of the flute; the recorder* is blown into directly through the mouthpiece. Oboes, clarinets, and saxophones are equipped with double or single reeds fitted into the mouthpiece. These vibrate as air is blown over them. (See also *Instruments*.)

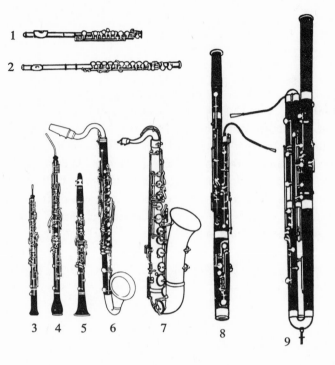

1. Piccolo, 2. Flute, 3. Oboe, 4. English Horn, 5. Clarinet, 6. Bass-Clarinet, 7. Saxophone, 8. Bassoon, 9. Contra-Bassoon.

⮐XYZ⮑

XYLOPHONE. A percussion instrument consisting of hardwood bars, tuned in a chromatic scale, and arranged like a piano keyboard. The bars are held in place by tightly stretched cords mounted in a horizontal frame over metal resonators that are firmly anchored beneath the bars. The resonators vibrate in sympathy as each note is struck with hammers. The xylophone has a compass* of three octaves upward from Middle C. The instrument can be traced back to very ancient forms, some of which are still used in Africa and Asia.

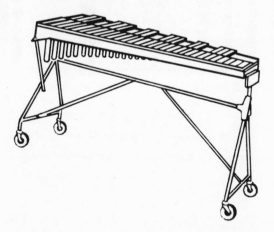

YODEL. A special type of singing heard in the Swiss and Austrian Alps. The singer uses both his chest voice and a falsetto,* switching quickly from one to the other.

YSAŸE (ee zah ee), **Eugène.** Belgian violinist, conductor, and composer, born in Liège on July 16, 1858; died in Brussels on May 12, 1931.

Ÿsaye began to study music with his father when he was five years old. He later studied at the Conservatory of Liège, and when he was fifteen had the good fortune to study for a short time with Wieniawski in Paris. A year later, Vieuxtemps* happened to hear him perform one of his concertos in Antwerp and was so impressed with the boy's talent that he made it possible for him to receive a special government subsidy for three years of study at the Brussels Conservatory. During that time Ÿsaye had a number of private lessons with Vieuxtemps, and by the time he was twenty-one he was ready to concertize. He performed with some of the finest orchestras in Europe. In 1886, when he was twenty-eight years old, he accepted a position as professor of violin at the Brussels Conservatory. He remained there for eleven years, during which time he founded his own string quartet and directed a series of orchestral concerts at which many famous artists appeared. He concertized widely, both as a violin soloist and as a conductor. For four years, beginning in 1918, he was in the United States, serving as conductor of the Cincinnati Symphony Orchestra. After that he remained mostly in Belgium, where he was extremely active in the musical life of his country, as a teacher, composer, and performer. He left many compositions for the violin, mostly in manuscript, but also including the published *Mazurkas,* Op. 11, six sonatas for unaccompanied violin; some smaller pieces for violin and piano or orchestra, and an opera in the Walloon dialect, *Pière li Houyen.*

ZARZUELA (tharr thoo AYE lah). A type of Spanish opera dating from the seventeenth century. The modern zarzuela is usually a comic opera in one act or a serious opera in three acts. A special theater for the performance of such operas, Teatro de la Zarzuela, was built in Madrid in 1856.

ZITHER. A stringed instrument native to Central Europe, but popular in other places. It consists of thirty to forty-five strings stretched over a flat wooden sound box. The five strings nearest the player are plucked and serve to play the melody, while all the others are strummed as an accompaniment. The melody strings are stopped, as on the violin. The instrument is held on the knees or placed on a table while it is being played.

The zither has been used as an effective instrument for playing background film music and for accompanying popular singers of folk music.*

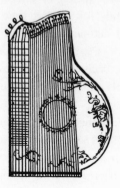